RESOLVE

RESOLVE

A Story of Courage,
Healthy Inquiry and Recovery
from Sibling Sexual Abuse

ALICE PERLE

BLUE BORAGE
Publishing

First published in Australia in 2023 by Blue Borage Publishing
Copyright © 2023 Alice Perle
Designed by Nada Backovic
Edited by Matthew Earsman

The author and publisher acknowledge the Gubbi Gubbi people, the Traditional Owners and Custodians of the lands upon which we work, live and sustain ourselves, and where this book has been written. We pay our respects to their elders, past and present, and recognise that First Nations sovereignty was never ceded. This continent always was and always will be Aboriginal land.

Cataloguing-in-Publication entry is available from the National Library of Australia: https://catalogue.nla.gov.au

Paperback ISBN: 978-0-6457497-0-0
e-book ISBN: 978-0-6457497-1-7

Barcode 9 7 8 0 6 4 5 7 4 9 7 0 0

All enquiries to: enquire@blueboragepublishing.com.au

Dedicated to my husband and our daughters.

If my love for you were an ocean, there would be no more land.
If my love for you were a desert, you would see only sand.
If my love for you were a star - late at night, only light.
And if my love for you could grow wings, I'd be soaring in flight.
JAY ASHER, AUTHOR

Contents

Don't hide the darkness. Don't hide the pain.
It wants to be hidden. Thrives on it.
It can do most damage from the shadows.
It can make you feel like you're the only one.
Crazy. Alone.
And you'll never forget about it.
Not the way you really want to.
Instead, call it out. Acknowledge it. Validate it.
Drag it from the shadows, unwillingly.
Force it into the light.
You might be surprised by how much smaller
it looks when you see it unobscured.
You might also be surprised by how much
others recognise it from their own battles.
There is no shame in this. No stigma.
Secrecy manufactures these feelings.
SCOTT EILERS, PSYCHOLOGIST & AUTHOR

Content and trigger warning

This memoir has been written to connect the dots between the recollection of my childhood experience of sibling sexual abuse and the repercussions of that abuse beyond the time it happened. It contains references to sexual abuse, incest, PTSD, bullying, alcohol abuse and other coping mechanisms and behaviours, which some people may find distressing.

Helplines

If anything within this memoir raises any issues for you, there are counselling services who can help. If you require assistance or would like to talk to a trained professional about the issues described in this book, each country, state and territory have listed helplines to call.

For instance, throughout Australia, the counsellors at 1800RESPECT are available 24 hours a day, seven days a week, by phone on 1800 737 732 and web chat via their website at 1800respect.org.au. The Kids Helpline is available by phone on 1800 55 1800 or Lifeline on 13 11 44.

The Australian Government's Australian Institute of Family Studies (aifs.gov.au) state that if you believe a child is in immediate danger, call the Police on 000.

Terms used

I have used 'her' in referring to the victim; and 'him' and 'brother' when referring to the abuser throughout.

I shift between the word 'victim' and 'survivor'. For all intents and purposes here, they are the same thing, yet 'survivor' is a term most often used when we are out the other end and no longer at risk from our abuser.

Similarly, the words 'abuser' or 'perpetrator' are used throughout. They have pretty clear meanings.

The actual abuse I experienced is 'sibling sexual abuse'. I personally knew it to be 'incest' when I first matched a word to the actions as a child. That's what it was called back in the 1970s and 80s. Most research and data I came across was on child sexual abuse. I will mostly use 'sibling sexual abuse' unless the content is from an external source, and 'child sexual abuse' or the word 'incest' is what was used in that context.

In terms of my adult relationship, the words 'wife' and 'husband' are used because that is what we call each other.

Why share?

Until I began writing this book I, like many survivors of sibling sexual abuse, had never shared what happened to me outside of the closest personal and professional relationships. Little by little, I began writing my story out of my body, and uncomfortable as that felt, it has led to many moments of freedom that have transformed my life from grey and fearful to an explosion of life and colour!

In my search for information about sibling sexual abuse, the answers didn't come easily or in abundance. What I did find was mostly between one and two decades old and was almost exclusively focused on child sexual abuse generally, rather than sibling sexual abuse. Thankfully as I came to the end of the publishing process, there were research papers surfacing that are more current, and solely focused on sibling sexual abuse.

This gave me hope for change in the future and I am more than happy to add to the conversation about sibling sexual abuse and how we might approach recovery from it and aid the prevention of it.

How this book is written

This memoir is about my experiences and my own perspective on them. My intention is to reflect on my experience for the purpose of understanding and learning, for myself and others whose lives have been touched by abuse.

I have been through many phases along the way, slowly opening up to my painful past and releasing it with the help of many wonderful people. It is incredible to think of how my life was before, compared to the peace and freedom that I experience now on a daily basis. It has taken courage, time and a lot of vulnerability to get to where I am today, but it has been an extraordinary journey, laden with unexpected gifts and surprising outcomes. To demonstrate how I have travelled along this path, I have structured this memoir into three sections:

Section 1 is based on my recollection and reflection on my experiences as Young Alice. Beginning with a vivid portrait of the dark days of abuse, it moves through a deep dive into demystifying sibling sexual abuse, with facts, definitions and investigations into the circumstances that these forms of sexual abuse develop in. We investigate the process of disclosure, from my own tentative and disastrous first steps through to other more successful attempts to share my experiences that led to the most amazing and supportive relationships I have found in my life. In chapter three the fierce lioness emerges from within me in a moment of great conflict, and I make the decision to give up people pleasing and establish the first real safe boundaries for myself and my family.

Section 2 is about the birthing of my intention to own my story. I work hard at establishing a new life, becoming a professional businesswoman and company owner. Embracing the choices of personal and professional growth, I begin to find success while avoiding dealing with the deeper issues but I am weighed down by the unseen effects of my abuse. Through many struggles and difficulties, I finally prevail and give more time and energy to dealing with the effects of the abuse and trauma.

Section 3 is an explosion of wonderful acceptance of all I have learned, as I begin opening myself in earnest to the possibilities and options available now. It is about the choice to take responsibility to change my life, as a forty- and fifty-something survivor, because it is never too late to begin. This section explores many tools for healing and personal empowerment, a magical attachment releasing visualisation and the four gifts I gave myself that are still serving me well in showing up as my truest self. Combining the lessons learned from consciously choosing to shine the light on the abuse, and the ties that held me back for so long, this section is powerful and life-affirming.

Mixed in is the biggest dollop of pure heartfelt love, empathy and compassion for myself and fellow survivors. Over the years I have become a down-to-earth realist and can easily find humour as well as optimism in my experiences. I do occasionally swear, and sometimes I may come across as irreverent, that's what feels most authentic to me: the adult Alice. The younger version of myself has well and truly done her time holding on to heavy emotions, way beyond her years.

Sharing respectfully

In the evolution of this book, I got stuck many times in fear and concern of whether or not it was safe to share my story. What if I embarrassed someone or made them uncomfortable, or triggered someone else's painful memories?

My hope is that my 'noise' creates a ripple effect in breaking down the silence and quiet shame, and that through saying 'no' to silence I can help survivors and their loved ones open into a freer life. We cannot change the past, but we can influence the present and the future.

I would love to think this book could:

- change what's happening right now or in the future for one child;
- help us understand how it begins and change the ways in which families operate and communicate important issues;
- make one parent more aware of what might be happening now in their home and think to check on that closed bedroom door;
- help one other adult survivor say, 'Thank God! It wasn't only me';
- give options and information to others who want to understand their partner, family member, friend or anyone who has survived this.

Only one small memory of the actual sexual abuse is shared in this book. Aside from that incident, no graphic details of the sexual abuse I experienced are shared.

RESOLVE

Section One

SPEAKING

the

UNSPOKEN

1

Young Alice's Story

You don't learn how strong you are until you are pushed beyond what you thought you could handle, and you emerge on the other side with more bravery, grace and determination than you realised you even had.

RACHEL M. MARTIN, AUTHOR

Alice could hear someone whispering. She didn't dare turn her head to see who was disturbing the sacred silence in the classroom. She had completed the set reading before her classmates, despite having slept poorly the night before and having trouble keeping her eyes open and the daydreams away.

After finishing her work, she continued to stare at the page as if she were still reading, but her mind flew away. Away from the long tedious hours at the strict Catholic school she attended in southern Sydney. Away from the grand church beside it, majestically overlooking the town where Alice lived, and far, far away from the nuns who exerted severe control over her school life. She became lost in a magical world, drifting through delightful memories of the school fete the previous weekend.

She had wandered for hours, sucking on a sweet sticky toffee, the scent of lavender potpourri sachets and happy sounds of children all around. She stood gazing at Tupperware containers overflowing with homemade chocolate crackles, honey joys and coconut ice and lingered by the gift stall of homemade crafts and embroidered handkerchiefs.

Searching the bursting tables, her eyes had found her favourite prize—a wicker basket full of chubby plastic dollies with tidy moulded plastic hairstyles. This year some of them had painted gold hair. How beautiful they were! Each one wore a colourful skirt fluffed up in layers as high as their necks, some had glitter and sparkles sprinkled on the netting or fairy wands glued to their tiny little hands. They were just like real fairies with their happy faces, kissable little lips, and long black eyelashes painted under their great big eyes.

Immersed in happy memories, Alice sat quietly, as required by the strict school rules enforced by severe and unforgiving nuns—but her moment of peace was soon broken.

Drawn from her inner world by slightly too loud giggling and fidgeting, she looked forward over her classmates' heads, bent over their rows of timber double flip-top desks where an imposing figure dominated the front of the class.

Behind a large desk, wearing a full-length black tunic, sat Sister Adelia. She was an impressive and frightening woman, her neck completely covered by a headpiece with a white wimple and black veil. Her face and hands, the only parts of her body exposed to the eye, were poised as if in prayer, but Alice knew better than to trust appearances when it came to the nuns.

A sudden burst of loud laughter broke the spell, and against her will, Alice's head jerked violently to the right, where she saw two girls hurriedly putting their heads down and studiously tracing their fingers across the lines of text they were supposed to be reading.

Sister Adelia boomed: 'Alice Smith! COME UP HERE! NOW!' Her voice echoed off the bare classroom walls. Still lost in fragments of her daydream, Alice almost jumped out of her seat, immediately regretting whatever it was she had done wrong. She knew that disobedience in the classroom was viewed as a sin, and punishment was inevitable, but still she considered saying, 'Sister, it wasn't me'. She had been sitting quietly and had done nothing wrong, but instinctively she knew it was better to just do as she was told. The Sister's word was law and complaining would get her nowhere.

Mortified, she closed her book and stood up, stepping timidly onto the nun's stage at the front of the large classroom, the interested eyes of her classmates burning her skin as they watched expectantly. She stood nervously just out of reach of the imposing figure, who stepped forward instantly and grabbed Alice's right arm, drawing her closer, and holding on firmly at the wrist, expertly pulling it straight. Sister Adelia roughly turned Alice's hand to face upward so that the soft underbelly of her forearm was exposed.

The punishment was quick. Whack! Down came the ruler, angled with the metal insert to hit the inside crease of the child's elbow. Alice received two more whacks for good measure.

'Laughing is not permitted in class!'

With her arm smarting, and her face reddening, Alice went back to her desk with her head down. The two girls who'd laughed aloud now avoided her eyes as she sat and opened her book, trying to focus on what the nun was now talking about. 'School is not a time for frivolity!' she said, 'Distracting other children is a sin, and a disrespect of the other students, the school and even God himself.'

Once she had settled in, her face red with anxiety and embarrassment, she saw her two friends watching her, whispering. Alice had met them in kindergarten, and often played elastics, jacks or hula hoops with them at lunchtime, but she never talked to them in the classroom. Friendships were tenuous at school.

If you only had two friends, there was a chance that one will be away sick, and then you had only one friend to play with. If that friend chose to go play with someone else that day, or was away at a sports competition with other schools, then you had no friends. As little lunch began, you'd have a fairly good feeling for how social playtime would be.

The days she was alone, Alice would see other girls walking and sitting eating their lunch in small groups, laughing and talking about things she could only imagine. She was quite a solitary child, spending most of her time alone, where she often daydreamed about happy and fun things.

She loved having tea parties with her dolls for their birthdays, where Kitty the cat got invited as a special guest, and sometimes dressed up in a dolly's frock too. She loved New Year's Eve, it was so noisy and fun. Mum played the big piano in the lounge room and all the adults stood around her singing songs out loud and laughing.

All the kids from the neighbourhood would play murder in the dark in one of the bedrooms, before grabbing two cooking pot lids each from the kitchen drawers, to clang together up and down the middle of the road, yelling 'Happy New Year!' when the clock struck twelve.

Memories danced in her head, the endless hot days of summer, playing in the pool with all the rules of life forgotten—the heat wave nights where they'd stay at the beach until the wind changed with a huge paper-wrapped fish and chips dinner, feeding leftovers to the seagulls. Then there was Christmas, and Santa Claus visiting, and of course, birthday cakes…

Alice caught herself dreaming again and looked up quickly, just before the nun's severe gaze swept across the classroom like a spotlight, vigilant for any inappropriate activity. Snapping back to reality she felt the sting still burning her forearm and saw the raised red mark glowing livid on her skin. Apart from instilling fear in the rest of the class, the welt would be there for the rest of the day as a humiliating reminder of the wicked child's transgression.

After eating their sandwiches at big lunch Alice and her new friend Mary sat on the bench along the side wall of the assembly area. Scrunching up her paper lunch bag so it didn't fly away in the wind, she put it beside her to throw it away later. Mary was a new girl at school so she didn't have any friends yet and she looked like a shy girl, not a sporty girl.

Alice had smiled at her on Monday, asking if she'd like to sit next to her at lunch. They had already played elastics at little lunch that day, over in the shade of a tree beside the tuckshop. Now it was big lunch and it felt like they must be friends, naturally gravitating towards each other when big lunch began.

Standing up to shake off her lunch crumbs and straddle the long bench to face Mary, Alice scanned the school grounds, watching the netball girls clustered in the centre of the netball court, telling another girl she couldn't play with them. Sometimes they were so mean. On the other side of the assembly area Alice spotted her big sister, sitting alone, and not looking happy. Alice felt like that sometimes too, sitting alone just felt right some days. She and her sister didn't talk at school. Her big sister was going to graduate and go away to high school next year, and girls in fourth grade didn't speak to sixth grade girls, even their sisters.

'Come on, slow coach, are you ready?' Alice turned and saw her new friend sitting ready, back straight, hands palms pressed together as if in prayer.

Feeling important, Alice quickly took her seat and counted them in: One-two-three!

'A sailor went to sea sea sea, to see what he could see see see, and all that he could see see see, was the bottom of the deep blue sea sea sea.'

Starting slowly, the clapping sped faster and faster, ending in a crescendo of laughter. Mary yelled, 'Haha, I did it!' Both girls were pleased and proud they'd made it all the way through, and Mary said 'Let's do it again... and this time faster!'

When the bell rang, Alice picked up her lunch bag to toss into the bin, ran to squirt some water into her mouth from the bubbler that shot water off at crazy angles and, noticing her sister was gone from her seat, did a quick happy skip to get in line ready to march off to afternoon class. *Maybe she really does want to be my friend*, Alice thought. Big lunch always went faster with friends and fun.

Every school day ended the same: the whole school was absolutely silent. The girls sat at their desks. Nobody moved a muscle. A little knot began nagging at Alice's stomach. She looked at the hands of the big clock turning at the front of the class, its tick-tock rapid as her heartbeat. Part of her wished they would go slower.

Suddenly the bell rang from outside in the playground. Like soldiers arming their weapons, in unison all the students stood up straight, then looking down they clacked their school case locks shut, 'snap, snap'. Bodies moved from behind desks, chairs were pushed tidily into place without a hint of a scraping sound. Row by row the children waited their turn to file out the door, trying desperately not to speak too loudly, or do anything wrong— the risk of Sister telling the class to sit back down and do it quieter this time was real— and freedom so near.

Into the corridor Alice and her classmates tumbled, finally able to breathe out loud, or to speak and giggle, a stream of uniformed little girls, pouring out into the golden afternoon light.

Children milled about on the sunny concrete playground between the class and the high walls of the church, some standing around talking or eating as others headed in their separate directions towards home. She looked towards the gate where her mother sometimes picked her up, although Alice knew she wasn't coming today.

She'd told Alice this morning to walk home from school because she had an interview for a new job in the city and didn't know if she'd be home early enough. The knot tightened in her tummy. Getting picked up usually meant it was swimming lesson afternoon at the local pool, or they were going shopping, or to get a haircut. She loved seeing her mum smiling at her from just outside the gate. It felt special to get picked up.

She couldn't see her little brother or big sister either, just the excited chattering children heading for home or talking in small groups, and the netball girls gathering for practice. Fully aware of their own importance, they'd drop their school cases in the centre of the playground, chatty and full of energy, eating home-packed snacks whilst they grabbed their colourful lettered netball bibs for afternoon practice.

Netball girls were like the special club. Alice sometimes wondered how you'd get to be someone on a netball team. She thought that if she was, she'd be the one to do something wrong on the netball court, like forget what the letter on her bib meant, and what she was supposed to do with the ball or worse, what not to do. Maybe she'd throw the ball the wrong way or drop it, because she was new and didn't know how to play. Shuddering at that thought, she put signing up for netball out of her mind. That was okay, because what Alice was best at was swimming and athletics.

She reluctantly turned and headed for the other side of the school where the pedestrian crossing opened to the long narrow lane that led down the hill towards her home. Alice was a good runner, she usually came second because the girl who always came first went to Little Athletics, and she had really muscly calves that made her legs run and swim faster than Alice's. Her mum said coming second was good, and that it was because the other girl was tall and had longer legs. It worried her mum though that the swimming would make her shoulders get too big to look nice on a girl, and the boys wouldn't like it.

Alice crossed the wide stretch of playground sandwiched between the red brick buildings of the school and the tall imposing church. No matter what the season, in the morning it cast a cold shadow over the playground, but the school year would soon be ending and now the afternoon sun was lighting up its windows and walls from its high steeples to the side steps the children used to go to school mass. She lingered, looking up at the beautiful stained-glass windows of adoring saints, of Jesus on the cross, his mother Mary, and little lambs, slithering snakes and apple trees. Every colour of the rainbow was in those pictures, they were an interesting distraction whilst the priest gave his sermons in mass.

Golden light warmed Alice's face as she headed past the line of slender trees that cast long skinny shadows up the church wall—poor sad trees that struggled for life in their tiny squares of soil—islands of nature in an ocean of cement.

Alice drifted past the church, dragging her feet as the school children moved around her, shouting, skipping and running, all heading towards the back gate and the freedom of a spring afternoon. Some walked with their heads up, purposefully striding towards home, snacks, and maybe some TV, but Alice walked more slowly than the rest, letting them pass around her.

She wasn't in much of a hurry to get home, her eyes on the ground as she watched the cracked cement change to sunburnt grass, then the black bitumen of the road alternating with the white stripes of the crossing and onto the footpath of the long alley that led down the hill to her home. A cascade of children crossed the road behind her, and flowed laughing all around her.

She walked slightly faster to keep on the edge of the group, as walking alone meant you might get stolen by that bad man that the police talked about.

The lane ended near a big dark pool hall. Motorbikes were parked everywhere, loud music was blaring and men were laughing, the air reeking of ciggies. Alice sped past to get to the next crossing, because they were probably the bad men in the stories.

When she finally got across to the long main road that led all the way down to her street, Alice worried she was alone; was she a sitting duck for a baddie to get her? There were no other school kids going her way, or they were already far ahead of her, and it was too soon for adults to be walking home from the train station after work. She knew all about stranger danger.

Sometimes she'd run if she knew her mum was home, other times she distracted herself, taking her time. She tried walking to the same beat the big red rattly trains made on the tracks across the other side of the road, bringing students home from school. Her mum may even be on one now or coming back from her interview if she wasn't already home. She tried walking with one foot landing on each concrete square of the path, and she gathered up some colourful leaves to do something crafty with because they looked especially beautiful.

Coming around the corner into her street, Alice felt her stomach drop and her mouth go dry. Her mum's car was not in the driveway. As she slowly made her way towards her house, she looked around for things to do, stopping to pick yellow dandelion flowers to make a daisy chain later, taking up a little more time. There was no one out in the street to talk to and so she kept moving towards her house where Kitty was absorbed with stalking some grasshopper or bird.

The cat was walking slowly along the grass, back flattened—all her attention focused forward. She looked up when Alice called her, somewhat annoyed for having her hunt disturbed. She came over anyway at the chance of a treat, tail raised to rub herself on Alice's legs, who picked her up and cuddled her, talking softly to the cat and feeling a little better.

Alice told her about her day and her new friend, and the beautiful smell of the rose bushes in the Italian families' gardens up the street—already forgetting the details of today's punishment and Sister Adelia's severity. After a short while though, Kitty struggled to return to the ground and resume her hunt, and Alice reluctantly put her down, turning towards the front door of the house with a feeling of dread.

She walked up the few steps to the porch, and quietly turned the handle of the unlocked door, and with her nerves jangling entered the cool darkness of the hallway. In the shadows, Darryl, her big brother, was leaning against the brown and cream papered hallway, waiting for her to arrive. Alice's heart turned to ice, when she saw him. He looked smug and confident, like a dark, menacing, curly-haired troll from an olden-days fairy tale book, grinning a dark smile of welcome.

She quickly gathered her senses. Not looking at him, Alice walked with purpose to get past him to where the hallway door opened into the loungeroom and the kitchen beyond, pretending she had no idea what he was doing there. If she could just get a snack, then at the right moment, run back through to her bedroom and close the door like so many other days, she would be okay—but today Darryl had no intention of giving her any personal space.

Swinging himself back across the door frame, blocking her path to the loungeroom, he threw his arm out to touch the other side of the narrow space. She found herself trapped standing face-to-face with him, his body too close, his hot and smelly Devon meat sandwich breath on her face as he pressed her backwards across the hallway towards her bedroom.

An hour later, Alice sat on her bedroom carpet studiously focused on twisting her dolly's hair into lumpy plaits. She heard her mum's car pull up in the driveway. As she walked to that same right-hand turn in the hallway Alice had tried for when she'd returned home, her mum called back over her shoulder, 'Alice, how was your day? Have you fed the cat? Homework done yet? Get it done and you can come to do the shopping with me.'

Shaken out of her trance, Alice lay her dolly and hairbrush down and followed her mum to the kitchen to pour Kitty her bowl of dinner biscuits, at the same time helping herself to a cupcake afternoon tea. She'd completely forgotten about late-night shopping with her mum. Thankfully there had been no homework this afternoon, which was a rare treat, so Alice knew she was going shopping.

Waiting for her mum, who was buzzing around between the pantry and fridge with a pen and paper to write out her shopping list, Alice sat quietly on the kitchen floor beside Kitty and watched her crunch her food, picking at it with intense concentration like it was the most important thing in the world. She was totally prepared to go when her mum was ready to leave, but her tummy still felt as if it had butterflies bumping around in there. At least she knew she would be out of the house, and not left at home with her big brother in charge. She didn't want that to happen twice in one day.

The morning sunlight shone in the window as Alice stood looking at herself in the mirror. Her piggy tails not quite at the same level behind one ear as the other, but Alice still nodded satisfaction. Proud that she'd given the piggy tails her best effort, Alice jumped, startled as her mum popped her head in the bathroom.

'Out you get or you're going to make us all late.'

Alice scooted out of the way, glad there was no mention from Mum about the standard of her hair styling efforts. Everyone was busy and distracted in the mornings, getting ready for school was a routine that she performed more or less by herself. Slipping her little blue prayer book into her case and closing the locks, she stood in the hallway waiting for everyone else to get ready.

When it was time, the kids were set free to walk together up the steep hill to school. They didn't usually talk nor walk together in a line, it depended on whether you liked to walk fast, or if you stopped to look at the drains over a handrail or were a dilly-dally dawdler and got left behind. As usual, Darryl rushed off ahead to catch his train to high school, one suburb along the train line.

Reaching the two big open drains that passed under the street near her house, Alice paused. She usually dashed across, thinking of the video the police had brought to school warning of 'Stranger Danger'. The scary images flickered in her mind of the girl being followed through the forest, the 'bad' man and the storm drain. The police gave them a stern lecture and told them to be careful walking to and from school. Then they left. Alice cast a quick nervous glance down over the rail as she crossed to see if she could see anything.

On the left of the path were all the neat and tidy gardens, where Italian grandparents sat on front porches in the sun and waved hello while watering their flowers. Alice felt a nice feeling and smiled at them before crossing the railway bridge and starting up the long hill to the church and school. She tried not to think about Darryl, already speeding away from her along the railway line towards his school. *At least until this afternoon,* she thought.

She felt hopeful today and had a little skip in her step. Today is the day she thought, checking in her mind again that she'd packed in her little prayer book.

This particular hot Friday morning, Alice sat with the rest of her class in the church pews. The other children sounded like chipmunks, quietly chattering amongst themselves. Pulling the small pale blue prayer book with gold writing on it from her pocket, Alice relished the feel of the cover. It felt like soft suede. It was a very precious possession to hold in her hands. It had little holy cards as bookmarks slipped between some pages. They were treasured gifts from her great aunt and grandparents, with pictures of Jesus or Mary or one of the Holy Saints, on the front. A prayer or a note written in scribbly old person's writing filled the back of the card.

The children from St. Genèvieve's Primary School had just finished the benediction mass at the church. The mass was always mid-morning, the sun burning through the tall side windows onto the children's heads. The scent of frankincense felt suffocating as the priest waved it about in prayer. Alice tried to hold her breath, so she didn't get woozy, vomit or topple down from her knees to disappear below the church pew.

Mass ended, and most of the school exited the church in a quiet and orderly manner, back to the school day, one row of seats at a time. One grade of children would remain behind, taking their turn to fulfil the sacrament of Confession, one of the Catholic religion's Seven Sacraments. Confession was what we used to call it back then, nowadays it's called Reconciliation. It is second in importance, the first being the Baptism of little babies. The idea was to attend Confession, tell the priest your sins and seek forgiveness and the love of God through the priest. Then you'd go away and say a few prayers and get back to being good or mess up and do the next thing wrong, so you had to confess again. Then repeat, for the rest of your life.

That Friday, the children in Alice's row were sharing ideas of what sin might be a good one to confess today.

'Maybe it'll be good to say I used God's name in vain,' said Mary.

Alice's friend Belinda, the girl who could run the fastest,

shared her idea; 'I'll tell Father, umm...' she looked up as if the church roof could give her inspiration. 'I know! I'll say I didn't help Mum with the washing up.'

Belinda's other best friend, Bernadette, who never played with Alice, spotted a flaw in the plan. 'Didn't you say that one last time?'

'Yeah, I did. Oh, fiddle sticks!' Her face lit up in triumph, the problem solved. 'Oh! Now I have a real one; I just used a swear word.'

They laughed and spun around with interest to hear Alice's plan for the day's confession, but she had seen the priest arrive and was already up on her feet, disappearing into the lavatory-sized confessional box.

As the heavy door closed behind her, she pulled it hard to ensure it was closed. She didn't want it to pop open and reveal all her sins to her school friends. In the dim light, Alice knelt onto a low, dark green felt-covered timber step and faced the ornately grated gold window, its timber shutter pulled shut.

She carefully placed her little blue prayer book on the ground beside her for later, thinking to herself, *Be careful, don't forget and leave it behind.* Alice's heart was beating fast in her chest. She brought her hands together in front of her lips and chin as if in prayer. Her eyes closed, she lowered her head and waited in anticipation for the priest to open the shutter.

Bang! Her eyes flew open with a start. Father had slapped the timber shutter slide back; it was now fully open. She could see the right-side profile of his face through the gold metal grate.

In those days, the rules of Confession meant a priest must only look forward at the door in front of him. He could not turn his head to look at the parishioner confessing their sins. Never. That way, anonymity in sharing the sinner's worst sins was assured. The priest, by rights, also couldn't claim he knew whose sins were whose.

Father, a tall, wrinkle-faced man with grey and white hair

scared the children most of all the priests at St. Genèvieve's Catholic Church. He had big googly, bloodshot eyes that either peered deep into your soul or any place else to avoid looking you in the eyes. His forehead intrigued the children; deep vertical lines ran between his brow, a reliable sign of his perpetual frown.

He spoke clearly and to the point.

'Yes, my child.'

She knew the correct words by heart: 'Forgive me, Father, for I have sinned. It has been one month since my last confession.'

'Yes, my child.'

'Father,' she took a deep, shaky breath and blurted out a stream of words that sounded like a wobbly light wind. 'Please, Father, can you please tell my big brother to stop coming into my bed at night-time?'

Silence. Breathless silence.

'Your brother? Is he older than you?'

'Yes, Father.' She caught his sideways glance: he knew who she was, her family, and her big brother.

Oh good, she thought as relief flickered in her chest. *I knew he'd help.*

But her jaw tightened suddenly, her eyes widened, and she found herself taking a big gulp of air. Father's face had turned beetroot red, and his nose snorted as he took his own sharp intake of air. With a slower, disappointed rush of breath out, he reaffixed his gaze straight ahead at his door and boomed:

'You stop that! That's bad!'

His voice then recoiled, but only a little.

'Now go and say five Hail Marys and one Our Father,' but he thought better of it. 'No, make that two Our Fathers, for your sins.'

'Yes Father. Thank you, Father.'

What else could she say? It didn't matter; he wasn't listening anyway. He made the sign of the cross in the air in front of him and mumbled at no one in particular, 'In the name of the Father, and the Son, and the Holy Spirit, Amen.'

Bang! The shutter window was closed, and she was alone in the box again. She felt tears prickle in her eyes but couldn't let them leak onto her cheeks. She had to stay strong. The others would ask what happened if she cried. Her head felt numb and tingly, like a nest of pins and needles. She didn't know what to think next. *Oh, that's right*, she remembered. *I must say my Hail Marys and the Our Fathers, so God will forgive me.*

She wobbled as she stood up. There was a strange empty feeling in her legs. She bent down to gather up her little blue prayer book. There'd be trouble if she forgot that.

She stood still, collected herself, turned the round brass doorknob and pushed open the heavy door, leaving it slightly open for the next child to know it was time for their turn.

She didn't raise her eyes. She couldn't allow herself to catch anyone else's gaze; they would see what Father had said as clearly as if it was written on a placard and hung on her neck. She walked to a seat in the back row and ignored the other children, who turned around to ask whether Father was in a bad mood today.

Alice kneeled at the pew and took her rosary beads from her school tunic pocket, then began reciting the Hail Mary to herself:

> Hail Mary, full of grace, the Lord is with thee.
> Blessed art thou among women and blessed
> is the fruit of thy womb, Jesus.
> Holy Mary, Mother of God, Pray for us sinners,
> now and at the hour of our death. Amen.

Then again and again. Five times.
Then the Our Fathers:

Our Father, who art in heaven, hallowed be thy name.
Thy kingdom come, thy will be done
on earth as it is in heaven.
Give us this day our daily bread, and forgive
us our trespasses as we forgive those who
trespass against us; and lead us not into
temptation but deliver us from evil. Amen.

And again. Twice for her sins.

Alice was used to feeling alone, but if there was a feeling of being more deeply alone, it was now pouring over her like molten lava. She shook as she waited for the remaining children to complete Confession. Her cheeks flushed red with shame; her eyes brimmed with tears. Her lips were zipped shut, and short, ragged breaths came through her nose. After an interminable amount of time, all the children had finished.

At the instruction of Sister Adelia, Alice marched in line with the rest of the children, her eyes still averted to the floor, quiet, wishing to become invisible. Back across the school playground to the classrooms they marched. She put away her prayer book and got her lunch bag out of her school case. It was big lunch time, and she took her paper bag to sit on an empty bench against one of the side walls in the school's assembly square.

With her back to the cold brick walls, Alice was finally alone. Her face was cooling down, but her chest was searing with a deep, resigned sadness. She wanted to cry. She put a corner of her homemade white bread and corned beef sandwich into her mouth and chewed bit by bit. There was no taste, but the distraction of doing anything was good.

Her new friend Mary didn't sit down next to her, but came and stood in front, as if she knew something was wrong. She whispered, 'If you'd like to, I'd like to play elastics with you?'

Whilst Alice liked playing elastics, today, her legs didn't feel like playing elastics. They felt like elastic bands all by themselves.

She shook her head and kept her mouth held tightly closed. She could feel tears trying to escape her eyes and she wasn't completely sure whether the roaring sound she could hear in her head would stay inside if she opened her mouth.

Mary made it easy, and as if she understood, gave a little smile, and with a tiny nod of her head went and sat with her other new friend Belinda.

No one else came to ask her if she wanted to play, but she didn't mind. She was glad to be alone and shrank into the walls to make herself less noticeable. Alice was good at being quiet; being invisible.

Father's words repeated in her mind, turning this way and that, and folding themselves over like a piece of paper.

You stop that. That's bad. She already knew she was bad, she didn't need someone to tell her that.

What her big brother did scared her. That's why she had pushed away her fear, gathered up every ounce of resolve and courage in her ten-year-old body, and asked Father to help her stop him.

Instead, it was confirmed. She knew she was going to go to hell, and nothing would stop Darryl, ever.

As Alice turned the corner into her street that afternoon, she caught sight of the tail end of her mum's car in the driveway. Realising she'd been holding her breath, she exhaled a whoosh of air and her feet broke out into a little skip. Mum was home. She trotted diagonally across the road and the front lawn. Kitty, all snug and warm lying in the sun up on the boot of her mum's car, took a lovely big stretch like she was reaching out with a little hand tap to say welcome home. She stopped to tickle the cat's chin.

Up the steps and through the door she went, into the cool

darkness of the hallway, then Alice headed straight for the kitchen. Dropping her hard school case by the dinner table, she flashed a smile at her mother, sitting in the corner chair just below the kitchen servery where the phone was attached to the wall. Her mum didn't see the smile, she was looking at her nails and nodding her head as she listened to someone on the phone.

Alice rummaged in the fridge for something to snack on, popped open the locks on her school case and pulled out her favourite chair at the dinner table, the one at the end of the table, with her back to the green fern patterned wallpapered wall, under the high windows. She liked that seat the best. She could see who was down the other end of the room watching TV, she was close to the kitchen, her favourite room in the house—and she could see across to her older brother's room. She cast a glance around the corner into the loungeroom, not sure if she saw a shadow of movement there. She couldn't see Darryl at his desk and wondered if he was lurking between her and her bedroom. She unpacked her things from the case and started to work.

Studiously focused on making beautiful curves with her pencil, Alice wrote the word 'mountain' tidily on its own line in the exercise book, for the fifth time. It was the last of her spelling words today. Finished! Relaxing her shoulders down, shaking out her writing hand fingers, she gave herself a little nod of satisfaction at all the mountainy letters in the word mountain.

She started packing away her pencils for school next week, seeing one needed sharpening, she whizzed it around inside her metal sharpener. Leaving the homework book open so she didn't forget to have Mum sign her homework, Alice didn't get up, happy to be where she was for the moment, in her favourite chair, with her mum sitting arms-length away. Mum was laughing now and twiddling her fingers in the curly cord of the phone. Then, standing up to stretch and look at the kitchen clock, she wrapped up the chat with her friend, saying 'Oh my, look at the time! I'd best get started with making the dinner, it's not going to cook itself.'

After dinner that night, Alice got ready for bed without much to say to anyone in the house. Brushing her teeth, she looked at herself in the bathroom mirror as if under a spell. Her mind flicked back to a memory of her big brother's first approach two years earlier, in the Christmas school holidays just after her eighth birthday. In her mind, it was like an old black-and-white film, scratchy, with the edges blackened.

The film depicted an event that happened at her Grandma's semi-detached two-bedroom cottage in Botany. It was the school holidays. Her grandma had taught her how to make the beds and fold the corners under just right, reminding Alice all the while that it's a girl's job to make the beds, and boys have more important work to do. 'Boys don't make beds,' Grandma had said.

The black-and-white film comes into focus as Grandma is leaving the bedroom, just as her big brother Darryl comes in quietly. Alice, admiring her hospital corners, looks up at her brother. He is now standing with his back to the wall. He doesn't say anything, he just watches. The film flickers as Alice studies his face, wondering what he is doing. She challenges him with an annoyed, 'What?'

The images slow down, and the voices become dull and deepen into a lingering slurred sound. With his chin pushed out, Alice hears her brother's voice in a slow, distorted almost unrecognisable tone.

'Show me your vagina.'

Her eyes widen, and her nose scrunches up, as if there's a bad smell in the air. 'My what? Oh, yuck, no way!'

A feeling of wrongness fills her body. She takes off like the Road Runner, sidestepping her brother and the bed near the door. She runs down the hallway and through the lounge in slow motion, and seeing her grandma sewing on her machine, enters the sunroom to the side of the kitchen. Time slowly returns to normal as Alice sits nearby and breathes a deep sigh, pretending to be fascinated by what her grandmother is sewing.

Finally, the film stopped. Avoiding her own eyes in the bathroom mirror, Alice tried to breathe slowly, her toothbrush forgotten beside the soap and fragrant handtowels.

There was no way she could have ever said such a thing to Grandma.

Her grandmother would have been angry, and at the minimum both brother and sister would have been dragged by their ears down the back stairs to the laundry in the backyard to get their tongues scrubbed with a big bar of yellow soap.

The old film had stopped, but her mind still had clouds of thoughts that she couldn't shake away quickly. She recalled trying to fathom that a small insignificant part of her body she couldn't see, always tucked safely inside her big white cotton undies, had a new name. Her mum and dad always said it was rude not to have your undies on, even in bed with a nightie on.

Darryl's request was yucky. It was in the way he said it. Her brother called it that name out loud, but he made it sound like he was asking for more than, say, let me see your sore knee. Her big brother knew what he asked was naughty. She didn't know why he wanted to look at that, and why now?

Why would he say that to me?

That was a long time ago now she thought, spitting out the toothpaste and gulping a couple of handfuls of water to rinse her mouth. Alice changed out of her uniform, hung it on a hanger on the cupboard door, and pulled her nightie on over her undies. She didn't bother keeping her bedside lamp on, and switched off the bedroom light. She just wanted to be in the dark.

Slipping into her bed, she lay quietly, running her fingers over the now much softer homemade lemon and white flowered cotton sheets, the same favourite sheets she'd loved back before she'd turned eight. Alice found herself tossing and turning, unable to drift off to sleep.

Her mind was trying to make sense of her confusion that Father did not say 'Yes', that he would help her, after all. How could that be possible? Alice lay still and tried not to think about it anymore. Instead, she tried to think of nice things that made her happy or that used to make her happy before Darryl put the idea of being in her own house on her list of not-so-fun things to do.

She closed her eyes, imagining she had one of those bright-coloured plastic View-masters, putting the circle of cardboard with tiny photos into it, and holding it up to her eyes, looking at all the photos one by one in full colour.

She saw a fete table stacked with sweet treats, toffees and chocolate crackles, the fairy floss served as a big fluffy pink ball on a stick. Easter Sunday morning with bright eggs shining on the end of her bed, the Tooth Fairy sneaking her tooth out and slipping a coin in beneath her pillow. Those last two images made Alice's eyes pop open again and stopped her happy thoughts because they reminded her of Darryl, coming into her room in the dark at night-time.

She shook her head clear of that thought, closed her eyes, and pictured herself giving Kitty the cat a cuddle, then pictured her favourite doll, Emily, who had the prettiest cornflower blue party dress, lacy socks and black shiny shoes. Emily's long blonde hair could be wound out long, or made short, using the wheel hidden under her dress.

She clicked the View-master in her mind and thought of a birthday cake shaped like a pretty bell, with the doll standing in the middle and the bell was her skirt. She loved that cake. *Click.* She saw the kids' adventures in her favourite books, the 'Enchanted Woods' or visiting their friends up the 'Magic Faraway Tree', and the dolly on a stick she had prized from the annual school fete.

Her tired eyes opened again with the realisation she had become Darryl's dolly, glued to a stick, her brother doing whatever he wanted to her, and she didn't know why. That made her think another bad thought, about her other plastic dolls Darryl had ruined—her cheaper hollow dolls, not like her one beautiful, very expensive Barbie doll. He liked the hollow ones, sticking Mum's sewing pins into their boobies.

Too tired to keep thinking up good pictures, her eyes wanted to go to sleep anyway. Hoping it would be a night where there was no night-time visit from Darryl, Alice's thoughts drifted away, with an acceptance that nothing was ever going to change.

Without Father's help, there was no hope—no one would save her and she was destined for hell.

Latchkey kids

For me, home was not the safe haven it was supposed to be during my childhood, coming home from school was not the happy occasion it was for other kids. I have tried to describe it as well as I could, to help you understand the feeling that I had as a ten-year-old, although I was only eight when Darryl first began to use me as his personal sex doll.

There were many bad days and also plenty of good days, when Mum was not out working. She was home as often as not, but as I turned that front door handle, I never knew if it would be one of those afternoons. I never knew whether Mum would be just about to head out when I got home, or if Darryl would corner me one way or another. This pattern of stalking and the threat of sexual abuse was repeated regularly until I was nearly twelve and was soon to get my first period.

Like so many other kids in the 1970s, at times, we were latchkey kids after school. In those days, Dad and Mum both needed to work to support the family. In the earlier years, Mum ran a sewing business from home, and Dad had a full-time office job in a government department in the city. Mostly Mum would work as a secretary in the suburbs or the city and get home later in the afternoon.

Latchkey kids are children between the ages of five and thirteen who come home (usually from school) to an empty house and are left unsupervised to fend for themselves for a few hours until a parent returns home from work. It was normal for kids like me in the Generation X era, as mums were expected to get out of the home and join the workforce to contribute to the household finances.

Darryl, as the eldest son in the family, had the ultimate responsibility or privilege to hold the front door key to our house.

According to a report from Darkness to Light (2017), 'one in seven incidents of sexual assault committed by adolescents occurs on school days between three and seven pm. Within this time frame, the peak of assaults occurs between three and four pm.'

I dreaded coming home from school. Our house offered no sanctuary, no safety. It didn't occur to me at the time that it wasn't normal for a child to feel that way about their home. I have since learnt that this sense of 'home being unsafe' is related to an overactive trauma response – getting stuck in fight, flight, fawn or freeze, and is common among survivors who experienced long-term abuse. The important right to feel safe in my home, was taken from me during those childhood years.

As an adult, gaining clarity about that made me feel the loss of childhood. I should have run happily through the front door, got a snack and relaxed, fought about which afternoon TV show we would watch, or begrudgingly got on with my afternoon chores and homework.

But no, it wasn't like that for me.

Family holidays

Throughout those years, the family holidays were held in Coffs Harbour. The Coffs Harbour holidays were the big annual family getaways where we kids weren't shipped off to stay with our grandparents. It was when Mum and Dad took two weeks off together at the same time as the family. We'd always book into holiday apartments in the cheaper streets a long walk from the beach.

Sometimes we had one apartment, or when Grandma joined us, we'd get a second apartment for her. One apartment was upstairs, and one was downstairs. Sometimes, the girls' room was upstairs; in other years, the girls' room was downstairs in the second bedroom of Grandma's apartment, and that meant the boys' room would be upstairs with Mum and Dad.

For Darryl, 'holiday sex' was his personal and distinct contribution to the fortnight.

In the middle of the night, I'd be shaken awake. I realised immediately it was Darryl and would pretend to be still asleep, though it never made any difference. Darryl knew he'd woken me up, and besides, for him there was no time to waste; he already had his pants off.

I could smell his musty boy genital smell. He'd sit with his shins pressed down on each side of my pillow, straddled over me across my chest. I would continue to pretend I was asleep, his scent filling my nostrils and a sickening feeling travelling into my chest and stomach. I'd lay with my eyes and lips firmly glued together; jaw clamped tight, teeth locked shut.

He would start by banging his erect penis against my mouth; then, he'd try to prise open my lips with his fingers to see my teeth. I hung in there, jaw clamped shut. *See!* I pleaded silently, *See! Look, I'm sleeping, sleeping!*

Not to be deterred, Darryl would make one of his signature moves. With one hand over my mouth, he'd use the other to pinch close my nostrils hard and long so that I'd eventually have to gulp air through my mouth. A sharp breath in through the mouth was all he needed to get what he wanted.

Having your mouth raped is not something any child should ever be subjected to. He'd cast his penis around in my mouth as long as he chose to while I lay prostrate, struggling to breathe, crushed and gagging. I also had to try to be silent, so I didn't break his rule about not letting anyone else know or there'll be trouble.

Then he'd be gone.

I'd be left to attempt to drift back to sleep, searching for the 'Sweet Dreams' Mum had sent me off to bed with. I could never find them again—they had always disappeared somewhere sweeter earlier in the night.

Quite often, I would lie with my eyes open as words ran through my mind repeatedly: *What did I do wrong. How come he's doing it to me?*

My inner voice, or what I have come to call my inner critic, would replay that question over and over in my mind. She'd do her best to keep the shame, self-blame and guilt suffocating me at any chance she could—for many years to come.

I have tried to comprehend what Darryl's thinking must have been like. Did he plan all of that when the lights were on, even at the family dinner table, anticipating the moment once darkness had arrived?

I pictured Darryl as he sat in bed, in his shortie pyjamas. He'd stand up, bare feet to the floor, cautious not to wake my little brother in the same room. He'd creep out across the notoriously creaky timber floorboards, up the hall, and past Mum and Dad's bedroom—Dad was a snorer so maybe that supported Darryl's mission. He'd open their apartment's front door and close it. Next was the tiled stairwell; he'd open Grandma's front door, and creep past her open bedroom door—she was also known to snore after taking her nightly Valium pills. Then, he'd work out which of the two beds in the girls' bedroom I was in.

By then, it didn't seem like he thought it was bad, apart from him telling me not to tell anyone. He had chosen me, and now I was dirty.

I was the bad girl. *Why did he pick me?*

My childhood between eight and eleven years old was a blur of frightening demands:

'Take off your clothes.'

'Take off your clothes but leave your school tie on.'

'Get on the bed.'

'Get on the floor.'

'Get in that room.'

'Be quiet!'

And the final instruction, threatened with teeth bared and nostrils flared: 'If you tell anyone, you'll be in big trouble!'

It was a blurred expanse of time, of feeling trapped and unsafe. Flashes of rooms, clocks ticking loudly, movement, hurting, pinching, prodding, touching, *urky* body smells, and fear permeated those years. Everything about it was dirty and nasty. Everything about it was wrong.

One morning, before school, I blurted out to Mum that I had a nightmare, and she looked up at me, so I continued with, 'The bogeyman comes into our room in the dark. He scares me'.

The bogeyman was a scary fictional character parents threatened kids with when they wanted good behaviour. They'd warn:

'Watch out! The bogeyman will get you.'

'That bogeyman does awful things to naughty children.'

'The bogeyman is coming!'

Mum laughed dismissively, turning her attention to the toast she was buttering and said, 'Oh Alice, don't be so silly. The bogeyman isn't real. Are you ready for school yet?' I didn't say another word, and I went to school that morning, and every other morning, like usual, like an ordinary, happy little girl from a regular happy family.

Resolve

At eleven, it dawned on me that it mightn't just be me going to hell if this kept on going.

I knew through the limited sex education stories shared at school about girls having periods, and reproduction. I knew that if I didn't stop Darryl now, I was destined for a very special place in hell, with a 'bastard' on board.

It's not something any young girl should need to be plotting, just as she is coming to understand there is a thing called a period and a monthly cycle, and babies were somehow involved with that cycle. The images the school education showed us gave a good enough hint that it had to do with Mums and Dads hugging, kissing and sitting down on their bed together, and I intuitively knew what Darryl was doing to me was the same thing.

On Thursday nights, I'd walk along with Mum doing the shopping, pushing a trolley stacked high with groceries up and down the supermarket aisles. I'd slow down as we passed by the sanitary pads and whatnot packages on the shelves, wondering briefly how you used them or how I would get them if I needed one.

The only other place I'd seen them was on the toilet cistern lid, looking out of place beside the crocheted toilet roll doll who smiled cheerily back at me. Tightly wrapped up in sheets of toilet paper, I guessed that the parcel belonged to Mum; and that she'd forgotten to take it with her to drop in the kitchen bin.

I concluded that with regards to all that womanly stuff and Darryl, it would be up to me to save myself: and I needed to stop Darryl before I got my period.

I found a firm resolve rise within me. I had to stop Darryl. No one else could. I said it over and over to myself. *I must stop him*. I had to do it, and I kept shaking my head *No more*, drawing on my courage like I had done that day when I asked Father for help.

I made no loud announcements, nor did I give violent push-back. There was no one moment where I stood up, put my hand out like a traffic cop in Darryl's face, and diplomatically stated, 'NO! Stop it. Don't you dare touch me again!' Instead, I utilised a more subtle, passive approach, engaged my instincts and the finely tuned sense of hypervigilance I had adopted by then.

Whenever I felt unsafe, and Darryl was coming near, I would spin away and move in the other direction lightning fast. He didn't know what to do about that; he didn't chase after me, so that worked.

I next came up with a plan to minimise the moments that I was open to danger.

My enjoyment of crafts had diminished long before then, unless I was with Mum or Grandma. I didn't sit and watch TV unless someone else was in the lounge already. I was a sitting duck inside the house if I was still, seated and alone.

My eleven-year-old motto became: *Stay Busy, Keep Clear*.

Rather than be left at home, I would ask if I could go to the library with Dad when he swapped his books over on a Wednesday evening, or offer to be Mum's helper for late-night shopping. When we were on our Coffs Harbour holiday, I'd happily be up before daybreak to go fishing on the lake with Dad.

Whether as a latchkey kid or even if a parent were at home, I'd go out into the street and ride one of the boy's scooters, do cartwheels and practice back arches on the front lawn, or be in the pool until dinnertime. Any outdoor activity was safe, just so long as I wasn't inside the house with Darryl.

I did everything possible to stay out of his way, making it as hard as possible for him to corner me again. I was hoping that somehow, I'd magically slip out of his mind.

I began to visualise feeling safe at home, imagined and pictured that he would forget about me and stop.

And then suddenly, he did.

2

Demystifying Sibling
Sexual Abuse

*The international media tends to represent child sexual
abuse as a problem of 'Stranger Danger', focusing on the
individualistic nature of sensational cases (Weatherred,
2015). The reality is rather different: most child sexual abuse
is carried out by people well known to the child and often
by other family members. Moreover, it is rarely reported
that these other family members may themselves be children;
indeed, it is likely that sibling sexual abuse—the sexual
abuse of children by their brothers or sisters—is the most
common form of intra-familial sexual abuse, estimated to
be up to three times as common as sexual abuse by a parent
(Krienert & Walsh, 2011; Stroebel et al., 2013). Nonetheless,
it remains under-researched and is the least studied form
of intra-familial child sexual abuse (Tener et al., 2020).*

EXTRACT FROM SIBLING SEXUAL ABUSE: A
KNOWLEDGE AND PRACTICE OVERVIEW,
S.ALLARDYCE & P. YATES, CENTRE OF EXPERTISE
ON CHILD SEXUAL ABUSE (JANUARY 2021)

When I began sourcing information for this book in 2019,
I was already aware that sibling sexual abuse (SSA) was
a topic that most people know very little about. It is almost
never even mentioned in everyday society. I soon found, however,

that even in scientific circles there was a scarcity of up-to-date information specifically focused on SSA. If child abuse in general is somewhat taboo in our culture, SSA felt to me as if it existed in an almost complete vacuum in terms of awareness and knowledge.

In my lifetime, I couldn't say I had seen any news stories at all in mainstream media that focused exclusively on SSA. I do recall on one single occasion seeing a movie that depicted an older teen brother abusing his younger sister in the afternoon before their mother came home. However, the vast majority of what I had seen shared on the topic, in news or in movies, was child sexual abuse: where it's an adult abusing a child. The only information I found about SSA came from purposefully searching for reports or stories on the web.

One article I came across in 2021 that mentioned sibling sexual abuse, featured Chris O'Connor, a former detective senior sergeant who'd dedicated his thirty-six-year career to protecting children from sexual abuse. Titled 'The last social taboo: how an unspeakable crime against children remains largely hidden', (ABC News 13 Nov 2021), it was focused mainly on the general topic of incest, but mentioned that 'older siblings were frequently involved in the incest cases he dealt with, but that was something most parents did not want to think about.' The article went on to raise the question: 'Where has an inquiry into intrafamilial sexual assault occurred?'— and provided a telling answer—'The answer is: it hasn't, and yet it's one of the most pervasive, soul-destroying and developmentally disaffecting types of crime that could ever be brought on a child.'

People shared this article across their social media feeds, the first time I had seen that happen with an article mentioning SSA, and I heard people speaking about it at womens' breakfasts I attended around that time. It was a beginning, and even though it was generally about incest, not solely about SSA, at least it would begin to raise peoples' awareness about the subject.

To bring the SSA taboo out into the light, I realised, we're going to need to increase public awareness one way or another. Dispelling myths by sharing definitions, facts, and recommendations that come through credible sources about the circumstances and extent of SSA is a start. I trust that whatever we do will improve the quality of conversations—perhaps even allowing for greater sensitivity towards those who have survived enough abuse already.

Before we dig around in the facts, findings and definitions related to demystifying sibling sexual abuse, I'm going to address two topics that people frequently bring up when I share my story. They used to upset me deeply, but I've finally learned not to take them personally, although I will admit it took some time and self-work.

It's just doctors and nurses

I recall one experience during a local womens' fundraising lunch, when a participant came up to introduce herself while I was making myself tea, waiting to listen to the keynote speaker. She slipped her business card under the saucer balanced on the palm of my hand and asked, 'What's the topic of your memoir?' She'd heard the event coordinator share the news that I was writing my story.

I responded, 'It's about sibling sexual abuse, it's my story, and I'm writing to speak up.'

She replied, whilst giving a little shake of her head and smiling simultaneously, 'Oh, your brother was playing doctors and nurses. He was only pretending to be an adult. Boys will be boys; he wouldn't have meant anything by it. You'll see on my card that I'm a healer if you'd ever like to talk.'

As soon as she opened her mouth to speak, I could tell that she was going to share an opinion with me. I was intrigued by what she said because I realised that this kind of response would probably not be isolated, in my journey of speaking about my experiences. I paused my tea bag dunking, not exactly shocked by the lack of acknowledgment of the sibling sexual abuse, given it's an awkward topic for many people, but with the feeling that I slipped into a kind of time warp.

Whilst neither of us physically shifted our feet or any other part of our bodies, I felt as if my body was tilting, rebounding away from her—the space between us stretching out in a slow-motion kind of way. I had heard her clearly say the words, then my hearing got a little buzzy, so the noise of the room dimmed, and my vision became misty, making me want to take a long blink or just let my eyes close a little while until she was gone. I could feel my heart beating like a drum in my chest, warming as it did sometimes when emotions arose. In the end, all I did was blink once, and then I came back to where I was in the room. I was OK. It was not about me.

I understand and fully appreciate when someone expresses their lack of understanding. However, was I hearing that I must have misinterpreted my brother's abuse? That's just a little wrong. I let out a heavy sigh, gave my tea bag one last dunk, swung it into the little tidy bin on the table, and replied, quite clearly, 'No. No, I don't think that was the case at all. They weren't games. I didn't have fun. It was sexual abuse.'

It was her turn to look slightly stunned before an awkward silence enveloped us. We turned simultaneously away from each other, scanning the room to see if there was anyone else to talk to, then thankfully we were being summoned to find our seats, ready for the keynote speaker to begin.

I don't really know what inspires people to have these opinions, perhaps partly it's the desire to avoid awkward or painful topics, leading to a cultural perception that it is all 'child's play'. I had read that 'the taboo goes as far back as the ancient Greeks' (Pasco,

A.H., 1995), and 'there was evidence that sibling sexual abuse had been somewhat romanticised in the past, mainly in Romantic literature' (Rowntree, M., 2007). Also, unfortunately, 'there is a popular misconception that sexual contact between siblings has been thought to contain innocent elements of age-appropriate sexual exploration, reflecting the belief that this 'exploration' is consensual, benign and without malice or harm' (Welfare, A, 2008).

That is a belief I have heard many people express publicly, despite it being incorrect, based on a lack of information or experience, and potentially very hurtful to victims and survivors. I know for a fact that I did not misunderstand, nor desire to try out my brother's 'exploration' of my mouth with his erect penis, whilst I was forcibly held immobile. That did not have an element of what is called playing doctors and nurses. Whatever the case, I do feel the reference to even age-appropriate sexual exploration as playing doctors and nurses needs changing; it's inappropriate, outdated and disrespectful of two honourable professions.

What made Darryl do it?

Over the years I have met many lines of curious enquiry from others, hoping to excuse my brother's unrelenting sexual predation:

'Oh, what happened to poor Darryl for him to have done that to you?'

'Did the priest bugger him?'

'What happened to your mum? To your dad? Were they abused?'

'Were you poor and had to share one bed so he couldn't help himself?'

'Was your mum abused by her father? Did she think it was normal family behaviour?'

'Did your dad or grandpop abuse Darryl, and that's why he did it to you?'

'Oh… So it's just like in *Game of Thrones*?'

I don't know, I've never watched Game of Thrones.

Maybe because the questions came so randomly, often indelicately, and always lacked authentic empathy for a little girl that her older brother had abused, I rarely could find words to reply to these comments. I would feel emotional triggers switch on; I wanted to disappear, and I felt alone all in the space of a moment. So, in writing, I have explored some of those questions—rather than leave them hanging unanswered forever.

What Darryl said

In answer to the concern for the abuser, I was informed by a close family member, that Darryl shared that he was never abused as a child, neither by a family member, a family friend nor by the parish priests. His reason for abusing me was that he was highly sexed.

Darryl's ex-first wife shared that he told her he gave up abusing me because, 'He said that you weren't that much of a goer'. Now 'goer' is an interesting term that I had to look up as I felt like I'd heard it as Aussie slang back in our teen days. The Urban Dictionary shared the derogatory meaning of 'goer' as being: 'an easy to get female or male. A girl that is easy and slutty. Someone who would have sex or perform sexual acts instantly.'

Very true Darryl. I'm glad that I made it onto his not much of a goer list.

Having chosen to inform myself more fully about the conditions surrounding sibling sexual abuse, I have found that I don't react as much to ill-thought-out enquiries, and don't feel like I want to disappear or be alone. Not taking things personally has been a powerful agreement to keep with myself.

Was it just me?

In my recovery journey, and in writing this memoir, I dug with curiosity into plenty of research, online support organisations' data and annual reports with the question 'Was it just me?' ringing in my ears. Even though I knew in my heart it wasn't; partly because by then I had heard first-hand about others' similar experiences; it took a lot for me to dislodge that question after having repeated it to myself for so long.

It was helpful and therapeutic to read whatever I could find about the topic, something I had not realised would be so beneficial to me in letting go of the misplaced guilt and self-blame. I soon saw that sibling sexual abuse was a far more common issue within our society than I had ever imagined.

Reading from reliable sources helped me find answers not only for myself. It has also supported me when I found myself in situations where others started asking me questions. I could pause and think about how I would best respond and know that the information I had available to share was relevant, honest, and not solely my opinion.

What is sibling sexual abuse?

It was confusing at first to read all the ever-changing different definitions and titles governments and organisations have come up with for the various forms of abuse. Even as an adult it has been difficult to access accurate information to understand clearly what happened. It made me curious about how confusing it must be for children seeking help to find the right avenue for support about SSA, not just sexual abuse. A big part of this problem is the common convention of lumping sibling sexual abuse in with all the other forms of abuse that exist, especially incest. I want to be as clear as possible here, to do my part in helping to break the taboos and fill the vacuum with the most accurate and useful information I can find.

I'll have to dive into some academic definitions here, so bear with me.

The idea of facts and definitions can be challenging for some, so they have been shortlisted to the top few I found helpful to me. You will find more detailed information in the Appendices at the end of the book. Some might choose to use this data as conversation starters: a conversation with yourself or with loved ones; a therapist; or a way to begin talking more about this kind of abuse in your community.

Definitions

Sibling sexual abuse has been defined as:

> 'sexual behaviour between siblings that is not age-appropriate, non-transitory and not motivated by developmentally appropriate curiosity' (Morrill, 2014).

If, in reading this, you require further clarity on what is not age-appropriate sexual behaviours, please refer to Appendix 1.

I learned that there are different forms of sibling sexual behaviours, including some that are considered not abusive, simply inappropriate; and others that are clearly defined as sibling sexual abuse.

It was enlightening to come across a report from the Centre of Expertise on Child Sexual Abuse which included these definitions:

'There are normal sexual interactions between siblings – behaviours between young siblings that exist within expected developmental norms. Then there are inappropriate or problematic sexual behaviours involving siblings – behaviours between siblings that fall outside developmental norms and may cause developmental harm to the children involved. The third description is that of sibling sexual abuse – behaviour that causes sexual, physical and emotional harm, including sexually abusive behaviour which involves violence' (Allardyce & Yates, 2022).

I have included in Appendix 2, a greater depth of descriptions of these different forms of sibling sexual behaviour.

I realised that the answer about what was and what wasn't sibling sexual abuse was something that I still needed to resolve. I had never felt comfortable asking anyone that question before. The characteristics and impact of Darryl's sexual behaviour was most definitely the third description—sibling sexual abuse.

In this mission of healthy inquiry, I became aware that it finally allowed me to find words to describe the feelings, emotions and experiences Young Alice suffered, but could never verbalise or even understand.

'Incest is a reprehensible form of abuse not just because it is cloaked in shame and stigma but because this type of sexual abuse, in particular, affects young victims by implicating and damaging their primary support system. This can be very confusing for children who have been taught to be wary of strangers but to trust in the family. Because they are in the beginning stages of developing their value systems and trust models, the betrayal of incest can be utterly confusing, if not permanently damaging, to a child's delicate psyche' (Babbell, 2013).

Further, the relational trauma of child and sibling sexual abuse leads to:

'Significant loss of trust in others and increased anger, hurt, and confusion about their family relationships. Changes in beliefs about the safety of close relationships in general, and negative views of the self in relation to others' (Kluft, 2011).

As I read more about the impacts of this kind of abuse, the 'Aha!' moments became more frequent and more comforting. The following, regarding the sense of betrayal the trauma of child and sibling sexual abuse encompasses, left me in tears:

'[It is a] unique hurt associated with violation by those who have a basic obligation and duty to protect and nurture. This extends to those who refuse to believe or help the victim, adding to the victim's traumatisation' (Freyd 1996).

I was gaining much greater insight into the unhelpful and hurtful reactions of those I had disclosed to, as I began to understand the involvement of family and society leaving a victim to carry misplaced shame, guilt and self-blame.

Sibling sexual abuse is not limited to certain types of families. I can only assume that many families do not believe it could happen in their home, and it can go on for a long time in many households before parents are made aware of the issue. Sadly, some parents don't take appropriate action, even when they're made aware of the problem.

The following is a convincing summary of how the conditions were ripe for sibling sexual abuse to occur in my family home:

'Sibling sexual abuse victims often live within dysfunctional family environments that subtly foster incestuous behaviours, and are not conducive to disclosing the secret. Sibling incest appears more likely to occur in large families and is characterised by physical and emotional violence, marital discord, explicit and implicit sexual tensions, and blurred intrafamilial boundaries. Emotionally and/or physically absent parents may empower older siblings to assume parental roles. In short, these families are chaotic and unlikely to recognise the significance of behaviours occurring between siblings. If sexual behaviours are noticed, they are likely to be minimised and misinterpreted as a normal aspect of childhood development. Lack of adequate parental supervision provides perpetrators with ongoing opportunities to offend, and protects the secret, leaving the victim vulnerable to continuing abuse' (Ballantine and Soine, 2012).

I cannot count the number of times my inner alarm bells would trigger at the sound of our Mum bustling around, gathering up her handbag:

'I'm just going shopping.'

'I'm going to be a few hours.'

'I'm going to get my hair done.'

'I'm going for my weigh-in at Weight Watchers.'

The worst part of those statements was the instructions that followed. I'd wait, my breath held because, yes, here it comes. It always did, no matter what I'd hoped. Holding up her pointer finger, wagging it at her audience with eyebrows narrowed, Mum would say, 'Now, you be good. Darryl's in charge.'

Saint Darryl would look on, lips pursed, a slight nod, raising his eyebrows in earnest, faked innocent agreement. 'You do whatever Darryl tells you, or there WILL be trouble.'

That sentence drained all the warmth out of me and left nothing but goosebumps and a jangly pulse.

Protected by the silence, characteristic of child sexual abuse generally, adolescent abusers learn they can get away with it.

This was certainly the case in my childhood home, and I have wondered, sceptical: 'Where were Mum and Dad, and how could they not have seen or heard anything? Over those almost five years when at the very minimum one of their children was being regularly sexually abused, one or both of my parents must surely have smelled a rat but didn't think to act.'

Mum and Dad's bedroom and the girls' bedroom sat side-by-side, across the house's front wall, with windows overlooking a standard lawn and garden beds that were the same as all the other neighbours in the street. The girls' bedroom I slept in was just four footsteps, door to door to Mum and Dad's bedroom door. My bedroom shared a common internal wall with my parent's bedroom. We slept with our bedroom doors open at night. Yet,

Darryl, whose bedroom was down at the back of the house, planned and snuck past our parents' bedroom door to get to my bedroom regularly without ever being caught.

> 'Due to the mostly close relationship and physical proximity between siblings, sibling sexual abuse is considered an opportunistic form of abuse… Abused siblings often do not disclose being abused due, among other things, to fear of not being believed, fear of upsetting parents, or confusion over their role in the abuse' (Stathopoulos, 2012).

I recall early one Sunday evening, close to the time the abuse ended, Mum knocking at my closed bedroom door not long before dinnertime. The aroma of Mum's signature beef casserole, my most unfavourite meal of the week with its mushy stringy meat and fat turned to jelly, filled the house with a ready-to-serve or be-burned intensity! At that precise moment, Darryl had me pressed against the other side of the door rubbing his genitals against my nightie. I'd not long before that had my bath.

With a hint of hesitant curiosity in her voice, Mum enquired, 'What are you kids up to?'

'We're just playing a game, Mum, ha-ha. We'll be out in a minute, ha-ha,' Darryl responded light-heartedly, all innocence, his eyes narrowed, nose flared and darkly confident in his power.

There were no further questions. No attempt to turn the door handle. It was time to get dinner on the table. I listened in silence as her slippered footsteps fell away from the door heading back to her duties in the kitchen, past the TV blaring in the loungeroom, where the rest of the family were laughing uproariously at the antics of whatever show they had on.

It didn't matter where the family was; at home, at my grandma's place, my great-aunt's when Mum and Dad were helping with her garden tidy up, or in our holiday apartments at Coffs Harbour; we would be left to our own devices, with one instruction: *Darryl's in charge.* He would preen about being reliable and trustworthy in front of Mum, but as the front door closed, his mocking eyes would shift to the faces that had just had Mum's finger pointing at them. Not long after that, he would come and find his prey.

For my parents' part, I would like to believe that a lack of presence, their own childhood conditioning, and their naivety kept them ignorant of the extent of abuse in their household.

'Easy access to siblings makes it more likely that an adolescent abuser (who can be just as predatory as adult abusers) will choose someone within the household. Their abuse is often well-planned and thought out' (Morin, 2022).

The latch-key kid generation I was a part of was like serving a little mouse up on a platter to a cunning cat. Mindful, of course, that cats don't like to eat their prey; they prefer to stalk and play with them a little first. There was plenty of time for the cunning cat to play with his little mouse in the hours after school and before a parent arrived home by around five or six pm.

Thankfully, the latch-key kids became a bygone era after my generation. A few decades of children were saved from being required to be independent before they were ready.

I read that with the increase in after-school care programs, by 2011 the number of kids left alone dropped by forty percent. What troubled me throughout the time of writing was the effect that COVID-19 lockdowns and changes to how organisations operated may have on school-aged children.

One news report in the United States shared that millions of children had become latch-key kids in 2020, as after-school programs shut their doors, and the remaining programs raised the prices or reduced available spaces. Dr Lynette Fraga, CEO of Child Care Aware, told the TODAY show that:

'7.7 million children in 2020 who don't have access to care and are left alone and unsupervised is undoubtedly a concern' (Kait Hanson, Source: TODAY, 15 Nov 2021).

Darryl came back for more

Life had carried on with no further episodes of stalking or abuse since I'd thrown Darryl off the scent at age eleven, just before I got my period. Then, when I turned fourteen, the routine of cat-and-mouse and the threat of abuse from Darryl returned.

I remember my stomach dropping and my scalp prickling with electricity as my mind fired off warning alarms at me one afternoon. I walked in the front door after school into the front hallway and paused; I knew something was about to happen. I could sense that old danger of Darryl's troll-like presence lurking out of sight, but close by—ready to pounce.

At the end of the hallway to the left was still the girls' shared bedroom. To the right was the lounge room that now led to a new, long family room and into the new kitchen. Darryl wasn't standing in the hallway like he used to. This time, he was waiting for me around the corner, standing in the dim light halfway across the loungeroom floor.

The lounge had become the darkest room of the house, no matter what time of day it was. After our renovations, the outside window didn't get any sunlight now. It was shadowed by a long carport for Dad's boat and car to park under cover. As my eyes adjusted from the bright afternoon sun outside, I saw Darryl standing in the dark.

I scoped the room for possibilities even before he said anything. I saw that I couldn't get to the door at the other side of the lounge room without passing him so that escape route was blocked. I could only turn back to my bedroom. I knew if I showed weakness and faltered in indecision over which path to take, he'd home in. I must have done so, or he was going to home in no matter what, because he walked fast towards me, touching the front of his body up against the front of mine.

With a strangely upbeat tone, he delivered a suggestion to which he anticipated I'd respond with an equally enthusiastic yes. With big eager eyes, he asked, 'Do you want to start playing those games we used to play, huh? Huh? Do you...?'

Every muscle tensed; I attempted a tight smile and retorted, as if I had no idea what he was talking about, 'Ha ha. What do you mean, umm... what, murder in the dark? No way!'

Using my old strategy, I spun back to my bedroom and closed the door on him, annoyed that I was starving for an afternoon snack. *What an arsehole!*

That happened every afternoon for a week. No one could ever say he wasn't determined or persistent. It would be the same question; I'd give the same answer, make the same dash to the bedroom and slam the same door closed. Each afternoon I would stand inside my bedroom door with my back to it to listen for sounds that he was closing in. He didn't press the issue, so I'd pull down the flap of my desk on top of my clothes drawers, pick up my chair, and place it in the short floor space that was mine, between the end of my sister's bed and the desk. I'd sit alone in my warm sunlit room and do my homework, vigilant to every tiny sound in the house. The lack of safety and the feeling that danger was present just outside my flimsy door was back.

I became acutely aware of Darryl's presence during dinner and family time. I knew he had much more tenacity than to give up after one week's failure. I varied my afternoon routine again. Without telling anyone, I made my return time home from school more irregular, so he didn't know what time of day I would be home. I'd go to the school library, not coming home until later, closer to Mum's train arriving at the station from work.

When I did come home, thinking maybe it was safe again, he was like an irritating fly. I'd hear him before I met him on my way to the kitchen. I'd divert my path, go to my room, wait until I heard the others come home and knew it was safe to come out.

This time around there was a shroud of moodiness about him, and I feared what new horrors he might have on his mind. It was as though Darryl disrupted the very air around him with a dark, seething bitterness.

He was living life by his motto now that rules were meant to be broken. He showed disrespect and disdain for Mum and Dad to them directly, and about them when they were not around. His face always looked red with acne. I knew that he had been having unsuccessful attempts, one after another, at finding a girlfriend who'd stay with him before they moved on to one of his school mates.

Even if Darryl had not considered his plan to reinitiate the abuse, our relationship was distant, if it's possible to be distant whilst living in the same house. I recall that I didn't initiate conversation with Darryl. I don't think I pieced that together with the earlier abuse; it was just that as a fourteen-year-old girl, being near him felt unsafe and risky, in a treading-on-eggshells kind of way.

Then, just as he had years before, Darryl appeared to lose interest in the chase. I couldn't drop my guard because I honestly didn't know if it was for good. If he'd decided once already that we might 'play those games we used to', there was a good chance it wasn't over yet. I didn't particularly appreciate that my desk was positioned just inside my bedroom door, viewable through the house from the back door. So, I started working at my desk with my door closed to ensure he'd not spot me and remember to re-initiate his attacks again.

It was only two weeks before Darryl began to ignore my closed door. He'd push it open and walk past me and sit on the floor beside or on my bed just to the right of my chair, so he was facing the bedroom door that I noted thankfully, he'd left open. Not that anyone was there, but at least I had a place to run to. He wouldn't say anything; he just sat there, a malevolent presence begging for a reaction.

I pretended everything was normal and looked at my home-work as if it was the most fascinating thing I'd ever read. Time went tick-tock slow; it was so distressing. I took quiet breaths to minimise noise and sat stone still, just my pen moving on paper, hoping to disappear—and then suddenly, without a word, he would get up and walk out.

That happened sporadically for a few months, and I could feel I was growing less distressed by it over time; I was getting angry instead. I was sick of feeling like stalked prey.

On the last occasion, he came in and sprawled across my bed. I could see him in my peripheral vision, my eyes trained on my homework, thinking, *piss off, will you.* I could see him fumbling with his pants and thought: *You've got to be kidding me; no way!* He finally managed to unzip his fly like one of those ugly, sloppy drunks I'd seen in some movies and slurred, 'I'm going to show you my penis.'

Enough! I stood up abruptly and knocked my chair over, crashing it into the end of my sister's bed. I loathed him and felt sorry for him; at the same time, I was disgusted and fed up. He looked comically surprised and was trying to get his bearings, wondering what I was doing. This was all in a matter of seconds, but they were seconds that held a sense of clarity and determination for me.

I could feel and hear a growl rising in my throat; I looked him directly in the eyes and spat out the words, 'Well, don't! Just don't! You make me feel sick!' and walked out of the room, slamming the bedroom door behind me.

As things go, thankfully, that final incident coincided with Darryl's escalation of disgracing himself and the family with drunken episodes.

Away from home, Darryl was that guy at every teenage party who'd end up the most shit-faced messy drunk out of all the drunks. He would end most parties with his pants off, waving his flaccid penis around with his hand, showing it off to everyone, offering it to the girls, and simultaneously running too fast for drunk legs. When his antics began, I would watch out of the corner of my eye from the circle I would be talking or dancing in. It was like he'd run and get shorter and shorter in height until he'd stumble into a garden, shoot back up again, head in another direction, fall down, back up and off he'd go in another direction.

His equally drunk friends would seek me out and appeal to me, their eyes full of concern, yet laughing at the spectacle, 'You need to do something about Dazza, Alice.'

'Do what? Help him back into his pants? Why don't you call Mum and Dad?'

He was a self-destructive disgrace, and I didn't want to go anywhere near him. Anyway, I knew those episodes always ended reasonably quickly. As a rule, and to everyone's relief, the penis-flashing performance ended with him passing out in a garden bed, from which at last he didn't get back up again. His antics became a hazy footnote of yet another weekend party where Dazza was plastered, wasted, hammered, drunk.

His fall from family grace became the talk of the street as his inebriation worsened.

If neighbours didn't find him passed out in the gutter, he'd be kicked awake by Mum or Dad at the bottom of the front steps, with angry hisses telling him to get up off the concrete and into the house before the neighbours saw.

The climax of his unacceptable behaviour came one afternoon when Darryl, reclining in a crumpled mess across the single bed in his room, was telling Mum he was sick and tired of her telling him what to do.

The house felt scary, and there was a new weight of unease at the bottom of my stomach as the moment unfolded. From where I was sitting in the family room, across from his bedroom door, I watched as, much to Mum's surprise, he lashed his hand out and slapped her across the face. For good measure, he also shouted, 'F**k off, you bitch!' Dad, standing with his arms crossed, giving Mum moral support from inside the doorway, launched himself across the room. He pulled Mum from harm's reach and roared down at Darryl, shoulders heaving: 'THAT'S ENOUGH.'

The next day Darryl came home from work to find his bedroom packed into a few black garbage bags at the bottom of the front steps. His collection of porn mags and half-empty spirit bottles wrapped in crinkled and undignified plastic. I was elated: he was gone, and I felt safe in my family home for the first time since I was eight.

My brother never touched my body again.

Use your instincts

When I started to research this book, I wanted to understand what signs I may have been exhibiting during the years of Darryl's abuse that would have raised concerns with parents or adults that something was not quite right for me at home. My childhood was clearly not normal, and so I wondered: *What part of what I remember was just me being a normal kid, and what was altered emotions or behaviours I experienced due to the abuse?* It was a search to see whether any of the signs resonated with my own experience of childhood, and they did.

I typed 'Signs of sexual abuse in children and teenagers' into a Google search, and plenty of information was available. One, an Australian parenting website called raisingchildren.net.au, set out helpful material; beginning with changes in emotions and behaviours; through to physical signs that an adult may notice in either a child or a teen.

As a child, some signs for me were quietness, crying for no apparent reason, never having friends around, and preferring to be alone at lunchtime at school. I had nightmares during the abuse and long afterwards, and that 'school day sick-bed lounge' routine with my sore tummy or head was a regular occurrence.

As a teen, behaviours fluctuated between incredible shyness and forcing myself to fit in—inadvertently putting myself at risk, both socially and sexually. I hung around with older kids mostly, and them being at a later stage of maturity, and sexual exploration, it made me often stand out as a next best option to wandering male eyes when all the hot girls were already making out with one guy or another. On many occasions, I'd find myself practicing similar escape tactics to those I'd used to avoid Darryl. Then I found drinking helpful to try to fit in more. My inhibitions would dissolve with the alcohol, and I'd put myself at risk, waking the next day trying to piece together the night before, and shower myself in guilt and self-blame talk.

I didn't want any boy touching my body, but sometimes when I got cornered I just froze.

It didn't matter that I had plenty of people around me, I felt alone.

I hadn't thought to search for signs before. It was helpful information to understand my own experience—and make me more cognisant of what I could notice in a child or teenager now.

One recommendation for adults that stood out to me was to 'use your instincts'. No, we don't necessarily need to go through a checklist of emotional, behavioural and physical signs. The advice to use your instincts struck a chord with me. The search made me see clearly that the adult guardians of my young life had their instincts and awareness dialled down to zero, in terms of what was going on in our family home.

I let out a heavy sigh and again shook my head in disgust at the injustice of abuse in any innocent child's life.

Where does responsibility lie?

In my opinion, there is so much opportunity in the education of parents and the abuser, now referred to in intervention language as "the person who caused harm".

Imagine a world where we would never have something as terrible as a child being abused in any way in the sanctuary of their childhood home.

Based on my own experience, making prevention the responsibility of the younger child victim, or "the person who is harmed", to stop a coercive and forceful older brother is like putting the little mouse in charge of telling the cunning cat, 'Please stop preying on me, or playing with me like that,' as whomp, down comes that cat's hefty paw once again.

What is the motivation behind the abuser's behaviours? What is the abuser planning; the thoughts just before it happens? There must be one or more thoughts in the abuser's head that seed the idea that their sibling is going to be their personal sexual plaything.

Validation

Much of what I learned in reading the reports and papers I was provided with or found through credible websites has helped me understand more about what I'd experienced and felt internally in response to the abuse. It also gave me validation. That was not the original goal of my book, however in the process of researching, I heard others speak of it, and read case studies about survivors' need for validation—to be heard and be seen. I wondered to myself if that is what this writing is about? Am I seeking to be heard and seen? I believe the answer must be a yes. The validation I felt was an essential step towards beginning to heal all that had been harmed, it helped me boost my self-identity, self-confidence and self-worth, and to strengthen my voice to speak out for myself and others.

3

The Problem with Disclosure

Within the context of abuse, sibling relationships make it possible for behaviours to be frequent and unrestrained and may make it difficult for younger siblings to tell anyone about abuse or have confidence that they will be believed.

FONTES, L. & PLUMMER, C. (2010)

Disclosure is when a victim or survivor reports their abuse to another person. They may describe in detail, indicate indirectly, or hint at the abuse. Or, as in my case, ask a trusted community member for help.

This can be incredibly difficult for children, young people and even adults to do during their abuse, or even after it ends. It is one of the most significant dilemmas victims and survivors face, and it is interesting to note before proceeding that 'children rarely lie about or imagine sexual assault. In 98% of cases, their statements are found to be true' (Dympna House, 1990).

In some cases, the affected people never feel able to tell anyone about what happened, or they allow many years to pass as they wait for the right moment. However, delayed disclosure has long-lasting and far-reaching effects on the abused.

'A study of seventeen women who had experienced abuse at the hands of their brothers indicated that those who were given the opportunity to disclose to their parents and found support from them were less burdened with post-traumatic stress disorder (PTSD) symptoms. In the same study, three sisters were not given the opportunity, or had the opportunity closed off by parents who did not want to hear about the abuse. The silencing of these women had a substantial impact upon the continuation of their severe symptoms and progress in recovery' (Welfare, 2010).

'Many children who are victims of sexual abuse do not report or disclose the abuse when it occurs. Due to the hidden nature and secrecy of sibling sexual abuse, the responsibility to end it by means of disclosure almost always falls upon the victim or adult survivor. In relation to sibling sexual abuse, it is often excused by parents as normal behaviour, as just kids being kids. As such, the symptoms of this form of abuse go undetected, and its devastating effects on the victim are often ignored' (Hatch & Hayman-White, (2001) & Welfare, (2010)).

The feeling of sinfulness and confusion I experienced from the way Darryl mistreated me, and from my body being involved in that sin, constantly played on my mind in the years the abuse occurred. It was those overwhelming feelings I believe that led to me find the resolve to ask for help.

Whether in a classroom, outside eating lunch, or playing with my friends on the school playground, I pictured scenarios of enlisting Father's help because I felt he could make Darryl stop his sinful ways.

Unfortunately, I hadn't foreseen the error in my ways in that first disclosure. I chose the only person I trusted to help me – the parish priest. The error was that I asked for Father's help during the sacrament of confession. That's where I went wrong! I didn't see it then, but it was obvious looking back on it as an adult.

Until as late as 2022, Catholic priests were not permitted to break the seal of confession when Australia's Royal Commission into Institutional Responses to Child Sexual Abuse recommended that religious confessions should not be exempt from the obligation to report abuse, where it constituted a criminal offence. They determined that the crime of sexual abuse of children is so serious that no one can be exempted.

The early pushback I read in response to that announcement came from interviewed priests' perspectives: That no-one would ever share that they had abused a child if that reporting were mandatory.

To be honest, I can't picture Darryl ever confessing to Father either. Still, I feel the missing element here is considering not the abuser's reticence, but the dilemma of a child who has experienced the abuse, asking for a priest's help. In this case, the argument that no one would confess such things is completely invalid.

Looking back at my past, I could not put my finger on any other opportunity, other than confession, where Father would have made himself available for me to ask for his help without me getting into trouble for bothering him, or feeling at risk of being overheard or interrupted.

I'd hate to think how many children felt the same thing I did. I am sure there were others who felt they needed that help from a trusted community member, and their hope died as mine did, leaving them feeling alone and unsupported.

The priest was a responsible adult man, and the so-called parish leader. He had as many other choices as any other responsible adult would have after receiving that disclosure from a child. He could easily have chosen to come up with a solution to help a little girl in his parish. He could have taken a responsible stance and devised a way to stop it from happening. He could have promoted the idea of the school running an education session for parents, or initiated boys' group conversations about what's right and wrong. I could think of many options here, but I won't get us lost in that rabbit warren.

It's not excusable for any adult to refuse to help a child who has risked asking for their help—so that someone will stop having sex with them.

Barriers to disclosure

The most common barriers that prevent or make it difficult for children to disclose sibling sexual abuse are varied. From my reading, I found that disclosure to parents may be affected by the following:

- 'a child's relationship and position within the family;
- awareness of the hurt and embarrassment a disclosure may produce;
- concern over protecting the feelings of parents from the offending sibling's actions' (Caffaro & Conn-Caffaro, 2005);
- 'lack of 'emotional closeness and affection' in the relationship between the victim and his or her parents' (Hatch, J. (2005);
- 'fear of authority, or getting into trouble either from a parent, teacher (or priest, in my case) and uncertainty

of the response and consequences of their disclosure'
(Crisma et al., 2004).

You'd think the Catholic faith was all about the light and love
of God, but from my recollection, it was much the opposite. As a
child of the faith, I was constantly instructed in sin.

'Don't do that! It's a sin.'

'It's a sin to use that word!'

'Only sinners do that.'

When I look back, living as a Catholic child felt like a constant
game of dodging guilt.

Our family elders passed down the Catholic faith, with Grandma, a strict believer in her religion. It was rare in the 1970s, but
I had to wear a white lace veil over my hair before walking onto
the church grounds when we kids stayed with her in Botany.
Thankfully, I only wore it when we stayed with her and not back
home at our parish church, where I would almost certainly have
been ridiculed by the other kids attending Sunday Mass. On our
knees on Grandma's living room carpet, all the kids would form
a circle with Grandma, heads bowed, and say our evening prayers
as we worked our little fingers around the rosary beads to count
down the blessings until we were done.

I remember standing roadside once with Grandma for hours
as we waited, and then caught a glimpse of the Pope driving past
in his cavalcade in Mascot. He was sitting in a big convertible
with the roof down. It was a standout, breathtaking moment, and
I remember feeling blessed. It also made Grandma very happy. She
was so delighted, she shouted each of us a takeaway KFC meal from
around the corner later that afternoon. It was a memorable day!

The Sacraments were also huge affairs and punctuated our
childhood regularly. For special days like our Holy Communion,
there were little white dresses with veils to be worn, and tables

full of fairy bread, toffees, and chocolate crackles afterwards to celebrate. It wasn't all hellfire and brimstone!

A good parish family would invite the parish priest for a barbecue lunch after church on Sunday, and it was an honour for the priest to say yes to our offer, over some other family.

We must have been a good Catholic family, or the priest liked Dad's steaks or Mum's potato salad and dessert, because he came to our place a lot. I'm not talking about Father whom I asked for help from; he never got an invitation. It was the younger junior priests that Mum would invite around. After lunch, ready for playtime in the pool with all the family, the priest would appear near naked out of his black shirt, white collar, long black trousers and shiny shoes, wearing only his baggy ill-fitting budgie smuggler swimmers. He'd energetically romp about, all pale-skinned and dark-furred, laughing away with the rest of us.

As a child of a good Catholic family, never, ever, in my wildest dreams would I have told my Mum or Dad, nor my Grandma, what my brother did. None of them ever approached me asking a question that would have supported that sharing.

To my young mind, only God could help with something as grave a sin as this. Grave sins could be varied, like not telling my grandma I didn't eat her burnt sausage that I'd hidden in my skirt pocket whilst she fussed over dessert. For much of my childhood the risk of going to hell felt like only a burnt sausage or night-time visitation from my brother away.

From that moment in confession and well into adulthood, my inner critic voice was busy running the soundtrack in my head, with variations on the same theme: *It must have been your fault because you didn't stop it. Father said that you had to stop it.* Even though I eventually stopped Darryl, it didn't stop the voice from telling me I was to blame, for much longer than I needed to be reminded of that message.

'Disclosure can also be affected through concern for the abusive sibling. Many victims and survivors may be reluctant to disclose their abuse because of:

- an incongruous sense of unease about their sibling being reprimanded;
- their innate love for their abusive sibling and concern they will create trouble for them if they tell;
- fear of the consequences of the disclosure, such as concern that the sibling would be banished, or the police would become involved;
- a desire to maintain the family unit and its status quo, regardless of the frightening abuse they suffer' (Stathopoulos, 2012).

'Directions and threats from the abusive sibling are another means of prevention:

- the abusive sibling may threaten their victim with retribution through violence or by implying the victim was complicit;
- shame and guilt are often enough to keep the abused sibling quiet' (Caffaro & Conn-Caffaro, 2005);
- 'as the abusive and abused siblings live in the same environment, threats are experienced as being inescapable;
- the requirement to remain quiet is often an additional source of pain for the victims' (McVeigh, M. J. (2003).

I personally experienced all of the above. Darryl approached every moment of the sexual abuse with purpose and power!

As I read each article or case study, any confusion I had about what happened to me was put to rest. Whilst some of the obstacles to disclosure didn't relate to my circumstances, I found it interesting to try to understand the experience of others beyond my situation.

> 'Confused emotions serve as yet another obstacle
> to disclosure. The abuse may be experienced as a
> nurturing element for the abused sibling, such as a
> sensation of intimacy or closeness, or feeling special
> or worthy of attention. This dynamic appears in
> many types of child sexual abuse and is why a victim
> may appear compliant and present little evidence
> of violence. One participant in a study of forty-one
> sexually abused young people was uncertain that what
> her brother had done constituted abuse, since the
> brother always pretended nothing happened'
> (Crisma et al., 2004).

Investigating all these barriers to disclosure helped me to dislodge years of self-blame and doubt about why I held my silence as a child, and felt it was not an option to ask my parents for help.

Lost and foggy memory

The most common barriers that prevent or make it difficult for children to disclose sibling sexual abuse are varied.

From my reading I found another considerable barrier to disclosure and asking for help is a 'lost' or 'foggy' memory blurring the events.

I'm confident I have purposefully suppressed plenty of my abuse experiences, given how they have randomly risen to the surface over the years. When they do surface I often see tiny flickers of an event, or a bad dream will be that little bit different to other bad dreams—and I know it's telling me something.

I recall the rooms, the ceilings, windows, wallpaper, carpet colour and texture, and the times of day within those rooms. I also remember that it always felt as if whatever room I was being abused in had somehow become separated from the rest of the planet—there was a sense of silence outside of the door, away from what was going on where I was, like no one was there—even if they were just through the door in another room. How could that be in such a large family? Where was everybody else?

I won't go into the details of what happened here. However, there is one memory I will share of what was happening around me, taking my focus off what was happening to me.

We were at my old Aunt Phyllis' house, my grandma's sister. The family was there to do a garden tidy-up on a Saturday. Mum and Dad were out the back waist-deep in weeds, with my aunt loving having the family there to talk to. I recall that at least Darryl and I were there to help for the day, along with my parents.

I can still hear Darryl cheerfully yelling to Mum that he and I would clean the loungeroom, so she could keep going with the weeding. I recall looking from the big doorway across at Aunty Phyllis' cluttered lounge, taking in the whole room, then hearing the big brass key locking the door from the inside. I remember focusing on my aunt's long deep antique lounge chair that faced the door and the mantlepiece. Smelly, old, dusty crochet rugs were strewn over it, I recall the bumpy feel of their wool on my bare back, and my pants not fully pulled off but down around my ankles, stopped by my shoes. I see the dust angels lit up by the sun on a dirty, round high window with the lead lines between the glass sections. The only sound in the room a loud ticking of the big clock on the mantelpiece. I watched how slowly the clock hand moved, one line at a time because I was staring at the clock thinking how loud it was and how quiet the world was outside.

That was just one day at my Aunt's house during a family spring clean.

No one came to check. No one doubted Darryl's word because he was such a good helper. Now I wonder why no one questioned why the room wasn't any less dusty than it was when we arrived that morning. I don't recall getting into trouble for not doing the work. Maybe we did do it afterwards, or maybe Darryl did, I don't remember. Perhaps it'd been a challenging and hot day in the garden, Aunt Phyllis had used up all her words on Mum and Dad, and everyone just wanted to go home for dinner or a cold beer.

Here, another survivor shares how lost or foggy memory felt to her:

'It's very cloudy to me. I was almost doubting myself. Even as I'm telling you, it seems like it was no big deal. But it stands out in my mind. I remember the feeling surrounding it, the dirty, bleh, horrible feeling surrounding it' (Mate, 2019).

Lost and foggy memory is said to be a common symptom of trauma. In essence, it is a protective mechanism, especially regarding children. We don't keep a firm memory of what happened or when it happened because it was traumatic.

There are plenty of matters regarding sibling sexual abuse that need to be addressed and spoken more about in our society, and these next words broke my heart when I read them. These two points Mary Stathopoulos shared in her report 'Sibling Sexual Abuse' for the Australian Institute of Family Studies are conversation starters at the very least:

'Families might accept that something has occurred between a brother and a sister, but give no credibility to the sister's protest that what occurred was forceful, and/or involved the brother making her available to his friends or cousins as may sometimes also be the case. If, and when disclosure by a child does take place, or a parent discovers sexual activity between siblings, it is often dismissed as inappropriate play. It is swept under the rug, not discussed, or is denied. In the latter, often, the abuse is minimised or denied because of the societal shame associated with sibling sexual abuse' (Stathopoulos, 2012).

Strong, clear words like that have power, and can be used to shape change: they certainly affected me deeply when I read them. Similarly, when I came across Stuart Allardyce and Peter Yates' paper, 'Abuse at the Heart of the Family: The Challenges and Complexities of Sibling Sexual Abuse', a more current report that a research connection shared with me: it felt like the rays of early morning sunlight lighting up a garden.

'Sibling sexual abuse must be understood as a problem of and for the family as a whole, and not just a problem for or about an individual child. The family as a whole needs to be involved in any intervention plan, and the strengths of the family – and potentially their community – must be harnessed in order to help them move on from harm' (Allardyce & Yates, 2022).

This may seem obvious to you, but as a child in these difficult circumstances, or a family member dealing with all the problems of life and the shame and secrecy associated with SSA, it is not so clear. There are often significant issues related to lack of communication skills that surround a family affected by sibling sexual abuse. For families such as these, this seems like an incredibly powerful exercise to work through together. What a brave family it would be that embraces such an opportunity for change, as models of what is possible now and in the future.

I was busy reaching for freedom

Estimates suggest that between 30–80% of child sexual abuse victims do not disclose before adulthood.
RAMONA ALLAGIA (2004) AS CITED IN BRAVEHEARTS, N.D.

As I ventured, dodging and weaving my way through adolescence, I eventually got to slip out of my old social circle. Until that time, I had mostly spent time with Darryl's schoolmates and a handful of girls we hung out with, always the same old crowd doing the same old things. I left school after Year Ten to go to business college and learn secretarial skills, which opened a new world to me.

Making that change gave me a city commute and a different uniform to that of a high school teen, along with a steep learning curve, and plenty of exams for shorthand, typing and other skills of the secretarial trade. It also was a fast track to earn an income and have a more independent life. One other girl commuted from my town, so we connected as friends, chatting all the way into the city and back on the red rattler train. We spent a lot of time together, as college homework was manageable during the week, and so weekends were mostly about lying in the sun in bikinis, baking ourselves as brown as our skin could go and dancing at night.

It was a good feeling to have some freedom, but it wasn't

without its challenges and dangers. On the dance floor we'd dodge the gropes of men, mostly in their twenties I thought at the time, although looking back there were many also in their thirties and forties. Covering each other's backs when a guy was making his move, we knew when it was time to make our safe escape to the taxi rank and home.

One weekend my girlfriend and I had been sitting in our bikinis, taking a break from sunbaking out by her pool. Our two kitchen chairs pushed back from the table, with our legs stretched out to rest our feet on the table edge, we were lunching on our staple diet of Cruskit biscuits with butter and Vegemite, and cold bottles of Diet Coke when my friend's big sister came in with her boyfriend—and someone new.

Adorned in only King-Gee shorts, tanned with wavy brown hair nearly to his shoulders and a beard attempting to find some form, this guy walked around the other side of the table to pour a glass of water from the tap for himself. There was something about him I liked; beyond his outward good looks he seemed different in some way. I tried not to let him see me checking him out, but I saw him sneaking glances at me, so I guess he saw me watching him as well!

At their friend's backyard twenty-first birthday party a week later, which I somehow got a late invitation to on Saturday night, I suddenly found myself standing opposite him. There was a tingling expectant energy between us as Troy gallantly offered to roll me a smoke.

It was a subdued backyard barbeque party. The dads and uncles were turning steaks on the barbie, laughing and slurping beers, and the mums and aunts were laying out large bowls of clingwrap-covered salads. My girlfriend and I ate sparingly, really only to avoid getting too tipsy from drinking without food in our bellies. The older friends, who were stoned, sat quietly with food stacked high on their paper plates balanced on their knees, devouring every morsel like a banquet.

After the standard twenty-first birthday speeches the birthday boy and his mates busied themselves trying to chug down a yard glass full of beer, their shirts drenched in the overflow down their chests. The music volume got turned up, and the youngsters removed themselves to the dance floor in the garage, coinciding with the parents' retreat indoors to enjoy a plate of Nan's signature pavlova.

Troy and I didn't cross paths a lot during the formalities of the evening, but as the party was wrapping up, our destiny was sealed. We sat on two garden chairs pulled close together and kissed from midnight until the birds chirped and the first light of day came into the garden, where the party had been in full swing a few hours before. It was the first time I felt whole-body tingling energy, and it stayed with me for days. Now *that* was an exciting feeling. I thought he was attractive and different, but I had no idea at the time that he would be the one who stood by me, who loved me and supported me—and was the key to my beginning to open up to all that I had experienced.

Troy was outdoorsy and adventurous. He abseiled, rock-climbed and scuba-dived. He was an artist and music aficionado, a traveller, motorbike rider and well-read, with the most extraordinary recall. He had fish tanks full of exotic fish who sometimes threw themselves out onto the bedroom carpet. He was gentle, kind, and a loving uncle to his small nephews. Born in Scotland, Troy was interesting, different to the suburban boys I'd known, who were mostly friends of Darryl's. He was the best kisser, and was as smitten with me as I was with him.

I came to learn that Troy's younger years were also chaotic; zigzagging across the world, shifting between many towns; living with or without his parents for financial reasons; and getting his share of beatings as he showed up to each new school as that new kid with an accent. In Australia, he'd get beaten up for his Scottish accent, and then in Scotland he'd get a Glasgow kiss to knock his Aussie accent out of his head. He came with his own set of amateur parents, but with a father who was more volatile than silent as mine was.

We didn't want to get stuck in any kind of deep-and-meaningfuls when we met. He did try to share his past experience of intimacy with me, but I'd freeze and shift the topic as fast as I could. I didn't want my turn to share to come up. It never did. I know he knew something was up. We were young and inexperienced at being in a boyfriend-girlfriend relationship, so we lived each day as it came, and partied each night because we could.

We were married when I turned twenty, because in my family the rule was that a good Catholic girl was not allowed to move out with a man before getting married. Of course! That's what good girls did.

Never in our budding relationship or early marriage had I told Troy what had happened with my brother. The guilt and shame fire stayed warmly lit in my core. My inner critic kept that fire stoked, poking me from the inside whenever she could, picking out one or another relevant topic from the list she'd been saving for a long while now: *How can you be the only person who let that happen? What sort of awful girl were you? Sinner! Don't tell Troy, or he'll leave you!*

The only way to dull her voice and the commotion I held inside me was to keep numbing it; luckily, our newly married twenty-something social life accommodated that well. We had a blast those first few years, living in a shabby rental, watching bands, drinking too much, and partying and dancing until the small hours before dawn. Whether it was a weekend or a weeknight, it didn't matter.

Life was all about fun and the two of us, in love and lust, together.

Disclosures and mixed responses

Three of the most important words anyone can
say are not 'I love you', but 'I hear you'.
OPRAH WINFREY, AUTHOR & PHILANTHROPIST

Eleven years after I refused to see my brother's penis for the last time, I finally told Troy what I had needed to share with him for so long.

I sat on the hand-me-down cream coloured vinyl couch in the first little house we bought, in a national park-bordered town at the far south end of Sydney. We'd been chatting about his workday; our first baby girl was wrapped up in a shawl and with the palm of my hand I was patting a soft rhythm on the curve of her back. I had given birth to this sweet cherub in 1990 and she was still in her first year of being adored completely by both sides of our extended family.

The conversation shifted to cover every clucky second of the baby's day, infused with a solid dose of deep abiding love. I was about to hand her into Troy's arms to go and make our dinner when I stopped in my tracks. It was time.

I recall that pause in the conversation. I'd leaned forward on the lounge to stand up. The pause lengthened, and I knew now was the time to talk. Even I was surprised to hear myself start to speak when I'd initially planned to get on with the busy events at day's end whilst the baby was asleep.

First came a heavy exhale of breath up from my belly, followed by words that seemed to rush, as if I was chasing them down but couldn't catch them: 'I have to tell you something....'

'What?'

As he waited for my reply, my chest and neck heated up, and my arms prickled with goosebumps.

'Darryl. He abused me when I was young.' I didn't look him in the eyes nor pause to catch a breath between my words, rushing on with, 'It's not a big deal. I just thought I should tell you because it's good not to hold secrets. I'm okay, I don't need anything. I just wanted to say something. I'll make dinner now....' I was babbling.

Troy had listened quietly, and I glanced up to see his jaw clench, his eyes dark, skin reddening with a range of emotions playing across his face.

He looked away at the darkening sky through the front window in silence. I got scared. *Oh no, I've done it again; I should have stayed quiet.* My body froze, nerves jangling, and my throat gulping without making a sound.

In my head, the inner critic was sing-songing at me: *Oh, now you're in trouble. I told you not to tell him! What were you thinking?*

The silence hung between us. I could feel the little lounge room expand as if the walls were stretching far away from me. My body felt empty, and I was suddenly exhausted.

Then, he spoke to me with care, softly saying, 'It's okay. I'm glad you told me that secret. What Darryl did was wrong. What can I do to help?' Disgust for my brother emanated from him.

Relieved, I took another deep breath and rained a deluge of words down on him. In that first conversation, as the sky was turning dark outside, I shared what I felt was enough, without going too far. For the first time since my early childhood I felt safe and it was an enormous relief. I cried.

Troy listened. He didn't move over to where I sat. He gave me space. He didn't try to save or tell me what I needed to do. He didn't question me or seek out details.

Amidst all that sweet relief, I knew there was another steel door tightly locked, holding back an entire glacier inside of me—and now wasn't the time to go any further than I needed to in my sharing.

Now I know I am not alone

Sitting on that couch opposite Troy, our baby girl in my arms—with Young Alice shadowing my every word, watching to see whether it was safe to come out—was incredible. The feeling of having someone who listened to me, who did not make up his own stories or offer justifications, whilst I shared my pain and my deep, dark and dreadful secret was a blessing beyond anything I could ever have imagined.

I had complete trust in Troy, and at that moment, I realised just how overdue the conversation was.

Trust doesn't come easily to abuse survivors, so I didn't beat myself up anymore about why I hadn't spoken earlier. Because now I had spoken, and that was enough.

For our first eight years together, I had kept my terrible secret, my shame, and the heightened feelings and emotions that rattled obnoxiously around in my body hidden.

That beautiful man had needed to interpret everything, with absolutely no idea what was happening.

Telling Troy had gone as well as I could have hoped. The following day I woke feeling lighter and just a little surer of myself. I decided my next undertaking would be to tell Mum. Troy offered to be with me when I went to see her, but I shook that off with a 'No, I'll be fine. I'll go to Mum's on Saturday; if you can keep bubby here, I'll be okay.'

I vividly recall summoning the courage to tell Mum as I walked in the same front door I used to dread walking through during all those school day afternoons. My positive feeling had slipped away on the twenty-minute drive over there, realising that this would be a tough conversation for both of us.

Unfortunately, disclosing Darryl's abuse to Mum didn't go very well at all.

I remember we were both standing in the now not-so-modern laminated orange kitchen with orange hibiscus flower-printed wallpaper and pine cabinets, just as we had many times before. I had called out 'Hi!' on the way through the house and headed straight to the kitchen sink, pulling out a glass to pour a glass of water to calm my nerves.

Mum came to the kitchen, leaning against one end of the kitchen bench, asking why I didn't have her granddaughter with me. I mumbled that she was having a little time with her daddy. Turning around and leaning back against the sink, I felt the heat of my nervousness rise through my body. It filled my chest and I knew I was blazing red, from my chest to my throat to my cheeks. The words came out in a few quick sentences, 'Mum, I've come to tell you something. Darryl sexually abused me when I was young.' Done!

The look on Mum's face was a peculiar mixture that took me back to that day in the confessional box with Father fifteen years earlier. I watched in confusion as Mum's face matched mine in its red tone. Her response to my disclosure was anger, doubt, cross-questioning and accusation. Mum pushing herself away from me and the bench, she crossed her arms tightly over her chest and with a sour look shook her head:

'You're lying!'

'He would never do that!'

'How could he have at that age!'

'What exactly did he do to you?'

I tried sharing some details, confusedly piecing together small instances to make her see it was true; how old we were, the times of day and the rooms or holidays where it happened. Mum was shocked and in denial:

'He did not. Stop lying!'

'What are you trying to do?'

I didn't hear any words like: 'I'm so sorry that happened. What happened was not your fault. I believe you. I hear you. I love you.' It was a short conversation that left me with nothing more to say.

I pushed myself away from the sink bench and slipped past her to get out of the kitchen without coming into physical contact. I took my car keys and purse off the dining table and walked back out the front door to head home to sanctuary and safety.

The connection mum and I had developed since I had become pregnant and a mother myself evaporated into thin air that day. I didn't know what to do with Mum's denial. All the earlier versions of me that had lived and played my roles in that family: the little girl, the abused child and teen, young woman and mother, were present at that conversation with our matriarch, trying to decipher what was going wrong.

There was no follow-up nor request to talk more about it from Mum. I felt anxious, shut down, shut out, unworthy of Mum's love and unsafe, and I didn't want to get hurt any more than I already was. I felt deserted.

I'd started something, though, and I kept moving forward and bravely decided to tell Dad.

I didn't want any secrets hidden inside of me anymore now that it was coming up. I didn't know what response I would get from Dad when he came to dinner at our place, but at least Troy was beside me for that disclosure.

My parents had been separated for a few years by then, and those years had been a rough ride for Dad. The family all took turns at being on Mum's side, or wishfully thinking they would have been better together, then snapping out of that daydream, realising who we were talking about. No way. This is how it should be! Dad began by living a swinging single life, but it wasn't long before he found a quieter solitary life was more his cup of beer.

We had added that extra family gathering as families affected by divorce do. Troy and I would invite Dad to come for dinner, he would have his turn at holding the baby while I cooked or Troy barbecued and we'd sit around the table talking and drinking wine until he was ready to get himself home. I could trust Dad with what I shared with him. He wasn't a gossip. He listened and would think before he spoke. He was not so great at conversation when he'd sunk too many beers, but I didn't try to talk about anything when he was like that.

Mostly what I did share was new mum talk, and details about work. The night he came to dinner, I waited to tell him about the abuse until after dinner was finished and I'd had a few glasses of red wine to fortify my courage to speak, if I could even speak—let alone get through it.

Dad listened and teared up, shaking his head, his mouth turning downward with distaste as if he'd just sucked a lemon. It was probably the most emotional conversation I'd ever had with Dad; the only other times I'd seen him choke up were as we were pulling up to the church on my wedding day, and when I came out of the birthing suite after the birth of my daughter, and he walked with me to my room on the maternity ward.

He didn't question me. Dad shook his head and said, 'I'm so sorry, I didn't know. How dare he do that to you. Leave this with me to think about.' His tone of voice shifted between empathy, contempt and protectiveness.

It wasn't the most in-depth conversation, but what was shared both ways was enough.

The anguish I'd felt about not saying anything for all those years was replaced by a feeling of being embraced by masculine strength. I had the unwavering support of my family's men, which felt good.

In writing this, I have sometimes cringed on reflection, and have been hard on myself, self-judging for how earlier conversations went with my mum. I went over and over the words that were spoken, what I missed out on sharing, the ideas for how we could move forward; what I did or didn't do as well as I could. So I try to remember that this is a historical account. Its purpose is to share lessons learned, mistakes made and aid change in how others may approach it when it is their turn.

These conversations happened over thirty years ago, and neither Mum nor I had the communication skills or life experience to navigate our way through to a healthy outcome. For my part, that twenty-something Alice felt the way she did at the time, risked making disclosures, and tried to pull herself back together repeatedly from hurts.

Whatever happened, whatever was said, it was better to have said something rather than say nothing at all.

Why do we tell our mothers first?

Why don't we go to our father first, or feel we could have trusted to ask for his help as a child?

I found in reading multiple case studies that disclosing to the mother first was the common preference of daughters sharing that a brother had sexually abused them.

Possibly, the feminine, the maternal, nurturing mother, the older woman who would protect her young daughter feels like it would be a safer conversation than talking to a father about something as awkward as sex.

Once disclosed to, the girls' fathers within the case studies shared what they'd decided to do without delay. My own Dad didn't take long to tell me what he'd resolved to do about Darryl.

Mothers, more often, were less resolved to act. Yes, they'd listen, but there would be the feeling of a drawn-out pause, of inaction. It was as if the action required of them to support the abused child was at another level beyond their comprehension. They'd instead shift into becoming the victim of circumstance because this was an accusation about their beloved sons, not some stranger to the family, who had touched or abused her daughter.

> 'Parents can feel that they are in an impossible situation, torn between the needs of the child who has harmed and the child who has been harmed' (Tener, Newman et al, 2020). The shame, self-blame, secrecy and stigma experienced by parents may be particularly acute. They may feel that some wrongdoing on their part has resulted in sexual abuse having taken place between their children. Parents need support and emotional containment in order to be able to offer appropriate support to all the children within the family' (Allardyce & Yates, 2022).

Parents can benefit greatly by checking the web to find what information is available to support them personally through such difficult times. In Appendix 3, I have shared some simple and helpful tips sourced from RAINN (Rape, Abuse & Incest National Network) in the USA, from their page titled 'Help for Parents of Children whose Family Members have Sexually Abused'.

It would be so helpful for parents to understand how they are (or were) supposed to react; how to manage the feelings that arise; the challenges when a perpetrator is part of the family; what they can expect from the abused child; and what to do to help.

I could only imagine how professional support would have helped Mum alone, and us together, to find a path to walk forward in solidarity, rather than on parallel tracks where we could not quite reach across to take a firm, loving hold of each other's hand in support.

It wasn't until a very long time later that I tried raising that topic with Mum again, asking, 'Would family counselling be a good idea for us, so we can talk about what we need to?'

She replied, 'What good would that do now? It's over. If only you'd come to me and told me back then, then it wouldn't have happened in the first place. There's nothing I can do to fix it now.'

End of story.

I reflect on what might have come about differently for us all individually and as a family if whatever needed to be tabled was talked through in a safe, neutral place, with unbiased professional support. It would have been anywhere from a smidge better, to an abundantly better outcome than the silence I was expected to hold onto; out of fear, guilt and shame.

Getting back to life as usual

After those three disclosures, my mind switched back to getting on with my own life as usual. Busy with a baby and a job in the city, somehow we all went back to playing happy families.

Darryl was still included in our family gatherings because to Mum, he'd done nothing wrong. I had been told not to say anything to Darryl about the disclosure. I yielded, conscious that others' fears of the repercussions of doing so were real to them, if not to me.

We all pretended everything was as happy as can be.

I had slipped straight into 'good girl' mode, doing the 'right thing' after being so disruptive with that whole disclosure distress I'd caused for my Mum.

My inner critic found herself a new script to whisper to me, reminding me: *Don't disturb the peace any more than you have, Alice; don't talk about it, Alice; remember to be civil, Alice.*

I was a young mum of a daughter, for whom my heart was filled with love, and my self-blame dial was cranked up as high as it could go, worrying that I needed to fix the hurt I'd inflicted on Mum. I did that by doing what I was asked to, shutting up about the topic, and talking about only lovely things. I didn't want to make our time together uncomfortable.

It was an internal challenge I can now easily see for what it was, but at twenty-five, I didn't see it. Beneath the surface, I knew my ability to trust and feel safe in our mother-daughter relationship was damaged that day in Mum's kitchen.

I still wouldn't allow myself to reflect on what had happened to me as a child. I had many things to do: work, washing laundry, housework, and mouths to feed! I could speak about some details openly with Troy, but not much. I wasn't comfortable sharing the words that solidified the slide show of pictures only I could see passing behind my eyes.

Psychologists were not on my radar at that time, or at least not for someone like me. I did a subject focused on behavioural psychology for my nursing diploma a couple of years before, and wrote an essay about certain behaviours related to Mum and Dad, mainly about the lead-up to the separation and the aftermath of emotions after they'd divorced.

I'd never known anyone who went to a psychologist.

If thoughts arose, I just pushed them straight back down. That had to be better than talking it out and feeling bad all over again, right?

Unfortunately, that strategy didn't, and couldn't work: primarily because we had maintained contact with Darryl. Every time I saw Darryl, I became more alert and on edge, feeling like this happy family sitcom was a farce—what were we doing? We were not a happy family.

I recall listening to what Darryl would be saying out loud and being fascinated by his incongruity, wondering if anyone else was hearing and seeing it apart from me.

I'd witnessed for enough years before adulthood that he was accomplished at feigning personas, and he still did it as a man, depending on his audience. I'd watch his eye movements and whether he was breathing only through his nostrils like he used to when he was angry or trying to stay in control. I was alert and aware of all the movements and body language going on whenever we were together.

Everything about him was still as much of a mismatch as it had been when he played his earlier roles of the good first son and trustworthy big brother.

I was comfortable knowing that Darryl's now ex-first-wife wouldn't have let anyone harm any child. She was very much in control, the mother bear who would eat you alive if you were to hurt a cub, whether the cub was hers or not.

If you've not yet disclosed

'The longer the time between when the episodes of abuse stopped (if they have) and when the child tells of the abuse, as abuse, the greater the damage that has been done to her personality.' (Levenkron, 2007).

'Due to the silence inherent in non-disclosure, it is difficult to estimate the percentage of child sexual abuse victims who have held that secret within them for their entire lives. What we do know is that many people have struggled with disclosure, and have maintained their secret for many years, causing themselves and their relationships damage in the process. The barriers to disclosure are many, as discussed previously; from fear of not being believed; the expectation of a negative reaction or response; to a belief that the disclosure will have negative consequences. Shame and embarrassment can also overwhelm a victim and have a silencing effect that lasts for many years and decades' (Wright, 2017).

'Crucially though, how a family reacts to the existence of sibling sexual abuse has been recognised as an important part of the recovery process for a victim' (Doyle et al., as cited in Caffaro, J.V. 1998).

Whilst I have shared how my disclosure went badly twice, as a ten-year-old to Father and again at twenty-five to Mum, I had at least an adult awareness that, as far as each of those was concerned, their response and resultant behaviours were theirs; they were not about me.

What would I do differently now?

Without a shadow of a doubt, an organisation such as 1800RESPECT would have been my first port of call to disclose to. 1800RESPECT is one Australian organisation doing good things in terms of supporting victims of childhood sexual abuse, family abuse and domestic abuse.

In the early 1970s, such organisations weren't discussed on TV, radio, or at school. Incest or sibling sexual abuse wasn't either.

In contrast, stranger danger was discussed at school, with police detectives coming to class to present horrifying educational videos. I remember sitting on the floor in the dark with the rest of the class, watching the screen as a little girl ran and tripped over in panic, being stalked in the woods by what must have been an adult man. That's based on the depiction only showing the villain wearing dark trousers, leather lace-up shoes, stepping off the path into the woods, and walking at a determined pace behind her. The educational session ended with snapshots flashed on the screen of a crumpled-up little body wearing a dirty torn dress, the police had found buried under the leaves by a drain.

I had nightmares for years that brought up images and fear of stranger danger after that and I was scared to death at crossing the sections of the path that were over big open drains, thinking someone might be waiting for me.

Even in the 1990s, no services or organisations were on my radar when I disclosed it to Troy or my parents.

A disclosure conversation with a professional support person or specialist would have helped me develop a family disclosure strategy. I'd also have their support and advice around what reactions I might expect, whatever steps they recommended next, and in helping us move forward to find professional help.

I have come to greatly appreciate professional support and going to people who are specialists in their field of study. As I didn't call an organisation like 1800RESPECT, my other best action in 1990, apart from telling Troy, would have been to make an appointment to see my GP and ask her for a referral to a trauma-informed professional or therapist.

4

The Lioness Appears

*Each of us chooses what is acceptable in our lives. As kids,
we don't get a lot of choice. We are born into families
and situations, and it's all out of our control. But as we
get older, we choose. Consciously or unconsciously, we
decide how we are going to allow ourselves to be treated.
What will you accept? What won't you accept? You're
going to have to choose and you're going to have to
stand up for yourself. No one else can do it for you.*

JAMES R. DOTY, M.D., PROFESSOR OF
NEUROSURGERY & AUTHOR

In the year I turned twenty-nine, something happened to shatter
the relative calm that had infused my life. We were at Mum's
home that she'd bought and renovated following the divorce, in
a new housing development west of Sydney.

Our second little girl was asleep in one of the quiet, cooled
bedrooms at the back of the house. Only some of the family's
women and girlfriends were present that day, out in the kitchen
at the front corner, far away from where she slept. From the
sunroom connected to the kitchen, the aircon poured cold air
while the fan-forced oven fought back with blasts of steamy heat
every time Mum opened the oven door to check on the roasting
lamb and her signature crisp roast potatoes.

I hung around the periphery of the women as they talked in the kitchen, keeping out of Mum's way, ducking and weaving amongst them as she swung between the oven, the fridge, and the dinner table, preparing to serve lunch. I felt uneasy in my stomach, on edge, and decided to take a moment to step out through the sliding doors of the sunroom and check the back garden to see what the kids were up to. I gazed out from where I stood on Mum's small back porch, scanning the yard from right to left and there, at the side of the yard, was my four-year-old daughter standing with her back to me, only just in view down behind Mum's garage. She was standing opposite Darryl's boy. Her bum was bare. She had her shorts down around her ankles, and our nephew was leaning in with something in his hand.

Something roared in my brain, and my vision was suddenly filtered red like I was looking through a sheet of red cellophane paper.

Like a bounding lioness, I headed straight for them and yelled. 'NO!'

The second I arrived at the two of them, I thought, *Shit! He's not my kid; I can't touch him!* Instead, I landed a big smack on my daughter's bare bum and grabbed her upper arm to pull her away from his reach, shouting at him, 'You stop that! That's bad.'

I was horrified!

The red filter to my vision had subsided, and now I was at a loss as to what to do next. My daughter was crying from the sting of my smack on her bum and fear was written on both of their faces.

Troy had heard me yell from where he was inside the house. The glass sliding door opened and slammed closed, and he was leaping from the back porch across the lawn towards us. The door opened and slammed closed again, and I saw Darryl had heard me and was on his way not far behind Troy.

I had mustered up quite a roar, which they heard beyond the kitchen and air conditioner's noise.

Troy and I communicated in broken phrases. My daughter now held tightly in my arms, I managed to splutter, 'She had her pants down, he had a big stick in his hand, he was aiming it up at her vagina...'

Troy put his hands on my shoulders, jerked his head and indicated I should go back inside and settle down. He scooped our daughter to his chest with a calm, 'I've got this' energy.

I couldn't look at Darryl. A strong recollection of his abuse had flashed before my eyes in that red-filmed moment between the back deck and where the children had stood, leaving me feeling dirty and repulsed at his presence. I tried to keep control, walked back up to the house, and slid open the door. I walked past the women, head down, and around the corner into Mum's bathroom and closed the door. I knew I needed to calm down. I was in shock, something I would only come to realise later. I rested my head against the cool bathroom wall tiles, both hands over my heart, repeating to myself with each ragged intake, *She's okay, she's safe, she's okay.*

Slowly, my heartbeat began to shift from my throat and slowed down, dropping gradually back to a regular rate inside my chest. I felt light-headed and sat on top of the toilet lid to ground myself.

Noises of the women bustling between the kitchen and table filtered through, pots and pans getting knocked about, and a nervous feminine laugh.

My mind was spinning with questions and responses: *Am I making a fuss over something silly? No. You know that what was happening had the same feeling you used to, don't you? Yes! I was not being silly, and she is my baby! Now, pull yourself together.*

Through the high, open bathroom window I could hear Troy and Darryl talking on the back deck. Troy was saying in a low dangerous tone, evenly and calmly, so as not to disturb the clucking women on the other side of the glass sliding door, 'No matter what just happened, we both know why Alice is so upset, don't we.'

Only three adults and two kids were aware of the event. However, it was a turning point that would soon cause major familial upheaval.

A minute later, Troy was in the bathroom, hugging me with our daughter squished between us in his arms. The pressure of his hug set off a waterfall of tears that seemed to have been holding themselves back inside my chest. I sobbed, washed my face to freshen up, tried to smile and not distress my little girl, and towelled my face dry, only to have the tears pour out again.

I knew I didn't have time for crying; I had to pull myself together. I rewashed my face and towelled it dry. Leaving Troy to wash our daughter's face and give me some space, I turned the bathroom handle, knowing the family were likely worried and wanted to know what happened. Also, our sleeping daughter would wake up and need to be checked on.

I did not want to be there. I just wanted the four of us to go home.

As I came out of the bathroom, pale and blotchy, Mum walked around the corner of the corridor, her eyes narrow with disapproval. She pulled up directly in front of me, pointed her index finger towards my face, and said in an uncompromising tone, 'Alice, don't you dare ruin lunch,' She turned and returned to the kitchen.

'No, of course not, Mum', feeling guilty and bad again. The world was still spinning and wonky, not entirely on the same axis as before.

All of us, the adults and children and our little one in her highchair, sat around the table for what felt like a tasteless roast lunch and pretended it was a lovely, albeit quiet, lunch at Mum's place.

I had no words, and no appetite, but I was seated at the table. It was a very uncomfortable meal. *Sorry, Mum,* I thought, *I ruined lunch after all.*

I knew with all my heart that it was time to stop playing happy families.

The lioness had been roused within me as I crossed that backyard. Young Alice had no protection, no safe sanctuary: but my daughters would.

Troy and I were quick to bundle our two girls into the car and exit stage right as soon as the plates began getting cleared from the table.

Once we were a few streets away from Mum's place, I said to Troy without emotion, but with incredible calm and clarity, 'I won't be seeing Darryl again. He and his family can never get close to our daughters again.' I said it without wanting a response, and Troy reached out to squeeze my hand, confirming that he was with me on that plan.

It was the safest and most correct decision for our daughters and me. It was well overdue, and I'd let my daughter be at risk.

I can look back now and see where the idea of whole family intervention fits into our family's puzzle. That day at Mum's was where it would have fit in: where a conversation could have been had, maybe not exactly on that day, but at least in the weeks after. None of us felt safe to speak of that day, what occurred and its loose relationship to the abuse that had gone on in our family home years before. The long-trusted silence and secrecy were honoured as our family's only safe way to operate together and move on.

Troy rang and asked the police what the options were to report Darryl's abuse. The officer said there'd be very little chance of anything being done, it was in the past, and they'd need to see evidence to prove it happened.

Troy and I got on with life again, back in our little home, busy with two little girls. Time spun by, and there was no time for much more than being parents and working.

Wherever we had the time and space, I shared with him memories that had started flashing before my eyes since the ruined lunch at Mum's place. I didn't share a lot because the emotions were a bit treacherous for me, and I was a mum of two little girls. I couldn't go and crack open at the seams in an emotional mess—for them or for me. I had held it all inside for so long, pushed down tight, it just had to stay there.

It felt good to have Troy by my side, and eventually, I accepted his counsel that I needed someone to help me talk through it when I was ready. Troy, working by now at a supervisory level of a large team, had come across all kinds of people who needed mental health support for one thing or another. He shared his knowledge that there were people out there qualified to help talk about this. During the lead-up to Christmas, I made an appointment to see my family GP, rambled on at her about having been abused by my brother, about what had occurred at my Mum's between the children lately, and whether she could put me in touch with someone to talk to.

The subsequent first visit to the therapist began with a round of rapid-fire questions directed at me. I didn't know at that time about the importance of building rapport or finding a therapist I felt safe with or could trust, as probably the most important thing in finding someone to speak with. We didn't click at all. Afterwards, I did realise she was trying to prioritise the order of the things she had to deal with. What I'd shared about the incident, involving two young children at my mother's place, meant she needed to ascertain whether someone might have abused Darryl's son. If so, the therapist would have the duty to report it to the authorities.

Right then, in that first session, I wanted to have the therapist tell me how to leave the abuse behind me. I also wanted her to help me come up with a strategy to reinforce, with Mum, my choice of setting safe and healthy boundaries. If she could help me with that in a couple of sessions, that'd be even better. During that first foray into seeking professional help, I had a completely unrealistic timeline of how long this 'healing' business would take. It was going to take much longer than that, that's for certain.

The strategy gained from that short round of sessions included a recommendation that I prepare and practice saying a few scripts for upcoming difficult conversations. Surprisingly, a script was handy and just what I needed. I was yet to tell Mum we would not be sharing Christmas for the first time that year. Christmas for our family was about to change forever. Darryl would be there, no question about that, and I had made a promise to myself and my immediate family. No question about that, either.

Dropping the Christmas bombshell

We can't have change without loss, which is
why so often people say they want change
but nonetheless stay exactly the same.
LORI GOTTLIEB, PSYCHOTHERAPIST & AUTHOR

I recall having my scripted conversation with Mum in the middle of an aisle of Toys"R"Us.

We were walking together doing our Christmas gift shopping. Thankfully, my two girls were not with us when Mum threw the switch that launched my scripted bombshell. As though she was commenting on the weather, she said, 'I'm so looking forward to us all being together on Christmas Day. It'll be so lovely.'

It went downhill from there.

My shoulders tensed, and I knew this was the moment. 'Mum,' I glanced at her and took a breath, 'Troy and I aren't coming to Christmas with the family. As I said before, I don't want to have Darryl in my life, or anywhere near my girls.'

The relief! *That was easy*, I thought to myself. *Short and sweet!*

We had both stopped in the aisle, bright smiling dolls towered over us on high shelves as busy mums and excited kids bustled past, their Christmas trolleys fully laden.

'Don't be so silly. It's Christmas. You don't want to ruin Christmas Day for the children because of that.'

I was unsure whether it was a dismissal, reprimand, or a statement, but I stood my ground.

'Mum, I've told you before that if Darryl will be at a family event, I'm okay not to be there. You go on without me. It's okay.' She stared, frustrated like I was a particularly agile fly she couldn't swat away from the lunch table. 'But that doesn't have to include Christmas Day? You're breaking up the family.'

'Oh Mum, I'm sorry but the family is already broken.'

That reply was unscripted, but we don't always need to write something down to know it is true. Afterwards, there was nothing but incredibly awkward silence.

I could understand her unhappiness, but I had to stand my ground then, and many times after that first conversation about many future events. In this, having a script was highly beneficial. My inner lioness and I felt our resolve unite, confidently protecting our cubs.

'We can move Christmas to a park, so we're not in a house.'

'You won't even have to talk to Darryl if you don't want to.'

'Just do it for me. Just do it for the kids.'

'No, thank you,' I replied. 'I'm decided on this. Enjoy your day without us.'

It was challenging to maintain, especially as I couldn't simply pretend the tradition of Christmas Day wasn't going to be a loss to me, too. Since I'd become a mum, not that many years earlier, Christmas had been a joyful time of planning gift-giving and menus, Santa sacks, singing carols, games, playfulness, and laughter.

I did not take the choice to break away from the family celebration lightly.

I found ways to persevere with making the change required—which opened new ways to make Christmas magic with everyone we still loved sharing it with. It was only Darryl that I was choosing not to be with. We needed to be more creative in planning gatherings with my family on other days when Darryl wasn't present. After all, there are another 364 days to make alternative arrangements in the year.

DRAWING
on the
LIONESS' COURAGE

5

~

Let's Move Someplace Beautiful

Wings are like dreams. Before each flight, a bird takes a
small jump, a leap of faith, believing that its wings will
work. That jump can only be made with rock-solid feet.
J.R. RIM, AUTHOR

Soon after I made that resolution, Troy and I became parents to our third little girl. With another new baby in the house life became a hectic mix of working hard to earn money, dance classes, Wiggles music, swimming lessons and night-time reading. Occasionally we would escape to the south coast for weekend adventures, but even then an intense rhythm prevailed. Then, one of my favourite life-transforming decisions occurred, and I saw the light.

It began with a simple but pointed question as I sipped coffee at the local shopping mall one Friday morning with my mother-in-law.

'What the f**k are you doing, Alice!'

It wasn't a harsh question; she was Scottish, and that's how she spoke. I wasn't even expected to answer. I just nodded thoughtfully at the time, but over the weekend I thought about it more.

My mother-in-law had tested me out a few times in the years before we had our first child. I could see her doing it, so I'd square my shoulders, take in what she'd said and sieve it around to see if she was being nasty, or if I needed to hear the message. I never backed down. 'Alice, you're a smart lass,' she'd say, but that could also mean 'Don't be daft'. In this case, 'What the f*ck are you doing!' meant the same thing: 'Don't put up with a mundane life; it's not about just earning money to pay the bills—go live, go travel. Life is short.' I always knew when she was speaking her truth. She was very forthright. When she had something to say, it didn't matter whether you wanted to hear it or not, you were going to. Then she'd leave you to think about it.

Troy and I had long commutes each day, so everything was meticulously planned. We knew exactly how long each task in our mornings and afternoons would take, so that we could complete them all efficiently and achieve our daily missions. In the evenings, I'd get home from work, and it would be about getting school and day care bags packed before bed, lunch boxes in the fridge, loads of washing done, uniforms laid out, homework sorted and baths enjoyed before dinner together. Finally, it was time to get the kids into bed, each to be read their favourite night-time story.

We'd not be long behind the girls' bedtime, setting the alarm to get up in the dark. Troy would be up and gone when I awoke, his workplace close to the city a forty-five-minute drive away; and he started at seven am. Mine, also in the city, began at eight-thirty. I would get out of bed and see if I could tell what the day held in store for us in terms of weather. Rain mattered in the running of the morning's plans, as extra time might need to be allocated to the morning list. On a frosty morning, I even needed to allow some minutes to hose the front car windscreen to dislodge the light layer of frost!

Otherwise, I'd grab a quick shower, get dressed up for my job in a city corporate environment, and then get everyone else clothed and fed. I'd wait until I got to the city to eat some toast and pour myself a coffee. In the mornings, if Troy had a lift with a workmate, I got to drive our car to the train station, so it felt like I had tonnes of time. Otherwise, I'd need to allow another twenty minutes to wheel a stroller with our three daughters on board or in tow. Drop-offs were made at the girls' before school care and the day care centre.

With one eye on my watch, and fingers crossed that the day care would let me in the door early, I'd know whether I would make the earlier train or have to wait until the later one. That depended on which teacher was on the early shift. They were all friendly, but some were that little bit more empathetic, giving me four or five more minutes so I could make the first train. I knew exactly how much time it would take for me to run up the hill to the train station for my commute to the city.

I loved my job in the office I worked at and once there, I'd put my mind to whatever was needed. I enjoyed walking the city in my hour's lunch break, and before I knew it, the clock showed I needed to head off to catch the train back to home and family, and repeat.

Troy's workday finished earlier than mine, so he headed to the after-school care and day care to collect everyone, bringing them home to have some playtime in the garden: and also repeat!

Indeed, I thought, *What the f**k is this all about? What are we doing? This isn't living a life.*

We got away for long weekend escapes with the girls, and on the other weekends we'd spend a lot of our time outdoors in playgrounds and parks with them. But that work/life cycle would continue for a long time into the future, and our cost of living wasn't decreasing, it was going up, so our work hours and income had to be maintained. But for what?

Troy and I began to talk about our options, and our conversations took us full circle, back to our earliest shared dreams of leaving our Sydney life behind. Step-by-step we seeded a plan to live life on our own terms. Considering where we would move to, I recall saying to Troy, 'If we're going to move, let's move someplace beautiful.'

It had to be affordable, with a healthy lifestyle and a new start.

Finally, we decided. The idyllic Sunshine Coast in Southeast Queensland would be our new home. It was the best decision we ever made! The timing was also lucky, as the kinds of house and land prices available in 1999 would never be the same again. We got in before the price hike, and just before GST began.

My Sydney days before the move felt incredibly empowered, because I knew this decision was much more than just a geographical shift. I'd dance around the house singing about sitting out on patios and breathing the humidity. I'd be working at my computer and high-five the air. It felt so good! I was deliriously happy that Troy and I were going to create a life we loved, for ourselves, and our little family.

Within six weeks, we took the opportunity to travel up to Queensland to explore the amenities, and ensure the two school-aged girls had places in the school ready for the upcoming term. Our exit from Sydney came together beautifully.

Between April and June 1999, we sold our house and a lot of our possessions, packed a truck with still far too many things, piled the car full of pillows, snacks and toys, and headed north with a back seat full of excited eight-, five- and two-year-old daughters.

The Sunshine Coast itself was magnificent. There was a joyful holiday spirit that began from the moment we arrived in the driveway of our new rental property, only a few streets away from the river. The removalist truck had beat us in the drive up from Sydney, and the garage had all our possessions stacked high.

We knew Troy would be on holiday for three months before he'd start searching for work and took advantage of the time. We splurged and bought pushbikes for all of us, teaching the girls how to ride. We could be across town in safety for a dinner picnic in jig time, and rode home along the river and through all the little bicycle paths that joined the streets.

It was time to have a break from the rat race and living on the Sunshine Coast felt like a long, slow holiday we'd earned. It was the first time in my girls' childhood that I didn't head off to an office in the morning, there was no more shipping them off to before-school care or day care. I was at home all the time. What a gift to give myself as a young mother.

I loved my simple routine, especially not getting up early with that city commute in mind. With no day care nor mother-in-law to help me with the three girls, I was very busy with family tasks: keeping house, helping with homework, finding new playgrounds, and splashing around in the local river and the pool. We decided to build our own house rather than buy, so I tackled that project with gusto. I spent many hours meeting with the house designer, and then the builder, and many months later, we finally had our own new enormous breezy Queensland home and pool. It was nothing like we'd ever owned.

I was getting busier, but I'd been in a rat wheel in Sydney and this 'busy' was a pleasure compared to that life. Thinking back, I apply colours to how I felt. The Sydney busyness felt grey, whereas this new busyness was sunshine yellow, and the colour of blue skies. I was very happy juggling all the new tasks that needed to be taken care of. I still didn't have much free time, but it was such a simple routine compared to Sydney.

Before long, Troy's parents followed our trail. Soon after, my dad also moved up. He had seen the light about the same time as we did and wanted to be close to his granddaughters. Within a few months, when Mum arrived, we were surrounded by the full complement of grandparents, and our daughters have a stockpile of happy memories to reflect on. We lived in an idyllic location, surrounded by family, and were far better off than when we were slogging it out back in Sydney. Four retired parents with us wasn't quite what Troy's and my vision had begun with, but we happily got on with living our new life in the sun.

Work and income

Troy found work sooner than planned. New Sunshine Coast locals, the ones who'd arrived in the year or two before us, liked to share their wise words: 'It'll take you at least three months to find a job, mate'. It rattled him, and he didn't feel like a three-month break was warranted. A couple of weeks of job searching and he had already found himself a new job.

I was still earning a small income, working short hours at home running a virtual transcription service for Sydney legal and medical specialists. It was my Friday side earner, which I had established during my pregnancies and maternity leave in Sydney. I sat at my desk typing furiously, preparing court and medical reports for doctors and lawyers. I quickly and accurately transcribed the documents from their voice recordings, before sending them back with an invoice to Sydney via express post.

Around those few intense hours of work, my weekdays consisted of dropping the two girls to school, sometimes staying with the Year One room to help with reading, or at the tuckshop. Most days I'd go to the aquatic centre to swim laps. My two-year-old daughter and I had a routine; she would go into the pool's creche, and when I'd finished swimming laps, she'd come out for her swimming lessons. Then we'd eat morning tea together and play in the water, before we went home for lunch and a much-appreciated midday nap for both of us.

I got to be at school for all the performances, ceremonies and sports carnivals. We went fishing at the river after school, had dinner picnics of fish and chips, and walked our dog on the doggy beach before sunset. We were living a very different life from the one we had in Sydney, and I often contemplated how I could make our life even better. Now that I had taken control of my own life and begun to make it my own, I asked myself: *What do I want this new life to look and feel like?*

Before long, money worries arose that catapulted me into action and set in motion a chain of events that would dominate the following years, and change the rhythm of our family completely.

We were doing alright financially, yet even though our expenses were less than they had been, Troy's work paid a pittance compared to what he'd earned doing the same work in Sydney. It wasn't the managerial role that had paid him so well before. I'd also been used to earning a very nice salary, so whilst we ticked along, I felt the building pressure—that on reflection came only from inside of me—to be responsible and get some real money coming in.

Typing was an excellent small business, but it had grown beyond my control. Academically inspired as they were, the medical specialists soon added long recordings of their theses to the list of reports I needed to turn around quickly. It was work that required me to sit typing and listening to their voices and concentrating hard to understand the complexity of the content. This meant a laser-like focus on a screen for hours and hours, and as the demand increased, I realised I wouldn't be able to expand with it.

I had to shift my work hours to after the girls went to bed or when Troy got home, because I couldn't focus on daily life and schoolwork, and work so intensely at the same time. I could feel my body breaking with the repetitive actions of my hands on the keyboard, fingers flying away at over a hundred words a minute.

My wrists and forearms felt the strain, and between a numb bum and swelling ankles from sitting on the seat for such long hours, it quickly became clear that it wasn't going to be a sustainable long-term business.

I could have just applied for a job, but I didn't feel that having three kids was compatible with only four weeks of annual leave a year. I knew instinctively that I was finished with having someone else tell me when I could and couldn't take a holiday. *What could I do to add to our income?*

I thought about it in all the small gaps in our routine, trying to tap into insights I imagined would suddenly surface one morning—and I'd just know exactly what my new work would be. *What had I seen do well before?* Sydney was seeing all kinds of new business ventures pop up. My mind was awakening with an entrepreneurial spirit at the myriad business opportunities here. I wrote a list of the types of small businesses I'd seen in the city that were simple, innovative and successful, and searched the local directory to see if such businesses had made it up here yet.

Did I want to try something like running a café, or a boutique, or a garden centre? Not really—that felt like I was buying myself into a job again. I wrote down all the things I was good at, all the skills I had used in my job in Sydney. I somehow knew the answer was there. Then I thought about my mother-in-law, who had become something of an inspiration for me with her strong no-nonsense attitude—and how she'd started a business many years ago in a laneway in central Sydney. She was bold, and it was a different time, but that business was still operating, and had grown over the years with my sister-in-law now at its helm.

I wanted to create something, and let my lioness sink her teeth into a project that would give our family strength. I knew there would be sacrifices, but I could visualise how the administrative, front desk, payroll, and people skills I'd honed serving the elite

Eastern Suburbs clientele of a law firm would be a strong base. In my heart I knew the kind of business that was already in the family was a strong option. I again checked the local directory, and such businesses were thin on the ground on the Coast, so I made the choice to go for it. I had my idea, I knew what I wanted to do, and that I'd be good at it.

During one beautiful autumn sunset, as the colours changed on the skyline, I said to Troy, 'I'm going to start my own business, one like your mum and sister have down in Sydney.' Troy agreed, and we made a toast as the sun went down.

The first inkling that this idea of mine, supplying 24/7 relief staff to the healthcare industry, would challenge me was the warning my sister-in-law gave me when she heard my plan: 'Oh Alice, the phone, it's like having a colicky baby. You never, ever get to put it down. It just consumes you.'

I remember thinking, 'Consumes. Now that's not a word you'd throw around lightly.' As she said it, deep down I knew it was true, but I didn't want to believe it. I was consumed with the idea: the sense of freedom, of self-reliance and making my own destiny. It felt so different from how I had felt as a child, before I began to make my own decisions to define my life. I just smiled, appreciating her well-meant warning.

I'd seen the family business in action during the years since I'd met Troy. When they took a call, they'd be unable to think about anything else until they were finished. You could be part way through a conversation, and you knew you'd lost their attention until that booking was taken care of. All their children were attuned to the sound of the phone ringing; as soon as it was picked up, every one of them knew to become silent. But was that busy? Was that consuming? I shook off my doubts. I had this picture in my mind that I could go to the beach, take the phone, and my diary, sit under the umbrella, and if the phone rang, I'd fill the shift. Easy peasy. *What else was there to worry about? Surely I would work it out as I went.*

I overlooked those wise words, possibly partly because I had never had a colicky baby and didn't grasp the whole meaning of what that might be like. On my merry way, I went to register my business name and placed an ad in the Yellow Pages for the following year. By then, I'd be ready to start my own business. Sweet!

I loved that the move away from one life was letting me feel what it was that I could deliver, that would finally make use of my mind, skills, creativity and experience—and that I would decide my own future. It was time to open my mind to an opportunity that was something much more than just working because I needed a job.

I knew it would be hard work, and I think I was secretly seeking something to distract me from the unprocessed memories that occasionally stirred deep inside me. I had no idea how quickly this distraction would rise up, nor how completely it would consume me.

Jumping the gun

At that time the world wide web was still in its infancy. We used it occasionally for work emails, but most people really knew very little about it or how it worked. I hadn't been aware that my Yellow Pages book listing was going to be searchable online six months before the paper copy of the Yellow Pages would be delivered to front doorsteps across the region.

Dad was in a dual-living arrangement with us, so he was home one afternoon as I walked in after picking up the kids from school. He poked his head in through the screen door from the deck to say hello to the grandkids and added, 'Oh, your phone

RESOLVE

rang. It was a woman who has just seen your ad in the Yellow Pages, and she wanted to book an interview.'

I stopped mid-stride and stood like that for a few moments, processing the information. I thought, *Wow, right now I've got to make dinner. I can think about that tomorrow.* The day after, I remember sitting and staring at my blank computer screen, bombarding myself with internal chatter:

Are you going to do it?

Is it something you want?

Because you are the only person that needs to decide that, you know.

You know you can make it work.

If you are, you better decide now. That nurse is expecting a return phone call.

Is it a yes, or a no?

Was the idea of starting my own business bravado beyond common sense? Part of me wanted to prove I could forge my own life as I wished. There were fears behind it, too.

What if I fail? What if I'm found lacking? What if it's too hard?

Yes, I had experienced the joy and feeling of accomplishment in making our move from Sydney a success. That gave me a sweet taste of new beginnings and starting over, plus the unique geographic location also had a little magic. No one here knew me, and I would be able to practice growing my self-confidence, whilst growing my own little business. I was making positive changes, and nothing could get in my way apart from me, but could I summon up the courage, confidence and grit to be a business owner?

My mind hadn't gone anywhere near worrying about the bigger picture of running a business, what the day-to-day life would be like, and whether I wanted that life. The question was whether I could do it at all. It was a daunting and healthy challenge at the same time, and I was determined to make it—and myself—a success.

105

I shook myself, smiled, got goosebumps, and said out loud to no one apart from the blank computer screen in front of me: 'Yes, I'm going to do it. I know what needs to be done.'

I'd already been busy gathering current information on the healthcare industry, demographics and other research from the moment I'd first thought about starting. I knew what I needed to do, I just needed to decide which day would be Day One, and take the next step—or should I wait until the following year as planned?

That first phone call was an unexpected spur of purposeful action.

I decided I wouldn't panic-start now just because of one phone call. I rang the woman back, a junior nurse, and told her I'd be in touch in the future. I sought insurance and the licence required to operate a recruitment and labour hire business, which is what the business was in effect. A folder of my back-office and recruitment paperwork came together quickly; I read the State Awards to understand the intricacies of casual work pay rates and scales, then brought that together into one-page rate sheets and client charges. I played around with how to create staff ID badges.

I was loving being busy and doing things that would directly affect the lives of others and bring prosperity to my family. It seemed like there was an inexhaustible source of energy that drove me forward. It wasn't long before I felt that the essentials were in place, enough that I could declare the business open for bookings.

I believed in myself, and I was scared at the same time. My mind was open, and my imagination, creativity and resourcefulness joined me at my desk daily. I enjoyed learning something new and working out what I needed to do. Getting this business off the ground made me feel strong and inspired.

I knew I would make it work, and was excited about speaking those words out loud to my family. But that courage and confidence would sometimes disappear, leaving me alone with my old doubts and fears. One day, walking across our local supermarket's carpark with my mother-in-law, pushing our trolleys of groceries to pack into my car, all my resolve crumbled into dust as I heard some news that brought back shades of the old me I thought I had completely left behind.

At that moment, in the late afternoon sunlight, I observed that my inner critic was with me, telling me uncomfortable things, and I felt uneasy; she'd had much less to say since our move north. It came to me that possibly it was because of all the positive, purposeful changes I was making and how much happier and freer I'd felt since leaving Sydney.

I felt so good that I had dropped the habit of second-guessing myself, at least as much as I used to. No one was bringing me down at that time, which made it more difficult for my inner critic to find chinks in my armour. I loved our move and finding my way around, making new friends at the girls' school, at the pool, and in our street.

Yet that afternoon, as my inner critic took her front-row seat for what was about to occur, I sensed my hypervigilance radar switch back on—as it used to when Darryl was lurking around the corner. What was coming? I couldn't see any physical danger, but I did have a gut feeling I was about to be delivered a bombshell.

'Ach, Alice, I'm just telling you for your own good. Your mother and father told me they're not happy about you and your new business. Your father said "Alice doesn't have it in her," and your mum said, "Who does she think she is?"'

The hurt of those gossiped words hit me like a blow to the gut.

My legs felt like jelly, and my self-confidence drained away in seconds. Hot air radiated from the inside of the car as I quietly helped load the groceries with a tight-lipped smile masking my true feelings. *Oh right. So that's what they think.* In the warm afternoon sunshine, I felt cold inside.

As we rode home, my inner critic and I both sat silently, weighing up whether it was a lie, or whether my parents had really said that about me. She eventually chimed in: *Maybe they are right. Whatever were you thinking?*

Their words resonated and reverberated around inside me, as if they felt right at home there and were glad to have returned after such a lengthy absence. I tried to shove them back down, to tuck them away with whatever else I didn't want to deal with from the past. But they'd triggered something in me that didn't want to be tucked away that quickly.

Feeling my anxiety building, I took a breath and tried to think about it logically, from outside my own perspective of past hurt and shame. I tried to sit with their words to see if the truth was there. After all, I'd been the bad girl breaking up the family before, ruining Christmas, ruining a roast lunch.

She doesn't have it in her. Who does she think she is?

Did they see me as being weak and incompetent? If that was the case, why didn't I see it? Was I blind to what everyone else could see?

Many years later, while I was researching this book, I discovered these exact phrases, mentioned in Brené Brown's book, 'The Power of Vulnerability' (Brown, 2012), as being the words that shame uses to speak to us. This time though, they had come not from my own inner critic, but from the mouths of the elders of my own family whom I loved and trusted.

On reflection, there was an increasing struggle at that time to keep all four retired grandparents in their respective corners. A sharp word here and there, and plenty of gossip was going on between them and about each of them. They all had way too much spare time for people who'd previously been very busy in their respective careers and businesses.

Unfortunately, it didn't cross my mind to go and ask them to their faces what they meant by it. It seemed safer to stay in that hurt state, rather than risk hurting more by hearing what they had to say. I bottled it up, and chose not to fuel the elders' gossip trail with a response. I wasn't interested in causing a fuss; I just got on with things that needed to be done, but doing so with a feeling of being just that little bit more alone. I had always believed that gossip was other peoples' fears being mirrored onto me.

My own parents would never have dreamed of starting a business, or at least not one that was anything more than a hobby. By getting busy with a business, I could easily see from their perspective that it meant I would have less time with them in their retirement move north, too. As my grandma would have done to us kids, I decided all three of those elders could have done with being dragged to the laundry by their ears to get their mouths washed out with soap!

It took a great effort to pull lightness to the surface from inside of me; reminding myself, *You know it's not true.* I tried hard to breathe consciously, get outside and walk, do some laps at the pool, keep going—but there was darkness rising up from inside where I had it pushed down, and many moments that felt too hard.

I went to ground and licked my wounds. It took several days to shake it off and get back to taking care of what I had to do. There were many moments I wanted to give up, but deep inside I knew I had to pick myself up, because it was essential to my family and myself to make this happen.

One morning, I woke up and just got started. Something inside me slapped a hard hat on my head and said: You didn't need to hear that, it was unkind; but seeing that you did, let's kick butt. Your butt, too, while you're at it! You will make this work, whatever it takes. It's roll up your sleeves time, girl. Prove to them that you can. Self-doubt had momentarily attempted to shroud the beacon of light I'd lit around this business I was determined to create, but I couldn't let it fail. So, I buckled down and pushed the dark feelings back under. There was no time for them after all with so many important things to do!

Face my fears until I make it

I had never run a business before, and I found myself suddenly surrounded on all sides by difficult learning curves and people who expected me to be a leader and solve their problems. Letting them down and admitting I didn't really know what I was doing wasn't an option, so I applied the start-up mantra of 'fake it until you make it'. It worked for a while, but the word 'fake' made me shudder. It felt wrong to me. It wasn't a sustainable or honest way to operate or show up as a new business on the block.

My earlier experiences with Darryl left me with an aversion to deception and manipulation. Faking it is the same as keeping unhealthy secrets, also known as lying. So very early in those first few months of business, I self-corrected my course, and with honesty and vulnerability, I decided to face my fears until I made it instead.

I'd faced many fears before and was reasonably well practised at that, so I was okay to be genuinely me and learn from every conversation I had: with healthcare workers, clients or patients. From there, both I and the business grew in a way I was much more comfortable with.

The long hours of operation and intense nature of the business triggered my fight, flight and freeze responses constantly, and my adrenals gave my body a workout seven days and nights a week. On a positive note, my thought processing capability expanded exponentially as I devised tactics daily for maximising the matching of staff to work placements and began slowly positioning the business as the one to call, and the one to work for.

In the quiet hours, there was a constant voice inside my head saying: *Those people you employed, you know they do want work, don't you? What are you doing about that? Nobody else is going to do it for you. There is only you. Move it!*

There were times I was in bed, and not woken by a five am call for relief staff. I'd sit up with an anxious tight belly, and within minutes be across the other side of the house, in my nightie, sitting at my desk in the pre-dawn light, making calls to see if any facility needed staff that day. Much hope was involved, including the hope that my people still wanted the work if I did get it for them. I did that repeatedly, every day until my day-to-a-page business diary overflowed with bookings.

Those doubtful words of my parents, unkind as they were, served a purpose I'd never expected. In a taunting way, and regularly, my inner critic would chirp: *Alice doesn't have it in her. Who does she think she is?*

Those two sentences did have the power to light a fire under me, causing me to leap whatever business hurdle I'd felt was beyond me. They'd make me think, *What haven't I tried already? Who else should I call? I know there's something I've missed. I will make this happen!*

Remember the sea change?

Well, this wasn't a sea change business in those first few years establishing a client base and a territory. The freedom and flow of our life we had found got altered for all of us. I was so serious about answering every phone call immediately, I stopped swimming laps at the pool as there was no one else available to answer the phone for me. Our girls dropped into silence as soon as the phone rang. That took away the feeling of presence we'd had with all the lightness of our new routines and the new life we had been enjoying. Troy stepped in to help before and after work, being with the girls and doing the housework, because I'd have a page full of shifts to fill.

One phone call could mean I'd be lost, back to my desk for a few minutes or an hour. If I couldn't fulfill a request quickly, I'd come back out to do what I was doing, but the girls knew I wasn't really with them. My mind was jerking around between where I was and what I still needed to do. I'd need to get back to the client soon with an answer either way. Guilt niggled at me as I'd see the time ticking away to get the girls to school on time, or couldn't get back to finish making dinner. They entertained themselves together, played out in the garden, bouncing on the trampoline outside my office window, and Troy's parents also stepped in sometimes to spend time with them and help us get everything done.

They loved being with the girls, driving up from where they lived a few streets away, so the girls had this newly altered extended family. Troy's dad showed them how to sketch, and then my dad began to pick them up from school and take them to the park. My mum showed them how to craft and sew as my grandma had taught me. We made it work, but it wasn't the same as it was when we had first arrived.

I'm all for quality time over quantity, so what time we did have in those quiet moments when the phone wasn't ringing was quality. In the little gaps, longer on Sundays, we played in the pool together, read books before bed, and cooked sweet treats. We'd sometimes escape for a fish and chips or pizza night by the river, and I think that steady way of living helped us stay sane. So, our family slipped into a routine of accepting that this was how we were doing things for now. The fewer distractions we had the better.

I'm so grateful the girls seemed to understand that we needed to do whatever it took, so long as it wasn't forever. I had no intention for that way of living to go on any longer than we needed it to. Thankfully it was the era before going out regularly for a meal was a thing, and having coffee in a café just wasn't something we thought to do. It was simple. That's all we needed, to keep it simple.

Outside of the impacts on my family life, it was working! Relationships with hospitals and their staff were being made, bookings flowed in, and we had more and more staff to find shifts for, which meant more money coming in—and more work for me to cover. I was thrilled and distracted as a wide range of emotions filled my days: anxiety, excitement, fatigued mind, and the incredible blinding flash of the obvious solution! Every day there were wins and losses, and lessons that I would take on board.

I was acutely aware that the ball was in the client's court more than it was in mine. There were a lot of uncertainties, but we had to keep going. A budget decision might be coming down through their ranks, to stop using hired staff. Holding my breath, I'd wait to see the repercussions of that. Those plans often failed as their team rebelled, declining to work the extra hours, so then suddenly even more bookings flowed in. Page after page of faxed rosters arrived for me to fill, more than they had ever booked before.

The people in my neighbourhood must have wondered about me, as I'd do happy victory dances across the front lawn when I filled that one extra booking I'd been working on for hours on a Sunday. Physically, my energy levels would zigzag all day, but it felt so good to deliver what I had said I would and I knew the work was paying off. I was making it happen!

Sometimes I heard myself add two more words to that sentence, *I'm making it happen— so there!* Quite often, I still felt like that in those early years. I knew inside that I was proving my parents wrong. It was incredibly satisfying, but it was an unhealthy way to operate.

After two years of hard work and crazy hours, I felt like a ragdoll flopping about the place, trying to keep the smile plastered on my face, my mind as fog-free as possible, maintaining business as usual no matter what. Looking back, it was manic. I was fully in this new zone of mine, and I had a long way to go before I felt I could take my foot off the accelerator. I wasn't coming into a new industry; it was a very long-established niche market and there was no giving up. There was no letting my clients know I was taking two weeks of school holidays. Competitors would be in there in a heartbeat.

Although my mind would say *God this is hard work!* I'd tell myself, *Suck it up princess, you're not done yet.* Even though I knew it was unhealthy, it filled a need in me that was seeded decades earlier, the resolve I'd found at ten years of age. I was determined to do what I said, no matter what.

The exploration into business unleashed in me a business-woman who was passionate about finding resourcefulness, working creatively, and expanding my tactical capacity as a leader. I found it hard to let others into the most important parts of the business, in my constantly stressed state it was easier to just do most things myself. Eventually, I began to see the light at the end of the tunnel.

A couple of years into the business, Troy left his day job and joined me to interview recruits. We were running the business from home, and the girls needed at least one of us always free to ferry them to and from school and all the other after-school activities— swimming lessons, dancing, homework projects. My dad came in to help without saying a word, in his resolve 'not to sit and rot' in his retirement. He took over doing the recruitment reference checks to help us move through from the interview to a first booking faster. Soon after, we began to add more office staff, and I was able to take a small step back and reassess what was important to me.

I treasured working with the incredible people who had chosen to be part of my business. It was very humbling to work with people whose job was to care for others. I had studied nursing before having our first baby, and my dream then was to become a midwife. Later, as things turned out, the birth of my daughter and a great job with one of Sydney's reputable law firms meant I didn't pursue my nursing/midwifery dream.

Yet now, whenever I walked through any hospital my company served, across a maternity ward, an ICU or a theatre, I felt nursing and care were in my veins. I loved that this business provided hundreds of thousands of care hours every year to the people in our communities.

It was so much more than I had imagined when I started my small business, just so I didn't have to ask a boss for four weeks of annual leave each year! We were creating a growing income, something Troy and I would have never dreamt was possible, and we were able to provide better for our girls. Still, I had the feeling something was missing, lurking just under the surface. I didn't realise it at the time, but what I had been avoiding was soon going to catch up with me and change everything.

What is success?

Most of our tensions and frustrations stem from
compulsive needs to act the role of someone we are not.
HANS SELYE, ENDOCRINOLOGIST

In the time since our move north, I still hadn't done anything further about healing from my abuse. I knew my recovery from abuse and releasing the need for affirmation from my parents would be intimately linked together, but I kept pushing only one part of that—to make the business a success.

Eventually, I got caught in a vicious cycle of working harder and longer hours again, despite the extra help. When was success going to get the tick it needed from me? What was ever going to be enough?

Before I turned forty, my body started to show me signs that if I didn't stop, it would stop me. I started taking some small positive steps, like seeing a naturopath or doing a weeklong juice cleanse at the start of each season. Then I would return to work, kicking my day off with two double shot coffees just to get the day moving. I was putting Band-Aids on my health and expecting things to get better.

The naturopath told me I was living on adrenaline, and to be careful because that would have repercussions on my health at some stage. I was becoming overweight from working and sitting at my desk for too many hours. I was tired, but too wired to waste work time on exercise or rest. I wasn't sleeping well, and was stressed most of the time, but that was normal in business.

It wasn't like I was physically ill, just not well. I woke up every day in the early hours of the morning, already switched on, my mind whirring. I was working the long hours I believed were normal for successful business owners, according to all the success books I'd been reading.

I had no 'off' button. I hadn't yet connected the dots...

From the age of eight, I had become addicted to living in that adrenal, reactive state of problem-solving, coming up with ideas and then better ideas. That was just the way I operated. It served me through those abusive years, but it was an unhealthy and unbalanced way to work—and live a life.

6

Awakening

*When we feel fulfilled, we have enough time
and energy for anything needed.*
DEEPAK CHOPRA, AUTHOR

For the early years of the business, I was locked into an endless cycle of work, planning and achieving. It was an exciting and exhausting merry-go-round I knew was unhealthy, but I didn't know how to stop. The answer appeared one evening in an unexpected place—at a business conference I attended on the Gold Coast.

Troy and I were both in the audience as co-business owners. Our eldest daughter was now old enough to oversee the two younger girls, using the beautiful resort facilities to entertain them until we came to relieve her on our meal breaks. At that time, this was our idea of a family holiday, a way to get a break from the routine of school and life and the-day-to-day running of the business. That evening we were going to be meeting them back in our apartment for a room-service dinner.

We were both feeling somewhat drained as the keynote speaker, Robyn Moore, got up to do her presentation. The topic was: 'What is most important in life?' Her presentation was the second last, with a senior leader of the Australian defence force to follow, the closing highlight of a long, thought-provoking day.

Robyn touched on how we show up at the end of our day,

once we leave our office, drive home, park our car, and turn the front door handle. How are we arriving at this precious home time with our loved ones? Are we coming home tired and distracted, tired and grumpy, or tired and loving?

That was a question I could immediately see the answer to: I was showing up at home tired and distracted all the time.

At the end of that session, Troy and I looked at each other with red eyes, picked up our notebooks, walked to the front of the room and thanked Robyn. We had intended to sit through the final address before returning to the room, but instead we walked out of the auditorium together to go and have some fun with our girls. We all hopped into the car, drove into town, and found what would come to be our favourite cheap but authentic Chinese restaurant for all our future Gold Coast getaways.

After dinner, we went to the TimeZone arcade and played on all the machines, laughing together. We ate ice cream and, when we returned to the room, put on our pyjamas and chose a funny movie, all piling onto the main big bed together. I decided that day that life was too precious to be absent from the people I loved.

Over the following weeks, Robyn's message stayed with me, and as I made time and space to explore it, I observed where I had lost touch with what was important.

Simple things, like when I went upstairs to the kitchen from my bedroom in the morning. I'd stopped raising my eyes to see the extraordinary 180-degree view we had of the ocean to the mountains, turning on the kettle and dropping bread in the toaster instead. We lived in an amazing treehouse-style home that looked out across the treetops of the National Park. We'd moved in not long ago, and I wasn't even appreciating the view. When had I lost the sense of wonder that view gave me?

I could see I was living on autopilot. Up before dawn, my thoughts were immediately on work, then I'd head down to the office and be home late. I was feeling it physically and wasn't getting much time for presence and intimacy with Troy because my mind was elsewhere, or because the girls took priority when I was home.

At work, I observed that I wasn't as effective as I could be either. My mind was tired. I would get caught up in other peoples' dramas, draining my energy but not resolving them. That felt ineffective and time-wasting to me, and it further affected my sleep. I would toss and turn with worry and self-doubt through the night, before heading back to work at first light.

It became crystal clear to me that how I showed up in my home, work, and personal relationships was way off course. I'd listened to Robyn Moore's message at that conference, and it had felt so good to take steps to break my pattern afterwards, but somehow, I'd already slipped back into my old habit, far too quickly.

I felt like crying at the drop of a hat, like I was beginning to crack at the seams. Then that reminded me I'd thought of those words before, back when I first wondered about therapy as a young mum. I'd known I needed to do some more work on myself, to heal from the abuse in my childhood. But I was too busy for that—for fear of cracking open at the seams.

I suddenly realised that it was time. I knew I needed to find out whether talking to someone about what I had been holding inside of me might be good for me after all.

Returning to the path of healing

Thankfully, now that we had a solid and reliable business team forming, I was able to look at my schedule and find a time I could give myself— just one hour a week for a start.

I stepped outside my work/life routine to look around and see what else was available to me. Not the successful businesswoman me—but the woman herself.

It was 2005, and I had felt a new sense of empowerment on turning forty, having made it through the first fifteen years of parenting, and seeming to have not screwed up too much. Now felt like the right time to give some attention to myself and find out what made me tick.

It was clear I needed to talk to a psychologist about Darryl's abuse, but that seemed too full-on. A little too risky, maybe. Instead, the healing work found its way to me along an alternative route, that began with a Bowen Therapy treatment—one hour a week for three weeks.

I had the pleasure of being referred to a healer called Helene. A tiny, white-haired woman I truly believed was a white witch, Helene had the best 'witchy-poo' giggle! At first, I went to her for a package of three Bowen massages, and as time went on and our rapport strengthened, I eventually opened up to her about Darryl.

For each session, I'd walk down the side passage of Helene's house to her small treatment room. She'd let me get my day's thoughts out of my head, and then we'd talk about what we would work through that day. I would lie on her comfortable massage table, and she would gently and kindly encourage me into a soothing hypnotic state. Each deep breath out was accompanied with a word, repeated like a mantra: 'relax, relax, relax', and soon I'd drop into a far more peaceful place than when I'd walked in her door.

Helene would only work on one area of my body at a time, one area per session. It was a painful and bruising massage. She would explain the types of emotions held in that area of the body, and what might have caused those emotions to get stuck there. Her fingers would feel for the knots in my muscles that were holding the stuck emotions we were going to shift. Helene would keep working and kneading away to clear the deep painful knots while memories would surface.

In some sessions, I'd find that I'd suddenly be overwhelmed with grief, and tears would flow off the sides of my face into my hair. If I could, I'd tell her what I was seeing, and she'd do healing work and gently close out that session. Then we'd do the same the following week on another part of my body. It was painful work, physically and emotionally, and I often needed to concentrate on breathing to stop myself from jumping off the table.

It felt like I needed to feel it at that level, though. Like I had to break through an icy layer of numbness in my mind, heart and all over my body. I would leave Helene's treatment room feeling calm, knowing something had shifted. When I returned home, it was sometimes a little shocking to find that life was continuing as normal: the girls, the business and the day-to-day tasks of being a parent and business owner. I often needed to give myself a few days of being quiet and treating myself kindly to integrate what had shifted.

Over time Helene introduced me to hypnosis, timeline therapy, and other trauma- and memory-releasing techniques. She also gave me information and blog posts to read, to open my thinking and help me relax my mind which was constantly running to make sure everything was under control at work.

I remember distinctly one day, sitting at my computer at home after seeing Helene, reading a blog post about the drama triangle. I found the idea immediately interesting: a triangle of roles commonly played out by families caught in the cycle of stress and drama, just as mine had throughout my childhood and adult years.

Dr. Karpman's drama triangle

The blog author started by explaining that the drama triangle, invented in 1960 by Dr. Stephen Karpman, describes roles that human beings default to in times of stress. The three points of the triangle apply to roles we subconsciously assume, to help us cope in dramatic situations. These situations can be work related, or among people in our communities or social circles, but as in my case, they are also found within family dynamics.

The drama triangle centres around the key role of the victim (not abuse victim, but someone playing the role of victim). There will also be someone or something that plays the role of persecutor, and another the rescuer role. The three roles are not fixed, and the same person can shift between the roles as the situation fluidly shifts and changes.

The author shared an example of how the drama could be played out in a family, which caught my attention immediately and resonated with my own family history.

It went something like this: Imagine a family where the father drinks regularly and is often absent. The mother feels that she doesn't have his attention, like she's being treated like a doormat. The father is then seen as the persecutor, and the mother is the victim. The mother may then become resentful, and resort to berating and belittling the father in front of the children.

Now, the mother is the persecutor, and the father feels like the victim. The rest of the family don't want to cause any further issues, and tiptoe around, making sure they either stay out of the way or act in certain ways to fix the situation. By pleasing and 'being good', or offering to help with the chores for example, they then become the rescuers.

When the heat of the problem settles down, the father buys mum flowers, and everything between the two of them might be happy for a time. However later on, the mother might flip into a persecutor role, micromanaging the children in their efforts around the home, nagging and controlling. As a result, the kids withdraw from their rescuer roles, thinking they can't get anything right and feeling persecuted. They then become the victims. Over time, tension builds in the air, and next thing you know, the father is back at the pub again—and the vicious cycle repeats.

I read over that family example a few times. I easily could see how it applied in my childhood home, and how the drama triangle could be seen in other areas of my life, and in other people's lives. I was stunned at how well it explained so many of my experiences both within my family and outside of it. At that time I remember thinking with relief, *This is not just my family then*, if Dr. Karpman had come up with this model before I was even born.

The blog author then explained that awareness of this triangle of roles and behaviours, and taking careful disciplined action can help us to break the cycle. As I meditated on it, I actually did find that I was able to let go of long-held resentments and stuck emotions I had felt about my family. I was able to see that they were just people, trying to cope in a difficult situation they did not fully understand.

The drama triangle was just one of the things that began to help me open up to viewing my past in a different way, but it is one that has stayed with me for many years.

Coinciding with that experimentation in alternative healing, we opened a satellite office on the Gold Coast, a three-hour drive south of our home. I had to be away from home often to meet the new clients, so I normally planned an overnight stay to get the most out of the day's business. I thought one of these trips might be a good opportunity for Mum and I to get away from home together and catch up.

We didn't spend much quality time together and I felt on edge with her at that time, unfortunately. She was surreptitiously talking about Darryl with my girls when she minded them, or getting them to speak with him on the phone. Mum was keen for the road trip, and she found an art shop and signed up to do a one-day art class.

I'd do what I had to for work, then we'd meet up for dinner and head back to the Sunshine Coast the following day.

We were at our favourite Chinese restaurant, when Mum said, 'You appear to have better self-esteem than you used to have, Alice.'

Ostensibly, it was a nice compliment. I could have murmured my thanks and moved on, couldn't I? I could have continued skimming the surface with light-weight conversation and remained silent about the abuse even though I was currently working on that with Helene. Oh yes, I could have! But I didn't.

I looked up from my plate. Angry heat filled my chest, and I felt my carotid pulse thump harder than usual. I deliberately put my fork down and said, not angrily or loudly, but firmly, like I was the only adult here, 'Mum, you do know that being sexually abused by Darryl when I was a girl had something to do with my low self-esteem. Don't you?'

There was silence from the other side of the table then mum replied, 'No, I didn't know that.'

I leapfrogged my way beyond the improved self-esteem conversation and into the void of unspoken words. 'Mum, I've been wondering, how come you've never acknowledged the abuse nor apologised for not believing me, and for telling me I was lying to you?'

The gates flew open wider than I'd allowed to happen before. I had had enough of holding my good girl's tongue.

'How come you didn't know Darryl was doing what he did?'

I put my hands down flat on the table, finishing with, 'No idea at all, for all that time? Come on, think, surely you heard or saw something.'

Nothing.

Thankfully, it was a night when only a few other tables were occupied, and they weren't terribly close to us. As far as restaurant conversation goes, it was an uncomfortable one.

Conscious of not being my usual polite and contained self and feeling a little surprised at having said these things, I suggested we leave and go back to our accommodation so that we could talk in privacy, if she'd like to do that.

We sat in lounge chairs across from each other, nursing mugs of hot tea until we'd both asked the questions we needed the answers to. Mum had never asked me anything more about what I'd told her that day when I was twenty-five, so I filled in what gaps I could for her. The questions and answers didn't all get asked with a relaxed tone of voice either; some had a hint of sarcasm, and there was venting, words that each of us had wanted to say for a very long time.

Mum did apologise for letting me down and for not believing me. The conversation's outcome was Mum wringing her hands in her lap, saying, 'You need to understand that Darryl is my son.'

That conversation with Mum was the first time my unexpressed anger and resentment about the abuse bubbled to the surface in a conversation. I think the healing work I'd been doing with Helene had prepared me to say the words. It was clumsy but I felt I'd said all that I needed to, and it released the poison of anger from my body.

Is forgiveness real?

Helene soon retired from her practice. Feeling buoyed by the experience I'd had with Helene, of opening up without cracking down the seams, I thought I would continue to explore options to heal myself. I was told about a local clinical hypnotherapist who had helped a friend lose weight. Despite the fundamental idea of it being helping me lose weight, very soon the sexual abuse came to the surface for attention.

I had read and heard from other sources that weight problems can be related to trauma. That could involve holding onto weight to keep ourselves comforted and safe, self-harm or subconscious attempts to not attract attention. Also, I knew many people had issues surrounding body image, caused by the diet-driven, calorie counting years we grew up in. What I felt instinctively though was that weight is never the problem. Therefore, it didn't surprise me when the issue of my abuse came up.

I asked the hypnotherapist if it was possible to forgive someone who had abused me. Can hypnosis help me do that? She said it wouldn't hurt to try if I'd like to focus on that, and we scheduled to work on forgiveness in the next week's session.

I remember one moment under hypnosis that I visualised both Mum and Darryl attached to cords tied around their waists. I was holding the other end of each cord. They were sent floating up into the sky like helium balloons. Mum was in full colour, wearing a flowery nightie, and a shiny red silk cord around her waist. Darryl was grey-skinned and in grey clothes, with a barbed wire belt for his cord. I was attempting a practice aimed at forgiving both of them, which I wasn't sure was possible at that stage, but it felt good to try.

I visualised Mum as soft, pale and clay-like. She was wearing her nightie as she so often did when we all lived at home. She floated back to Earth: she could be loved as she was. She was who she was back then, and now. I couldn't expect anything from her or change what had happened between us. The red cord dropped away from her waist, and I dropped my end of the cord to the ground. Free. Darryl came back to Earth, remaining grey, sour-faced, and stone-like.

The hypnotherapist suggested I cut the barbed-wire cord, which, considering what it was made of, would need a chainsaw. The most significant realisation I got from this exercise was that forgiving Darryl didn't have to look like what I had imagined forgiveness to be. I could feel inside me that it wasn't actually about excusing or absolving his actions. Forgiving Darryl was more about seeing the reality of something damaged about him, which made him sexually deviant towards his little sister.

Cutting through that barbed wire required focus and strength to keep me safe. But I did it.

The process was not sunshine and rainbows. I didn't rejoice and welcome him with open arms as if nothing had ever happened, but I knew that any bonds Darryl ever held over my heart were cut loose. Deep down in my soul, I knew he would never be someone I would trust. Through his actions, Darryl had forfeited a place in my life forever.

At the time, that gave me a sense of peace.

7

There Are No Failures, Only Lessons

I can be changed by what happens to me.
But I refuse to be reduced by it.
MAYA ANGELOU, AUTHOR

By 2008, those first dabbles in healing and hypnotherapy had made a small difference. I could feel myself shifting and feeling lighter, but I was not going to be able to give that part of me any more airtime for the moment. I didn't realise it at the time, but I was about to lead the company through a chaotic time of challenge that stretched me to breaking point.

Without warning, our company took a massive hit from the impact of the global financial crisis (GFC) on the healthcare sector. Funding and spending in the whole sector were drastically reduced within a very short time, decimating our clients' ability and readiness to spend on temporary staffing.

Our demand dropped catastrophically overnight, and we had no choice but to adjust quickly or close the business. We shut down three satellite offices we'd just opened and poured all our efforts and money into. We had to respond quickly and do whatever was necessary to keep the company afloat and survive the next few years.

It was a very tough time. Big changes and sacrifices rocked us every week, but we had to let go and accept them just to keep the business afloat, as many others folded at this time. We battened down the hatches and rode the storm, which had an effect not only on the business but our family too as stress levels rocketed at the same time as our budget was drastically reduced.

Eventually things began to stabilise, but just as we were coming up for air, an entirely new difficulty raised its head: the swine flu pandemic. We were suddenly tasked with helping to design and implement new measures to reduce the spread of infection, not only among our own workers, but all of the healthcare professionals. At the same time, due to many medical professionals getting sick and the need to enforce quarantine protocols, there was a huge extra demand for temporary staff.

That crisis shifted our relationship with the industry, requiring us to step up as partners to the government and other regulatory bodies, not only as suppliers of staff as businesses like ours had been thought of before. All the hard work we had done previously put us in a unique position to provide help to the industry and all the people working in it, or supported by it. We suddenly became important players, with a heavy burden of responsibility for the entire community in a time of crisis.

In a very short period of time, we went from one extreme to the other. I forgot all about high achieving, and my desire for success was thrown out the window.

I experienced survival, commitment to serve and plenty of hard work—digging deep daily for new ways to sustain our business and support the industry. Once again, I was thrown into a whirlwind of work that gave me almost no time and space for myself, but this time there was a sense that I was doing it for different reasons. The feeling that I was somehow avoiding my inner work by running from one crisis to another was still there, but definitely less. I actually longed for some time to myself, and a chance to reconnect with some of the healing work I had been doing before.

Sometimes without even looking, it found me!

I recall being incredibly tired on a Friday afternoon and taking an early mark from work, thankful for a Mother's Day gift voucher to the local spa, where I practically had a book drop into my lap.

I was in the lounge area, waiting to be called for my massage. On the magazine rack across the room from my lounge, I saw a small paperback. The title was intriguing, 'The Monk Who Sold His Ferrari', by Robin Sharma (1998). I read the back cover and thought to myself, *When the student is ready, the teacher appears.* It felt like a breeze had blown through me to free the cobwebs of tiredness. I placed it back where I'd found it to go and enjoy the massage, and before I drove home I stopped in at the local bookstore and picked up a copy. It was a short, easy read, and I flew through it cover-to-cover over the weekend.

Robin introduced me to journalling and meditation, and I set up my first thirty-day habit creator with some new personal, life-enriching activities. I felt an opportunity for change that hadn't been possible before. Not a difficult transition that required struggle, but one that was about ease and self-care, and giving myself the beauty and grace of new rituals.

All the new practices were about self-love, self-care, and self-awareness. I changed a lot during that time, largely because of my new habits, I believe. I'd never meditated regularly before, but I found especially visualisation to be a powerful exercise for me. It suited me. Afterwards, journaling what I saw in those visualisations set me up calmly for the day and even made me more productive at work.

The peace I was finding in my inner life began to be reflected in my business life as well. Our hard work and determination had paid off; we'd survived the GFC, and the swine flu had been a profitable time for agencies. There was still a lot of work to be done, and plenty of pressure and responsibility, but a time of relative peace descended upon us. We lived in a lovely house on top of a hill, our back gate opening onto the National Park. I'd rise early and put on my iPod, and as I walked through the forest at dawn for an hour I'd listen to Robin's lessons.

I hadn't listened to spiritual leaders such as Deepak Chopra and Osho before that. The slow pace at which they talked would drive me crazy. But now I was slipping into a space where my tolerance was changing, I was becoming more present, and I approached life with far more clarity.

Gradually I was led on a slow and intriguing 180-degree turn away from my drive to be a high achiever in business with these early dabbles in therapies, and reading the books of inspiring leaders. I'd return to the office from a personal or professional development event, and it wouldn't be long before someone would ask, 'So, do you feel like it changed you?' I'd smile and say, 'Yes, it did', but I didn't need to flash it around. It was an internal change for me. I felt clear-minded, purposeful, confident and empowered.

As inspired as I felt, I was conscious that I was still ducking and dodging asking for direct professional help to recover from the sexual abuse. I was secretly hoping all this self-nurturing I was giving myself was going to magically fix that 'stuff' for me without needing to speak about it.

How good would that be? Magic!

After the hypnotherapy I'd had earlier, I rarely thought about Darryl anymore—maybe releasing him in that visualisation of forgiveness was enough of a change for now?

I have no doubt now that exercise was a significant release for me. However, I hadn't given that healing moment much of a thought afterwards. It's only now when I look back at it years later that I realise the significance it had.

Darryl was gone from my life. My mum was the only person in my circle who ever mentioned his name, she couldn't seem to stop herself from sharing his news with me despite my many requests not to.

Letting go and blaming effectively

As the crises relented, I continued looking for healing in easier ways; reading inspiring material, practising self-care, and attending personal development conferences at least once a year. One event on the Gold Coast in 2011 though, would force me to look at myself and my personal history through a whole new set of lenses.

On the first morning, sitting in the conference room with about one thousand attendees, we were asked to visualise a person or symbol we had called upon to help us through some traumatic or highly emotional event earlier in our life. Before those instructions were even completed, I'd already drawn into my mind the indomitable lioness who'd appeared at that family lunch, the final one I attended with Darryl decades earlier.

In that exercise, I thanked the lioness for what she'd brought to my life, and told her that she was welcome to stay, seeing as she is a part of me. However, as I placed my hand over my heart, I immediately knew that I no longer needed to maintain such a high level of protectiveness for myself or my girls—who were now themselves becoming strong, independent women.

In the packed conference room, I sat in a long moment of deep appreciation for the changes I had personally put in motion. Troy and I had raised our daughters to explore their truths, make bold choices, and learn from their mistakes.

To me, at some stage, our role in parenthood shifts from being the managers of children and teens, to become the good loving friends and trusted advisors of the adults they're becoming. We support them as they correct their own courses, and watch them become resilient, loving and kind members of the community.

That lioness within me was a strength that arose because of the shock triggering of memories of abuse, and a resolve to act to protect them no matter what. I didn't have to carry those over-protective measures around with me forever. I realised I didn't need to be a fierce lioness anymore, and it was a delightful moment that made me smile as I let down my guard.

I felt myself relax deeply in that moment, my shoulders softening as every part of my body finally let go of another deep layer of protection. That was such a stunning revelation. Letting go of the tension that went along with that—with self-love—was an extremely empowering moment for me.

We all know that blame is part of life

At that same weekend, I was introduced to an intriguing mindset shift called 'The Power of Effective Blaming' (Robbins, A. 2011). The first question in that session was: 'Whom do you blame?' My answer was easy: *Darryl for his abuse.*

The point of this exercise was that if you're going to blame, then blame effectively, accurately and in a balanced way.

If you're going to blame someone for your pain, you should also blame them for your happiness. It was a completely different angle, one I'd never contemplated before, one I had to sit with in silence to see if it was even possible for me.

The process fired my mind up on all cylinders. I felt such a lot of old memories and emotions arise as I worked through it and concluded with three questions:

1. What good things can I blame my brother for because of his abuse?
2. What good has come from it—because that is his fault, too.
3. What's beautiful in my life today, and why?

A guardian angel

After that event, I hired a personal results coach—and that was one of the best gifts I ever gave myself.

My coach, Leanne, matched me well; she had the kind of maturity, business, and life experience that were relatable to me, and she paced what we worked through perfectly. I knew immediately that I had partnered with a coach who would challenge and support me to reach my full potential as I took my life and business forward.

I wasn't aware then, but a coach is different from a therapist or psychologist. A coach is forward-focused, whereas therapists look back at the origins of trauma and what might have caused life to skew off the desired path.

That fact was pointed out on the intake form I completed a few days before our introductory Skype call. On the intake form, I was asked to describe a situation I'd experienced in my life—and how I had contributed to making a positive change happen.

Given that the event I'd just been at had picked up threads of the lioness, and other events related to the abuse, I made mention of what I'd experienced and what I had done about it.

In the first phone call with Leanne, she responded to my admission of the abuse with 'and you dealt with that already?'

I didn't want to sound weak, so I heard myself saying with confidence: 'Yes! Of course.' I didn't want to ask, *Could you possibly explain what 'dealt with' means?* I couldn't admit that I was edging toward midlife and had not begun deep work on the trauma of the abuse in my childhood.

Even though I felt that I had not been completely honest with her, I went on that year to accomplish more than I could have imagined with Leanne's help, establishing a brilliant vision for my life and the company's plans.

One powerful coaching session that I recall vividly set me up to manage a massive change. It happened one morning while I was seated in my comfy reading chair in our house on the hill. I found this corner of our room was the best space for peace, where I wouldn't be disrupted after dialling in. I had my mobile propped between my ear and shoulder, my feet on the stool in front of me so I could write thoughts and notes into my notebook whilst we talked.

In the coaching call this day, I told Leanne I would like to map out one of my plans for myself and the business over the next few years. This plan was all about fulfilment, growth and contribution, all of which were becoming more and more meaningful to me. In my hand-sketched circles of the mind map, I had a few interesting possibilities to consider:

- Will I keep the company as a family-owned business long-term?
- What about merging it with the service that had approached me that only supplied locum doctors?
- Should I keep the company and bring in management so I can step up and out of the day-to-day management?
- Will I sell the company?

For each of those choices, I wrote down what each would give me and what each of those felt like for me.

Leanne asked me to think about it in silence—I sat for five long minutes without speaking, and in that space she held, I saw the answer. I put my pen on the outer edge of the circle and added a zig-zag line all the way around its edge, like it was the sun shining brightly at the very idea of it. It was a course of action that was going to serve the company, our people, and the clients, and what also felt exciting was that I could see it serving our family and me as well.

I looked up from my new sunny centre of the mind map and said out loud the outcome I truly desired: I am going to sell the company.

It gave me goosebumps saying it for the first time with confidence, knowing I would make that outcome become my reality. Knowing that the outcome was about more than just myself felt so good. I knew it would involve growth, contribution, and fulfilment for all involved, both getting to the point of sale, and afterwards.

It felt like a great solution that would honour what I'd created. I had started the business knowing it had to be a sustainable service. The industry was changing, making things harder not easier, and I just knew it was a time where what I had been doing was no longer sustainable for me.

I was giving myself the gift of permission to walk away, and on my own terms. I didn't start the business with the idea of being a national organisation. I started it as a sea change business, but it had grown far beyond that vision. I had launched into this crazy venture to better provide for my family, and I had done that—and more. It was time to let go and change. It was also time for me to let go of the past, get the help I needed, and move on.

I wanted to honour the whole of me in this one life I have. I realised there was much more to be, do and have beyond the time I had spent on this business. After I put the phone down, I stayed where I was seated. I put down the notebook and stretched my legs out across the footstool, laying my hands on the arms of the chair.

Here in this comfortable room, with the morning sun fragmenting from the treetops into endless shades of green, peace surrounded me as I felt a dream coming closer to being realised. I reflected on the many hours spent journalling about my dreams for my life. They had mostly happened right here in this chair.

Celebrating love

With decisions about the business made, they had to be temporarily shelved as joyful personal celebrations coloured our world in 2012. Our eldest daughter, so beautifully in love, got engaged and our family came together as we'd never done at any time before. Planning the wedding became an amazing celebration of love for us all, like a colourful sari of exquisite silk. Everything fell into place so easily as we made the plans for the wedding, almost as if the whole world had fallen into alignment.

I was no longer so worried about 'Doing the right thing', getting everything right, or pleasing anyone else'.

I felt free and fulfilled, and love welled between Troy and I, and all the members of our family. It was such a beautiful time, full of ease and grace. Almost as if this couple in love had been touched with all the goodness of the world concentrated and it radiated out, affecting everyone. It was such a wonderful way to begin this new life together.

The days of the wedding weekend were a joyful time, everyone talking and helping each other, love was everywhere you turned. We danced up a storm, laughed and cried and made many unforgettable memories in a unique place of natural beauty. It was a magical time, we were all together so open-heartedly, like nothing any of us had experienced before. We didn't know it then, but that special wedding weekend was to be the last celebration that all of us attended together—the following year, I would lose my dad, and Troy's family lost one of their beautiful young men. The stories we made and images we captured at our daughter's wedding have filled our hearts many times since.

The sale of business

It was soon time to get back to the realities of business life, and see what I could do towards my goal to sell the business. I put aside all the frivolities, and got right down to it, knowing that it is normally a lengthy process to sell a business such as this. I'd gone to great effort through the crises to maintain certain relationships and preferred supplier agreements, so that other competitors would look at us as a positive potential acquisition. In the end, it came about faster than I'd thought.

I received a call from a retired mayor one day, saying he wanted to come and talk to me over coffee about the state of our local economy. My instinct told me something was not quite right, although it could have been a legitimate thing to ask—I'd been a local government economic development advisory board director a few years earlier. I agreed to meet the following week and looked him up to prepare for our chat.

His name was listed in connection with an organisation that had recently purchased a big national competitor with its head office in Victoria. That competitor had been starting to make some moves on our local clients, so I had been watching and getting filled in about their antics by our loyal clients and our field staff for the last few months.

Knowing that this organisation had acquired that large agency not long ago, my interest in our conversation increased. I reached out to him, informing him about what I knew so it wouldn't make the conversation awkward when we met. He said he hadn't realised they'd bought an agency.

We met at a café down the street from our office. Rather than dilly-dally, I said not far into the conversation that I planned to sell the company in the next one to three years, but didn't know yet whom I'd sell it to. He said he'd go and have a chat with his team and line up a meeting.

The process of due diligence started four months later. Due diligence is where the buyer asks the seller to provide documented proof of what the business has in place, such as financial details and assets—what the business is really worth.

I recall my brother-in-law calling me saying, 'Alice, you're not selling a coffee shop. Get yourself a team of experts.' Thankfully, and coincidentally, I had recently met one of the top acquisition specialists in the field, the day before I'd received that first phone call from the retired mayor. She and her team of associates provided incredible support through that process. I cannot imagine how I'd have survived that process without them.

A boy and his toy

The timing of the due diligence beginning wasn't great. Troy's long-planned off-road motorbike trip was scheduled to begin two days into the process. He looked glum in the days leading up to it, knowing there was so much to be done to get the sale through.

We agreed there was not much for it; he'd planned his trip long ago and it was already paid for. With a kiss on the nose through his helmet, I waved him goodbye early on the Saturday morning. He was to be gone for three weeks. I was okay because I wanted to be fully in my focused zone of delivering what the purchasers were asking from me and the acquisition specialists had a superhero vibe about them, so I felt I was safe to get the job done.

Troy posted a photo of himself on Instagram on Sunday morning, standing in his bike gear, coffee cup in hand, looking happy as an offroad motorbike rider in the dirt! Sunday before sunset, I got a call from one of the other bloke's wives saying Troy had been in an accident.

He'd broken his collarbone and was taken to the closest rural hospital.

One of his mates sent a picture of Troy looking cheerful with his arm in a sling in the small emergency room, his mates pretending to feed him a beer in his hospital bed. I was relieved.

Our son-in-law, an emergency nurse, was at our place and offered to drive the six-hour distance to retrieve Troy. I rang the hospital to tell them that was the plan, and they said, 'Well, no, that won't work. We're flying Troy by air ambulance to Toowoomba Hospital tonight.'

For a collarbone? Really? That sounded like overkill, but where they were flying him to was closer than the town he was in, so it worked. I didn't question it, and stayed in touch with the hospital as they gave me progress updates on Troy's departure, and his expected time of arrival.

Our daughter and son-in-law took off at dawn on Monday morning to be there with Troy, allowing me the morning to delegate tasks to the rest of the office team, so I could leave and get on the road for my three-hour drive, my bag packed, in case I had to stay longer than one night.

I began getting messages dinging on my phone as I drove along the highway across the rolling hills west of Ipswich, to travel up and over the mountain range to where Troy was now.

The messages worried me; had something happened? Enough

dings were coming through to make me pull over because I couldn't concentrate on the road. My eyes kept straying, trying to understand what I was seeing on my phone where I had it on the dashboard.

Our son-in-law had messaged that Troy was in the ICU.

That message was followed by more messages detailing a long list of injuries Troy had sustained. I asked for no more messaging, so I could focus on the road, and kept my eyes on the road, knowing I couldn't do anything. I needed to be there.

What had happened was that on Sunday, the group of riders were having a great day, and Troy, used to the type of road they were on, didn't think twice about driving across a shallow ditch in the dirt. Unfortunately, it wasn't shallow. It was a very deep ditch filled to the top with fine bulldust.

Troy's bike's back wheel dropped into that hole, then catapulted Troy and the bike into the sky. Troy was bucked forty metres up the road. He later told me that he recalled it being in slow motion. As he flew through the air like a helmeted upside-down bird, Troy recalled watching the trees passing by as he turned his head to see whether his motorbike was on the same trajectory as him. Thankfully it wasn't, but that turning of his head, we could see later by the damage on his helmet, had him landing on the road on just enough of an angle not to break his neck. He said the thought that came to his mind before he hit the hard dirt road was, 'I know this isn't going to end well.'

As I arrived at the ICU, I choked up. Troy was surrounded by drips, all bandaged up and bruised.

He had broken bones and internal injuries.

He was alive but sore—up to his eyeballs in drugs, stinky and filthy dirty from his bike trip antics—but he was not permanently disabled.

We were both elated!

We looked like the happiest couple an ICU could have come through their unit. Possibly also like the craziest people, given the grubby and bruised state that Troy was in, and all the beeps and buzzes going on around his bed.

We were both so grateful that he was alive and not paralysed, and that he would eventually be fully healed. That's all we focused on. More injuries were added to the list after all the tests and scans were done. However, we kept coming back to gratitude that he was alive, making all the other messages about what needed to be done for him easier to process.

I stayed for a week in a hotel close by. We had to coordinate which hospital Troy would be transferred back to on the coast: he'd need surgery and rehabilitation for weeks to come in order to get back on his feet again. In moments like those, I truly appreciated the compassion and care of our hospital connections back on the coast, especially that one person who said, 'Leave it with me, let's get Troy home,' and took care of all the difficult arrangements.

In the meantime, I continued pushing the paperwork through to the proposed purchaser of the company from my hotel room at night, and my chair beside Troy's bed during the day, answering every question they threw my way. All that in between supplying Troy with pee bottles, snacks, conversation, and just the right amount of laughs. With his internal injuries, too much laughing was not allowed!

Troy eventually fully recovered. We have a few milestone pictures of him: standing up from the wheelchair one day before he left rehab; when he came back to work; and back to his old self or as close to that as he could wish for.

While he had been unwell, my superhero team of experts had done their job superbly, and the preparations we had made in the years leading up to the sale had put us in an extremely favourable position. The company sale went through without issue a few months later. There was just one surprise: I had to commit to a two-year earn-out as part of the terms of the sale. I hadn't been expecting that.

It meant I would have to stay on working for the company, to make sure that it kept rolling along more or less as it had when I ran it. It wasn't really what I had wanted when I decided to sell the business. Just when I thought I was free to leave it behind and focus on myself for once, it seemed I would have to stay chained to the driver's seat for a few more years. It could have been a deep disappointment, but we were still feeling so grateful that Troy was alright, that we just accepted it as a necessary price, and got on with things.

I was expected to grow the sales towards a target we agreed on for each year, and if I surpassed that target, I'd not only get paid the second and third instalments of the sale price but an additional bonus. I was to be paid a healthy salary to shut up and get on with what I needed to do, until I'd done my time.

Those two years were very difficult and tiring. I felt like I had already placed my victory flag at the very top of a mountain, only to see there was that little bit further to the ultimate peak that was previously tucked out of sight. The joy of selling, of achieving and celebrating that long-desired outcome, and then having to show up and grow the business for two more years for people my values were misaligned with... to be honest that was one massive mind f**k!

On a Thursday in October 2016, I woke up at 4 am to the sound of our many bird friends in the neighbourhood and thought, *This is it. We made it*!

I jumped out of bed, and Troy pretended to be asleep, putting his pillow over his head. I leapt back on the bed, knelt beside him, and bounced the mattress to get him up, saying, 'Come on, Troy, it's today. Get up! You've got to get up now! Hear the birds outside.

It's today. It's finally the last day. Let's go and swim and get a coffee. There's nothing left to be done. Tomorrow we can rest.'

Our swimmers were pulled on in no time, we grabbed a towel each, and we were off. It was the last day, before the first day of the rest of our lives.

8

A Personal Mission

*If you want to have enough to give to others, you will
need to take care of yourself first. A tree that refuses water
and sunlight for itself, cannot bear fruit for others.*
EMILY MAROUTIAN, AUTHOR

In the years after the sale of the business, I finally was able to
dedicate more time to myself. At first, I found adjusting to the
new rhythm of life beyond business difficult, but as it involved
more leisure and free time with Troy and our girls, it was not as
hard as some other transitions I have experienced! I will mention
some other details about this time later.

For now, I would like to focus in on the genesis of this book,
which in the fertile space that appeared after the business' sale, was
intimately connected with the appearance of my personal mission.

I had continued my ritual of meditation and journalling every
day, and at numerous times I would experience a complete sense
of clarity and great energy. I'd write in a stream of consciousness
without letting the pen leave the page for three, five or maybe ten
minutes at a time.

It was as though I was connecting suddenly with my inner
wisdom and didn't want to waste a moment or allow any space for
my habitual self-blocking to enter. I was writing as if possessed,
and the pen moved by itself. I explored what I truly wanted, why
I wanted it, what it meant to me, and so on, drilling deeper and

deeper. I wrote letters to myself to read in the years to come, sharing what I wanted in my life.

Free the world's daughters...
Free young women from the shackles of guilt
and shame now, not wait until they're forty, fifty
or sixty to find true peace, freedom, and joy.
I will be a voice in the silent landscape
of sibling sexual abuse.

Words to that effect would flow through my pen from my heart, time and again. A draft mission statement began to take form as, almost in a trance, I started seeing my life purpose appearing on the paper. I didn't pinpoint when I would start that mission nor what would be involved, I just wrote.

Whilst I was deeply moved by what I'd captured in that writing, I knew that Young Alice was there with me too, nervously pitching from one foot to the other, whispering, *Really? Why don't you look after yourself first? That's as good a place as any to start.*

It starts with me

This mission was a huge, impressive thing I felt I could accomplish for other survivors, but I was aware that it was, in part, just another bright shiny distraction. What about me? Don't I want to heal? Why was I feeling so passionate about freeing others and not myself?

Wasn't writing the words 'trapped in the shackles of guilt and shame' about myself?

I still felt nervous jitters in my chest whenever I even said the words 'I was sexually abused' or talked about incest or sexual abuse out loud. I hadn't attempted to understand or find out all that 'sibling sexual abuse' truly meant, let alone its repercussions on my life.

I sat with a sense of discomfort that my huge mission was just another thing keeping me away from taking care of myself first. When the mind has been determined not to look at certain things, it can be very difficult to see clearly and with perspective.

For that huge mission to ever be realised, I needed to start with me first. In this, my beautiful daughters were to become my non-judgmental, trusted confidantes.

Normalising the conversation

When they had been navigating their teenage years, I hadn't been sure when would be the right time to talk more in-depth with a young girl about my history of sexual abuse—or three young girls, as was our case. In the end, it had come down to their readiness, maturity and curiosity that led to each conversation occurring.

One by one, they'd ask me questions about what had happened in my earlier years. I told them that Darryl had sexually abused me as a girl, so I don't want him in my life, nor near any of you, and that was all I had shared.

Although it was ultimately very healing and supportive to connect with them in even that small way, when I found myself in those conversations with each of them it had made me feel like I was losing control emotionally. I felt an energetic and defensive forcefield surround me from head to toe.

I didn't respond defensively, I responded to what was asked, but I could tell I was triggered, and it would take me a few hours after each conversation for that feeling to recede and leave me to go about whatever the day needed of me.

Back then, it was hard to choose what to share. Sometimes small flashes of memories and dreams showed up like a dark personal slide show running inside my head that part of me was watching, while the rest of me was trying to remain in the conversation.

Although I didn't often think about it, the disbelief, ensuing silence, and unwillingness of adults to engage in conversation or offer support when I had first disclosed it at ten and twenty-five made it hard to trust that I could open the topic again.

Non-judgmental, safe and meaningful communication was not part of the base from which I'd been raised. I'd been branded as a liar, the one who broke up the family, and the emotions and hurt of those memories made me fearful of being the cause of it happening again.

Now, our daughters had become independent women, establishing careers, homes and relationships of their own. It was time for me to practice normalising the conversation about my experience of abuse, starting gently and in small portions. This time, I was ready and willing to take the lead and speak first.

When my eldest daughter and I spoke, I felt her protectiveness towards me emanating from her anger at my brother's abuse and how several of my disclosures to those who held positions of adult responsibility had flopped so terribly. Always a gentle soul with a kind heart, who can see people and situations for who and what they are, she has no interest in drama. We talked straight, and I felt I could share more, noticing that my voice shook a little less as I did. We also discussed the event involving her cousin, where my lioness persona became unleashed. She recalled knowing I was angry like she'd never seen before. It scared her. I asked her if anything else had come up for her about that event, and she said 'No, it was so long ago'.

With our middle daughter, I will always see an element of her, regardless of how old she was, as a scrumptious and happy toddler dancing and singing to Wiggles videos in the loungeroom back in Sydney. As a woman, she emanates mature feminine wisdom. I smile at how protective and loving she is with her baby girl and how she models kind and considerate communication and respect with her partner. She chose safe places to ask me questions, prompted me and listened. A beautiful, kind, compassionate soul, she often reminds me that tears are there to flow, not be held back.

Also reminding me that tears need to flow when they come is our youngest daughter. Back in the time when I first shared about the abuse with her two older sisters, she was finishing high school, about to set herself free to travel and find her place in the world. All she knew was that I'd been abused. When we spoke more openly later, before and along the path of my writing this book, she communicated that I had her love and support. This beautiful human being proactively chooses to lead a life on her terms, with a deep appreciation of vulnerability, authentic connection and a strong sense of justice.

The kind and quiet support I have received from these three women has been a salve. Not a cheer-squad or rescuer kind of support, instead a gentle 'You know we've got your back Mum… you've got this Mum,' sort of way.

From the moment the lioness appeared at that infamous family lunch, and the resolution that came after to protect any child of mine from a similar experience, I have only ever hoped that my relationship with my daughters would be open, loving, and supportive.

I still doubt myself a lot in that regard, so I must continue to work at it. Trust and boundaries go together, and I must trust that it's okay for me just to be me. As crazy as it seems, since they have grown into such amazing women, I worry about getting parenting wrong too. I have worked so hard to break away from my own family experience and provide a better environment for my girls, but that worry can still make me shrink back into my disempowered alone space.

When I find myself slipping into silence, I can see how it served me at first, but it's an unhealthy emotional place for me to stay for too long. It not only puts me at risk of sinking into depression but also does not generate the love, support and connection that daughters need.

Placing and then respecting boundaries is not something that comes naturally for many people, especially if we have not had them modelled for us by our parents. Trust and boundaries come with practice and feedback.

I love my daughters for who they are, and I'm incredibly proud of how they've found their own unique ways of being in the world. In relationships, the spaces they create and the ways they move in them—I'm so proud of them just for experiencing life their own way. I feel that I'm to remain open to their learnings about themselves going forward, and stay aware of how our family's past may have contributed to that, good, bad or otherwise.

I didn't discuss with them in those early conversations how the abuse impacted me in terms of the coping mechanisms I adopted, nor the repercussions of the abuse on me, either physically, mentally or in terms of sexuality. I didn't know about all of that myself yet, but my hypervigilance, my need to feel safe, my depression and my stress responses were in full view of my daughters all along.

I wasn't fooling anyone but myself.

Broader perspective

You are the author of your own life... Don't let others
define it for you. Real power comes by doing what
you are meant to be doing and doing it well.
OPRAH WINFREY, AUTHOR &
PHILANTHROPIST

I've had many amazing experiences travelling, interested in both the wonders and the challenging times others have lived through— and what they built, created and changed in response.

In 2017 I purposefully added to what I called our 'gap year' trip itinerary, that I wanted to pay my respects to those who had experienced the most unimaginable of horrors. Troy and I visited Krakow in Poland for five days to walk through that city and learn about the Jewish peoples' real stories, not only what we'd seen on the screen.

As a teen, I remember watching a TV series called 'Holocaust'. I sat on the floor in front of the lounge watching the stories in disbelief, that any human being could do such wicked things to another person. I don't know if it was just the time, in the late 1970s, but there was more and more being shared about the atrocities of World War II.

It always stuck with me, so visiting Krakow, walking through the Jewish Quarter, and taking a day to be guided through Auschwitz and Birkenau concentration camps was a time for solemn contemplation and prayer. In town, at Schindler's factory museum, I spent hours reading peoples' heroic and heart-wrenching stories, their personal letters of love and hope, and watching the film clips that showed the injustice, the reality, and the bravery of so many incredible people surviving, saving others and risking their own lives.

What incredible human beings the Jewish people were to endure what they did.

I went to Poland to pay my respects, but I hadn't expected to learn so much, so quickly. Our time there, combined with many months of travel to see places, art, architecture, and the wonders of nature that I'd never seen before, opened my mind.

That trip Troy and I took, just for us, let me return home with a broader perspective and greater appreciation of what's most important and what's worth spending my time on.

As Victor Frankl, the Austrian psychiatrist who survived the horrors of three concentration camps, wrote: 'No one can take away the last of our human freedoms: to choose one's attitude in any given set of circumstances, to choose one's own way.'

Section Three

SET
YOURSELF
FREE

9

Secrets and Abandonment

Hurts travel through time. From one person to another this unwanted heaviness moves from the past into the present and then into the future. One of the most heroic things anyone can do is break the line of hurt. When people heal themselves, they stop the hurt from multiplying and their relationships become healthier. When people heal themselves, they also heal the future.

DIEGO PEREZ AKA "YUNG PUEBLO", AUTHOR

In planning to write my story, questions arose that I wanted answers to. Questions floating around my mind about how my brother's abuse was possible led me to take a deep dive into the family history. I wanted to see how this could have happened in our family, and understand what had carried through from the past into my current life experience.

Rather than the typical family tree kind of family history, I wanted to try to understand the life experiences of my parents and grandparents. I wanted to see if there was a trail of behaviours that would help me comprehend my life, and theirs from a different angle. I needed to see what was back there, that had flowed into my life as a child so that I could understand and accept what I had to let go of.

That not-so-comfortable mission gave me a new level of understanding of the challenges they faced, and inspired a greater love and compassion for the women and men of the generations before me.

Mum

When I spoke with Mum about Darryl's abuse, her words were most often something like, 'I was naïve. I was raised like a princess. I had no idea such a thing could be possible. If only you had come and told me!'

For me, it was hard to fathom how Mum could have been so out of touch with what was happening between her children. The questions I asked Mum included some that others had asked me:

'Do you recall feeling an inappropriate touch from one of your parents, or was there an aunt or uncle that made you feel uncomfortable?' Mum said no, she didn't recall anything like that, laughing that she was never out of her mother's sight!

'Did you ever see Darryl looking suspicious?' That took a moment's pause and a less firmly stated: 'No, never'.

'Did you ever wake up at night wondering at sounds in the house?', 'No.'

My mum was adopted. Grandma and Grandpa would have been in their forties when they got her. Mum's biological mother was Anne, who worked alongside Grandma, as a seamstress, sewing well-designed business and dinner suits for a tailor in Sydney.

From what scant information has been put together, Anne had fallen pregnant to a man she had been fond of before he went off to war. The section for 'Father' on my mum's birth certificate was blank. There's no further information about her father's identity.

In those days, a girl falling pregnant outside of wedlock was not something to be celebrated or even talked about. Anne's circumstances required that she leave her modest family home where she'd lived with her sister and two brothers to keep the pregnancy a secret. Once she'd birthed her child, she had to hand it over for adoption. The honour of the family name meant a lot in those years.

In the short few months that Anne continued to work before her pregnancy showed, Mum and I have speculated at the image of the two women stitching garments whilst coming up with an arrangement that worked for Anne and my grandma. As an already married woman, free of possible scandals, Grandma would adopt Anne's baby.

Grandma, the nifty seamstress, a good Catholic woman, and clearly a very good friend, faked her pregnancy with padded baby bumps sewn inside her frocks until her 'due date'. It wasn't just Anne's secret anymore; it was hers. Once she gave birth, Anne handed my mum over to her friend at a close-by Catholic-run hospital; the gift of her baby girl who would be raised as Grandma's princess.

Mum was raised in a time when children were not expected to speak unless they were spoken to and should be seen but not heard. She had parents who doted on her but were strict and taught her nothing about open communication.

'Raised as a princess' are my mum's words that she uses to recall her childhood experience. Princess, in one way, refers to the beautiful frocks and hair set in ribboned curly piggy tails. Princess, in another way, validates Mum's assertion that she was always under the complete control and eyesight of her doting mother. If she wanted to ask her father a question or whether she could buy something at the shops, her mother would tell her, 'Don't bother your father; I'll ask him for you.'

Mum recalled that her father was a gentle, quiet man who was unwell, and that his solid Catholic faith had him believe he was on earth to experience pain so that he would find a place in heaven. She said that after he'd passed away, they found all his pain medication in his bottom bedside drawer that he'd never taken to alleviate the pain he tolerated daily.

Mum recalled that she never had a birthday party and wasn't allowed to play with the other children in the street. She says the kids in the street teased her at school, calling her the prisoner.

From my perspective, Mum's overly protected upbringing, the rules she navigated in her family home, and what she could say or not say did sound princess-like, but a captive princess trapped in an ivory tower would be more accurate. Also, looking at it now with the wisdom of hindsight, Mum agreed that was an accurate description of her life in that home.

Whilst Mum said she had always felt something was being kept from her, the adoption story finally confirmed what she knew to be true when she was forty. A cousin, Denise, shared with mum that she knew of a family secret. When she was in her late teens, she'd accidentally eavesdropped on some conversations between my grandma and her mother, one of Grandma's cousins. When Mum became pregnant with Darryl, she naturally asked pregnancy-related questions of her adoptive mother. Grandma, who had no idea what the answers were, was back and forth asking Denise's mother for titbits of maternal knowledge to share with Mum.

When Mum told me in the car about having just had it confirmed that she'd been adopted—one early evening before we walked into the house from shopping—she said it had come with no real surprise. Nor was it a surprise to her when she was told that the woman she had an intuitively strong connection to as a young girl, Grandma's friend who she called Aunty Anne, was, in truth, her birth mother.

The revelation by Denise of Mum's adoption, and her sharing it with us, was still a good few years before Grandma died. Anne had already passed away before I was born.

Mum and I had a shared hobby of sewing around that time. It felt comfortable for us both to talk about the mystery of the adoption when we were sewing together or up at the mall shopping for fabrics or grocery shopping on a Thursday night. It felt like it was a good thing to be there for Mum so that she could speak about it out loud. I was fifteen, and it was the first time we had a grown-up conversation as mother and daughter. It was also intriguing to hear about a secret from our past because it was the only secret I'd ever come across, notwithstanding my own secret of being abused.

I asked Mum a few times over those years before Grandma passed away if she was going to tell Grandma she knew about the adoption and Anne, so the secret could end. Mum would look up from what she'd been focusing on in her sewing or cooking and then shake her head with a sad, 'No. There's no point now and it would break Grandma's heart if she knew the truth had come out.'

Unfortunately, as family secrets go, anyone with access to information has since passed away, and with them, the stories they could have shared with Mum. Adoption, like sibling sexual abuse, was and often still is a taboo topic, surrounded by silence, guilt, shame and self-blame.

Mum has often said that she thinks about Anne every day and wishes now that she'd spoken to Grandma about it while she had the chance.

My Grandma, in holding onto that secret and in her way of treating my mum as a princess, modelled many behaviours that fed into Mum's own life as an ill-prepared young mother of four children. Be they the rules that children should be seen and not heard; or to speak only when they are spoken to; or the difference between being seen as a good girl or a bad girl; or what good manners are and what they are not.

Grandma's opinions and teachings also flowed through Mum to us, that boys were to be treated differently to girls. Rules were set for what was a boy's job to do and what were the girl's jobs to get on with. Of course, there was the rule that went without saying—the first son would be left in charge in Mum's absence. No questions asked.

I can see that my mum would have had her job cut out for her, being the good girl that Grandma expected her to be, and doing what she was told or else there'd be trouble!

Abandonment

Four decades since that first disclosure of the adoption in our driveway, Mum and I found quiet space together over lunch at a café overlooking the river, or when sitting opposite each other in her lounge sharing coffee and cake.

Mum's hollow feeling of being abandoned by Anne, and the blank space where her father's name could easily have been written on her birth certificate, continued to break her heart. So much secrecy and unspoken words, mixed with what were probably seen as necessary white lies, has to have been a confusing place for love to feel safe to bloom and flourish. Mum was abandoned through adoption and never knowing her father.

Our lunchtime ponderings have included speculation about Grandma's need to control Mum's life experience. By keeping Mum safe from harm, making decisions on her behalf, and over-compensating, or what I've heard referred to as being a 'helicopter' parent, Mum and I have contemplated whether that was also a form of abandonment. A mother operating from a place of fear of some kind or other, perhaps.

Control, possibly originating from fear of the secret ever

being found out, caused Grandma to mother from control, as a priority over mutual unconditional love, trust, and honesty. An abandonment of the deep, loving, and growing connection they could have had between mother and daughter.

Stacked on top of that was Mum and Dad's abandonment of each other as wife and husband throughout their marriage, ending with another layer of hurt, Dad telling Mum he was leaving her the year I turned twenty-one.

So much hurt.

'It's too late now to do anything about the past,' Mum often responds when I ask if it would help her to speak with a therapist rather than continue to ruminate over what could have been. Is it too late to attempt to heal when ever-present emotional pain and intrusive thoughts are taking space in our heart and mind every day?

Dad

How about Dad? Interestingly, Dad was from a similar family structure. He wasn't adopted, but he was also a single child, born to forty-something parents in the 1930s, and raised in Sydney.

Like Mum's family of origin, anyone with any knowledge of the family history of my Dad's side of the family has passed on, including Dad.

We have a few tidily presented photo albums and handwritten journals of the little family's travels by ship, written by my Grandpop. Aside from those, there are also some detailed sketches – my grandfather was a talented artist.

Reflecting on all our conversations over the years, I cannot recall Dad raising the topic of his mother. When we asked him questions, he'd quieten, and I could sense his heavy emotions rising to the surface. We'd change the subject, sensing that subject was private, or out of bounds.

From what I could see, his mother loved him dearly. That is based on the quality black-and-white photographs of mother and child in the family photo albums. Whomever the photographer was, the images captured a tall, elegant woman, beautifully dressed, sometimes sitting on a blanket on the lawn, smiling at her blonde-haired little boy as he played with his toys beside her, or ran across the garden. I know that Dad's mum died suddenly in the garden when he was a young teen. No information left behind gives us an idea of who she was as a woman, mother, or wife.

My Grandpop was a debonair man. His work involved a lot of overseas and interstate travel. I knew my Grandpop, he was a part of our childhood and passed away in my early teens. Grandpop would be one of the elderly crew that Dad ferried around in his Holden sedan, the elder's taxi, sans air-conditioning, on Christmas Days and other special occasions.

Grandpop would come to our place for Christmas lunch and sit quietly, patiently watching for lunch to be served. Sometimes I would spy him looking like he was dying to break out with something funny to say, but within seconds the light in his eyes would dim again.

Christmas Day for Mum was always stressful, and she swore she'd never do it again! Do what again? Christmas Day, or make lunch for everybody? I didn't ask.

Mum was always the one in the kitchen, serving the pretty plates full of Christmas delights, keeping everyone topped up whilst the main course was still in the oven. She made the best Christmas lunch every year. In that quiet chaotic kitchen, she managed everything by herself. She must have been cooking with love to dish up all the great food she did in those circumstances.

It was awkward having the grandparents and great-aunt there as our only guests.

Grandma would sit in the lounge around the corner from where Grandpop was seated. We'd watch as she alternated between pursed lips and talking loud enough so Mum could hear she was annoyed that lunch was taking so long. Her husband had passed away. Grandma would be giving Grandpop the evil eye, judging him for anything he said. In the lounge room, having the time of her life, was Aunt Phyllis, singing her favourite Christmas carols and tinkling the ivory keys on the piano.

Our job was to not be in the kitchen; it wasn't a safe place for a child to be with Mum snapping away at anyone who got in her way.

We had to be with the grandparents so Mum could be left to get the lunch served, so I'd try to think up something that broke the tension in the air. I'd ask Grandpop to come and draw with me, which at least shifted the dynamics of the small hungry crowd.

We got to draw at Grandpop's sometimes too.

Mum had Grandpop lined up on the school holiday roster. If we didn't have a school holiday vacation care to go to, we'd always be at either Grandma's or Grandpop's place, so Mum could keep working. She only got a few of the school holidays off, and for at least one of those, we'd all go away for a holiday to Coffs Harbour together.

Grandpop would have us over to his house, never to stay a night as we did at Grandma's, but for day visits. His house was tidy, dark and quiet. It wasn't a place that had ever had a breeze blowing through it in my memory of it. The light part of the house was in the kitchen and sunroom, where the long back steps outside the screen door went down to the backyard.

Mum's selling point to stop us whinging about having to go there was that we'd get a meat pie. We were sent there with a finger-pointing parental warning that we were to behave, not make a mess, be quiet, and keep out of Grandpop's way, so we'd get an invitation to return for a future meat pie treat during a coming school holiday.

I'd play in Grandpop's long backyard, swinging washing baskets full of teddy bears along his huge clothesline that spanned the property's width and picking the oranges and lemons from his trees if it was the right season. Every time, and at the same time of day, we would all walk in an orderly line one block to the corner shop on a busy road, to buy the prized hot meat pies.

We all had our own ways of approaching a meat pie. I'd carry mine back in a brown paper bag to sit at the table in Grandpop's sunroom and quietly but methodically separate the crusty round lid of puff pastry completely, taking infinite care not to break it. Then I'd turn that lid upside down so its soft inside was up and eat it like a piece of toast whilst the meat in the pie base cooled a little.

Mostly Grandpop would be sitting reading a book or the newspaper. He was tasked with babysitting, but wasn't expected to do anything, although sometimes he'd surprise us by breaking out his special box of lead pencils and sit patiently with us as we tried to sketch horses and dogs the way he did. Those stand-out moments made me feel the day was good after all. I liked hearing him talking about drawing, how to shape the legs of horses or a dog's tail and showing us how he did his beautiful sketches.

The family photo albums gave some other insights, showing Grandpop contemplating life in silence or surrounded by groups of well-dressed men, a cigarette always poised between his fingers or a packet in his hand, at the ready to tap out the next smoke. I could sense he had a cheeky spirit he kept solely for that man-about-town side of his life. He was a creative artist; he wrote and was a man much like his son became.

According to Mum, Grandpop wasn't a very nice father to

Dad nor did he help them out as a young couple with a busy household of four young children. I was told he had money but wasn't generous with it. He had a tell-it-straight manner, and Grandma shared plenty of her poisonous opinions about him with us as kids that I knew she'd need to go and confess for having said out loud, so she didn't have to go to hell.

I know that my dad experienced school life at a Marist Brothers Catholic school, which he admitted was a harsh rule- and guilt-driven school, up there with the best of them! Dad said nothing ever happened to him by way of sexual abuse at the hands of the priests or brothers there, and even if he had recalled anything, he would never have shared it with us anyway.

As a young man, Dad was handsome, played cricket, and went to socials, as I heard Mum call them.

Both father and son were men who lived a home life that was primarily silent and private. They could both converse well when in good company, or with a few beers on board. They were intelligent dreamers, artistic music lovers who couldn't quite get the conversations at home to be as comfortable as they could with others.

Love and marriage

When teenaged Mum fell in love with Dad, they danced and dated, were chaperoned by their married friends on trips away, and within an appropriate timeframe, married. Almost immediately, they became parents to Darryl. Mum fell pregnant another four times without much space in between to gather her wits, nor to grieve one of the babies she lost pre-term. Dad took a night job serving beers at the local club when we were babies and worked his city job during the day.

Mum has recalled that the vision she had of a happy marriage was a young girl's wishful fairy tale of living happily ever after. The emotional struggles and financial pressure they experienced together were sprinkled generously across our childhood. There were many tense moments, frustrated or angry words from Mum's side and non-reaction and silence from Dad.

I remember one night, Mum and Dad having one of their one-way arguments in the lounge room. Mum was yelling about something Dad needed to do but wasn't getting done, trying to get a rise out of Dad. I looked around the corner from the family room before pulling back to keep out of the way. Mum was standing with her hands on her hips a few steps in front of where Dad was seated, shrinking into the lounge chair. Dad maintained his silence because that was his role, until the verbal tornado that was Mum's frustration had finished tearing him apart.

Back in the kitchen, I'd already done the dinner dishes and wiped the sink clean until it was over. I didn't like people yelling at all, whether it was a schoolteacher, a priest, or a nun. It always made me feel nervous and sick to the stomach at home. I just knew that it would never be a good night afterwards, so whatever had been planned, to play a board game, or watch one of the funny TV shows Mum and Dad liked, got ruined.

Silence fell. Mum had run out of steam.

I put my head around the corner to peep into the loungeroom to see if the coast was clear to go through to my bedroom. Dad was staring at the blank TV, he didn't meet my eyes. Mum was gone, but I heard her in her bedroom. As I came upon her in the front hallway, she was angrily tightening the belt on her overcoat, which she'd just put on over her dress. Red-faced and upset, throwing her shoulders back, she stuffed her hands hard into her big pockets, making the car keys jangle in one of them. She was trying to maintain her composure as she grimly stated, 'Life isn't always a bed of roses, you know, Alice. You remember that when you get married one day!'

With wide open eyes, I nodded, thinking this was serious. Mum never put her coat on after she got home.

Without another word, she turned on her heels and stomped out the front door, slamming it behind her so that it rattled the hall mirror before she backed the car at speed out of the driveway. I ran to the nearest window to the driveway, the one on the other side of their double bed and pulled down one slat of the aluminium blinds. Phew! Mum had driven away into the night but pulled the car up out the front of our next-door neighbour's house. At least I knew where she was.

I didn't go back into the lounge room. Instead, I worried at my already bitten fingernails and went into my bedroom, thinking Mum wanted to leave us, even if she was parked just next door this time.

Thankfully, her girlfriends from her teen social days were there for her, all of them now with a plethora of little Catholic children they each juggled.

It was a time when telephones were in one location in the house. Ours, after we had the new kitchen and family room added to the house, was beside the kitchen servery, so Mum's happy place was sitting tucked away in the corner of the family room, under that servery. Mum would be there for hours, sitting in her flowery nightie, talking and laughing with one girlfriend for an hour, followed by the next. Those connections she had with her friends must have given Mum some venting room, though I doubt her secret worries or fears around the marriage would have got much meaningful airtime. That just wasn't done.

Mum felt she loved Dad, the handsome boy she'd married. She just wanted to make the marriage work and didn't know how.

Dad's place in the world as husband and father were that he worked to earn enough money to cover the bills. He held down a full-time office job, leaving early to be at the office every morning and either needing to work back late or go from his day job to his evening job, first the bar job and later shelf-packing at our local supermarket, to bolster the family income. Wherever he could steal the chance, he found himself sanctuary, drinking a few quiet beers, and sitting alone at our local pub before he headed home.

If he was having a night when he came home straight from work, after dinner he'd offer to drive up to the shop to pick up a treat: 'Some Marella jubes maybe, for the kids?' I'd be so excited at the idea of Marella jubes; they were my favourite! Feeling happy that Dad would go to such effort for us, we'd wait for him to return with the slim emerald-green rectangle of colourful sugar-coated jubes. Dad would eventually return from his five-minute errand an hour later, silent and without the treat. Either he'd forgotten that part of his mission, or the shop had closed by then. We were disappointed, but none of us said a word because we knew he'd messed up, and he felt ashamed at having let us down.

Dad's happy place was fishing. He'd bought a boat and the necessary fishing gear for our May school holidays at Coffs Harbour.

He could be scary in the way he parented us when it came to schoolwork. He'd use his deep stern dad's voice if we asked him for an answer to our homework. I don't know why we tried that on because Dad always responded the same way: 'It's in the encyclopaedias... if I have to go down there (to the other end of the family room) and I find the answer... there'll be trouble!' We never ran down the family room to those encyclopaedias so fast! Amazingly the answers were always there in the encyclopaedia, right where we could find them if we looked.

Dad never took a day's sick leave: that just wasn't done!

There was no chance of sympathy if we needed or wanted to take a day off school. When Dad walked in at night, it was always best to avoid eye contact so as not to receive the look that told us what he thought about how sick we were. Whoever the patient was, they did their best to look very ill, laying on the now stale, Sao biscuit-crumbed and crumpled up sheet Mum had laid out as a lounge bed early that morning.

Our life as a Catholic family changed along the way. At some stage, in my mid-teens, we stopped going to Sunday Mass together. Mum stopped going altogether, and no one questioned why that was so. She'd only now attend on Easter Sunday and Christmas Day. Whereas Dad would still dutifully drag us teenagers to the six o'clock Sunday night service that we detested having to go to.

He'd drop us off at the curb by the church and drive back down to the main road for a few beers at the pub to make the most of the hour. We kids would walk into the church to find a pew, and Darryl would disappear out the door on the other side of the church before Mass began, to smoke ciggies and miss the Mass too. Then, on the car trip home, we all pretended it didn't smell of beer and smoke. Dad would ask us which priest was there that night. That was so he could tell Mum what a good sermon that priest had given when we got home. It felt like such a double standard. Mum not going, us being forced to go, Dad and Darryl pretending to go and expecting us kids to contribute to an adult's fabrication.

Mum and Dad eventually split up in the year I got married and had my twenty-first birthday. Dad said he'd waited for nearly all of us kids to have moved out of the home. Mum was heartbroken over the split. She'd have done anything to fix it, although that sentiment rocked back and forth between, 'I love him', and sounding like she'd cut out his heart if she had the chance. Staying married for as long as they both shall live wasn't to be, and that was devastating for Mum.

There were many examples of holding onto secrets, telling little white lies, silence, both expressed and repressed anger, hurt feelings and fear of speaking, as well as rejection and abandonment in the inter-generational family tree, on both sides.

I wouldn't say it was a completely new revelation; it's just that I hadn't looked properly before to see so much of it come together as I have now.

This mini-exploration of the family tree made it easier for me to see some of the traits that ran through my family; secrets and unspoken feelings, avoiding emotions and hypocrisy were more the norm than the exception. I was beginning to see that our family was one where an opportunistic sexual abuser would have a field day unnoticed, as Darryl did.

10

Uncomfortable Truths

People need to name the truth before they can change it.
DAVID B. DRAKE PHD, AUTHOR

In August 2019, during the first year of drafting this book, the writing process was dark and heavy. At times I felt like I had to drag the words out, certain parts stirred things up inside and I started to not sleep well on a regular basis.

I'd become anxious about going to bed for the previous six months—perhaps a coincidence, it was the same period I'd spent writing the book at that point. I would turn over like a rotisserie grill all night, my mind spinning from one thought to the next, none of them happy thoughts, all were worrisome and made me anxious. It made me worry that I'd wake Troy. Then I'd be concerned that Troy would be tired, and annoyed that he was fatigued for work, although I never mentioned the problems I was having.

I didn't want to worry him. I just tried to stay awake as long as possible, listening for him to fall asleep first, before I allowed myself to drop into a deep, but much shorter interrupted slumber.

It was ridiculous. My body began to show up with new aches and pains. I knew intuitively it was the combination of thinking about and writing my story that had my emotions and trauma shifting around. Helene had made me aware years earlier with her therapeutic release of the knots of emotions, locked in my body. I knew something similar was happening now.

I felt uncomfortable in my skin and knew I had awoken the beast again. It made me cranky, snappy and on the attack. Finally, Troy turned one afternoon in response to a caustic remark I'd made and snapped back with equal ferocity, 'You need to get yourself someone to speak to!' He went on, a little more care now wearily eased into his voice. 'This writing, it's heavy on you. It's okay to get some help again, you know.'

Writing my story came from my subconscious when the words and memories flowed. Yes, I got all caught up at times in facts and the information I was gathering, but there were other moments when I shared my story and felt that my typing fingers would fly. Not concerned about the trail of typos—they could be taken care of later—my fingers had their work cut out just to keep up with my subconscious mind.

Caught up in the need to get the book written, I was overriding my need to slow down, take care of myself and process what I was learning so that I could do something about it. Troy's prompt led to an 'enough for now' moment that I needed very much.

Without that pointed prompt that forced me to look up and out of my bunkered hole, I wouldn't have seen my behaviour was unacceptable and erratic, and I wouldn't have gone to get professional support. I would have carried on, irritable, alert and exhausted, until something I couldn't ignore broke me down completely.

At first, I felt affronted that Troy said I needed help. I cried all through the night in a good old pity party that I didn't invite anyone else to. In the morning, I woke, desperately needing lots of cold water splashed onto my face, looking much worse for wear. Then even before I'd had my coffee, anger kicked in. I thought, *Well, screw you, buddy; I will go and find myself someone to talk to because I don't seem to be doing too great at talking to you!*

I didn't say that out loud, my internal drama tornado having soon died down, but I can imagine Troy would have felt it was safer to be in any other place on the planet than in my vicinity.

In the morning, I booked in to see my GP for a referral to talk to someone. I sat down and started trying to speak and cry simultaneously. I couldn't stop the tears from flowing, and all my worries, hurts and fears tumbled out as best I could express them. Thankfully, the doctor was a beautiful soul. She told me it was safe to cry in her space, to let it all out, listened to me a while and then referred me to a psychologist who specialised in childhood sexual abuse to get some help and find some coping strategies to manage my PTSD.

My what? PTSD? Who Me?

Welcome to therapy

When you begin to talk about the abuse, it is important
not to simply report it without emotion, which you may
want to do to separate the words from your feelings.
You have to hear yourself say it, feel yourself say it.
That will change you: you will have proclaimed who
you are. You will no longer be in hiding, disguised and
trapped behind a false façade that keeps shame alive.
STEVEN LEVENKRON, PSYCHOTHERAPIST & AUTHOR

When I first saw Rose, the therapist that year, I knew that this time would include exposing and dissolving long-experienced suppressed emotions related to the abuse. Outside of that, I had no idea what it would bring up or what we'd talk about.

I was surprised that what I had worried about being the topic we'd discuss the most—digging up more memories of Darryl's stalking and sexual abuse—would be only a minor part of the bigger picture. I could go there if I wanted to, but I wasn't expected to do so.

My inner wisdom told me I was about to find hard truths about myself that I would need to face and accept. Truths and matters that only I could change—if it was important enough for me to break the chains of abuse. To do that I was going to learn about parts of my life the abuse had touched that I wasn't even aware of yet.

By the end of the first two sessions of sharing all that was heavy in my heart, mind and soul, Rose handed me a piece of paper with a hand-drawn mind map she'd sketched as I'd been speaking. The session had left me completely drained, but this mind map lifted me back up again. It showed me a direction I could move in that was helpful, something I couldn't see by myself in the overwhelm I'd been experiencing.

The page was covered in small circles, each with a word or two or the names of people written inside. Each circle was a concern, responsibility, relationship, or story that I had just shared with Rose, all of them I had swirling around inside my head.

I think I laughed in both hysteria and relief when Rose said, 'Alice, that is a minefield! No wonder you feel a little nutty. Anyone would! There's way too much going on. You need to eliminate some of these or shelve some of them until later.'

She also pointed out that my self-blame and guilt dial had been turned up to the max. It was time to dial it back down so I could calm down. Rose recommended I ask myself whether each mind map circle was about fixing someone else's problem, or my relationship with them.

'Is that person an adult, and are they safe? If yes, then know they are okay for now. Let it be. It'll work out when the time is right.'

After that session, I realised I had to let go of what didn't serve me. I crossed out a few of the circles as being safe to leave for now, and I parked the book writing. I had by that time allowed the whole of Young Alice's story out of my body and onto paper, which itself caused an internal revolution that was monumental to manage.

I knew that the book-writing journey, along with having found a therapist I was comfortable sharing my personal pain with, was going to be a winding road of home truths and healing old and new wounds. It was important to pace myself and let whatever came up to unfold, without time pressure.

In a subsequent session with Rose, I recall telling her of a strange, pervading sense of feeling unsafe. My mind would snap to attention when the side gate opened and closed, and panic would rise in me, enough so that Troy would give me a look, wondering what was wrong, even though whoever was coming in that gate wasn't someone I needed to fear. Why was that?

When I was out of the house, I was often feeling overly alert. As I walked through the sliding doors of a shopping mall, I'd scan to see if the coast was clear – clear of what I didn't know, but that's what I was doing. I felt like I wasn't blinking my eyes as often as I'd liked. I wasn't taking full, deep breaths from my stomach and couldn't breathe deeper than the very top of my lungs. I hadn't said those words to a professional before. What could be making me feel unsafe and hypervigilant?

I laughed nervously, 'Is safe even the right word? Maybe not, ha-ha!'

Silly Alice, I thought. *It sounds strange even to say the word 'Unsafe' out loud. You're a grown woman!*

Rose looked at me, her gaze direct as she said gently, 'That's you experiencing what you did as a child, during the time of the abuse.'

It was a pivotal moment. Is it true that this was one of my subconscious coping strategies, and there was no *silly Alice* about it?

It was a moment when young Alice poked her head out from behind me on the lounge to see who this Rose woman was. Sitting across from her in the cosy and safe office, I suddenly realised I was holding my breath. *So I'm not crazy.* The feeling could be associated with something from my past. Rose knew. Thank goodness I came, and actually said how I was feeling, as silly as I thought it must sound.

It was so significant to me to be heard by someone who had the experience to listen intelligently and share what she could see. I breathed out, my shoulders dropped, and my throat did a few jumps, not knowing what to say next: so I didn't say anything. This was another valuable gift of therapy.

I bawled my eyes out noisily and used a big wad of Rose's tissues from the box beside me to wipe away the cleansing tears. Rose pointed out that those tears came from a deep place inside, and that they had been waiting a long time to come out. I could feel from the intensity they flowed with they were a different kind of tears.

Never had I connected the feelings I was experiencing now as an adult with what I'd experienced as young Alice. No one had ever shown up in my life to have this kind of conversation with me. I cried anew, because now there was a professional, caring, guiding adult in my corner.

I spent the remainder of that session with Rose, honouring young Alice, who still felt she needed space, who felt scared sometimes and alone in the world. Rose guided me to let young Alice know that her feeling that way was necessary and understandable, as a child in my family home. I symbolically knelt and welcomed the younger me to rest her head on my shoulder. I embraced her with a heart-warming hug, letting both of us feel a sense of comfort, of loving warmth. I felt into the moment of letting this child know that she is safe and secure, and she will always be loved, and that love is unconditional love.

Then I continued with a non-scripted internal chat with this little girl, a simple conversation that I would have with any child full of fear and resistance to doing something that risks her safety or losing love from someone she cares about. I told her that it is safe now, and that we are free to make new choices, but basically, that we both are safe. I am so happy she is within me, supported and secure, and always in my heart. It wasn't overwhelming, and it was enough for the first time.

Since that moment, when the feeling of hypervigilance or being unsafe comes up, I give myself a moment to walk away and be with it, then take a few deep breaths to reset before returning to what I was doing.

When I got home that evening, I shared what I had learned with my daughters and Troy. Sharing that was a vulnerable moment, knowing it was my journey and I didn't necessarily have to tell anybody what I was working on. I wanted to let the people I love in on what I was learning, if it was associated with how I had related to them or was something they'd witnessed as one of my odd behaviours.

Connecting the dots

You cannot connect the dots looking forward; you can only connect them looking backwards. So, you have to trust that the dots will somehow connect in your future. You have to trust in something – your gut, destiny, life, karma, whatever.
STEVE JOBS, CO-FOUNDER & CEO, APPLE INC.

Drawing on those wise words of Steve Jobs, I could reconcile the myriad experiences and lessons I'd had in life for what they were. I could also begin to see where PTSD fit into the bigger picture.

I had only heard about PTSD in terms of what I'd seen in the news: victims and veterans of wars, natural disasters, terrorism, accidents, and other people getting hurt or abused.

Given that I hadn't previously pieced together that I had Post-Traumatic Stress Disorder related to childhood trauma, I didn't connect how writing about my trauma would trigger it as it did.

The PTSD was unconscious, and writing my story came from my subconscious, leaving the door open for things I had suppressed to come rising up unbidden. As I began to reveal and relive these moments, the emotions and trauma that had been hidden inside began to be revealed. This in turn triggered my PTSD, something I had previously managed to keep quiet, mostly by avoiding going into any of the challenging feelings.

The symptoms of PTSD I experienced were often changes in my physical, mental and emotional state that would arise at any time of the night or day. They included: having trouble sleeping, being easily startled or frightened, being on guard for danger, frightening dreams, and overwhelming guilt and shame. My mood and thinking would feel like a roller coaster of negative thoughts about myself and other people. At times I would feel alone or detached from family and friends, or lose interest in activities I used to love. At other times I would experience dark thoughts that were a struggle to come back from.

It was strangely liberating to acknowledge that all of those could be explained in the context of PTSD. It was a blessing to understand that's where all those pieces of me fit together. That knowledge gave me a chance to address them, and possibly even do something about them.

Many of my bad dreams throughout my young years were of feeling unsafe or being chased. Dreams where I'd run from our house to the corner of my street, away from the 'bad guy', walking almost as fast as I could run a few metres behind me. I'd open my mouth to scream, but no sound would come out. I had to keep running, but it would drop into such slow motion that I knew I wouldn't get away. I'd fall in a heap and curl up in a ball, ready to be captured.

Even as an adult, I've had bad dreams of being under the covers in my childhood bed, sensing the rest of the house asleep. A dark shadowy presence in the room would be creeping along, a silhouette against the wardrobe door along the other side of my bedroom, and I knew it wasn't right, safe, or good. Waking from those dreams, grateful it wasn't real, I would get my bearings and eventually fall back to sleep.

I recall two separate occasions when Troy and I had been on holiday in Indonesia that I'd woken in the middle of the night, feeling that our bed and the room furnishings were shaking with earth tremors.

My reaction was instantaneous; I was dressed and had our passports in my hand in a few seconds. I shouted frantically at Troy to get up, trying to rouse him from his undisturbed sleep. By then, each of the earth tremors had already passed, and only I was trembling.

The first time, I lay back in bed, still dressed, worrying there might be an after-shock coming. Troy, aware of my distress the second time, kept the lights on and checked his phone for news of what was happening just in case there was something to be worried about, and at the same time, allaying my fears so that I could get back to sleep.

Sometimes now, I'll say out loud, rather than keep the feeling inside me, 'I'm feeling unsafe again'. That lets whomever I'm with know I need some space or a chat, or maybe a walk in the fresh air to break the circuit of energy I am feeling.

These reactions, moods and behaviours, aren't the natural version of me. What a stunning realisation that was, one that

I might never have had if I hadn't started to look at what this healing business was all about.

Stop downplaying what was

One of the landmines on Rose's sketched mind map was the book writing. Sometime later, in one of our sessions, Rose suggested I look at a memoir writing course to help me formulate an outline. I found an online course that resonated with me, short information sessions followed by exercises and journalling prompts.

One exercise was to write a poem about any challenging or life-changing experience. Immediately, this prompt brought to the surface of my mind a visual, an old black-and-white movie that was often playing right behind my eyes. I realised I'd never acknowledged it, nor said anything about it, this film clip that had played on repeat just for me for a very long time.

I sat with that writing prompt and wrote these words that I also had no idea were waiting to be written out from within me, but they came incredibly easily:

Alert, breathing, waiting.
Only she hears the quietest of footsteps.
No one else hears; does no one else have ears?
Why does no one else ever hear?
Heartbeat drumming, tummy churning, mind empty.
Going limp, waiting to be trapped.
Dread as footsteps stop beside her bed.
Then, Dad's cough from the next room.
Like playing 'Marco?' but no one responded 'Polo!'
Dad's subconscious screaming, 'Wake up!'
Ah, uncertainty, now hovering, risk of capture.
She can't hear him breathe.
It feels like minutes, yet parts of a second.
Slow, slow, slow; tick, tock, clock, tick,
tock, stop; please stop; stay stopped.
Her breath short, pretending to be dead.
Wishing for invisibility, to magic
herself through the bed,
into the dark beneath.
His feet shift on the carpet. Exquisite
awareness, her every sense alert.
Hopeful, is he going to scurry away?
The tiniest movement, the carpet
squeaking under bare feet.
He hesitates, uncertain, unfulfilled.
He's boiling mad. Will he risk it?
She waits, praying for a sign that tonight she's safe.
Then, dozing off, and, as if in a
dream, recalls a shadow.
Alert, the shadow looming was gone.
Heart and breath return to an even rhythm.
Body loose, she drifts into childhood
dreams of cloud lands,
of kittens and fairies and troll bridges.
The bogeyman fades from her mind.
Until next time. There's always a next time.
~8-year-old Me~

As I finished writing the words of the poem, I stared at how I had signed it off: *8-year-old Me*. My pen paused and then kept going as if it had its own mind or possibly its own soul. Be honest with yourself, the pen challenged as it wriggled in between my fingers. It's okay now to see what it was.

Stop downplaying it: that was your childhood experience.

That film clip running on repeat behind my eyes wasn't a fictional scene from a film. It was a memory of childhood nights in my little bedroom at the front of the house, a shared bedroom in which I was meant to be safe and soundly asleep.

My pen added four additional lines:

9-year-old Me.
10-year-old Me.
11-year-old Me.
12-year-old Me got my first period.

The first draft of the book I'd done before finding therapy was fairly dry and fact filled. Finally, this little exercise made me realise that acknowledging abuse was more than just saying, 'When I was a child, or between the years of eight and eleven, my brother abused me'. This visual I'd been having showed me it was about more than just the nights and days I was actually abused. I was affected in all the moments in between too, as tension, vigilance and feeling unsafe became a part of my daily life.

'Can't you just leave it behind you?'

Accepting the truth of the abuse and moving on without caring for myself and healing, to my mind, is not honestly leaving it behind me. I know in my heart that it is only suppressing or repressing it.

What we don't address stays with us, bubbling to the surface in small ways and key moments; in how we cope, live, communicate, and relate to others.

Have you ever looked at yourself at a tender age, in the first school photo of many more years of school photos to come? I found mine one day while rummaging through a storage container, preserved nicely for over fifty years in its solid white and gold Pixifoto cardboard frame and plastic sleeve.

It was a head and shoulders shot. In my school uniform, a dark blue winter tunic, white button-up blouse and necktie, I stood in the morning sunshine. My golden brown shiny hair in a little top fountain, with its dark blue ribbon to match the two piggy tails just above my poking-out ears. My brown and hazel eyes sparkled with the day's excitement, my chubby little girl cheeks meeting each end of an adorable, mischievous smile.

With it, I found the school photo of me at nine years old, a year after Darryl's abuse had begun. I can see a wiser look in that child's direct gaze at the camera. Her hairstyle—which was either a really bad home haircut or maybe done by a barber rather than a hairdresser—had short, straight edges framed around her face. A small, shy, uncomfortable smile said, *please stop looking at me.*

It was that little girl who was abused. Would it be appropriate or fitting if an adult dismissed a five-year-old or nine-year-old child with 'Can't you leave it behind you?' if they disclosed abuse, or were showing signs of abuse, or asked for an adult's help? I don't think so.

Choosing to experiment with this healing journey rather than keeping things buried inside of me is about my deep desire to be present to the good in the world, to laugh and to love and experience the wonders with all my five senses renewed. I want to feel fully present in my life, without the taint of abuse.

If that's even a slight possibility, I'd prefer that. Even though it hurts.

Maybe that's just me.

What I'd written in this poem as an adult represented a wound decades old and so sore to touch that until that point, I had never shared it with anyone. I thought of how often I'd permitted the abuse to come up in conversation and how incredibly wired it made me feel. I would be so wary of the other person's following comment. Even just sharing the small amount of information I did, I always felt like that was a huge moment. It scared me, and I'd creep back into silence.

A straightforward writing prompt on one ordinary day cracked open something in me that needed to be set free. What other silent movies had I watched play out? I knew that there were others.

It made me shake my head and sigh. If I did that exercise again, would more come up? Was I ready for it? Yes, I was ready.

I stopped running

That afternoon when I closed my notebook on that handwritten poem, I knew I needed to get outside into the fresh air. I took off my shoes and walked down the back stairs into our backyard to water the flower and herb beds and settle my nervous energy. I could feel a heat that I'd call grief under my skin, laying heavily across my chest. If I could have wailed or raged, I would have—but no one screams in their backyard with neighbours just beyond the side or back fence.

My usual go-to is to ask myself more questions to keep my mind moving forward, but I knew this was a significant, tectonic plate shift for me.

As I watered the garden beds, I wondered why I'd seen that

movie but never addressed it by myself or in therapy. It wasn't like the revelation was a shock. I knew I was looking inside and seeing what had been there all along. I had watched it before, always followed by shame. That film wasn't new, it had just found its way onto paper as a clumsy poem.

It wasn't a big decision that afternoon in the garden, but I just decided to stop running from my past. That's how it felt physically and mentally.

I looked down at the hose I held in my hand. I walked over to the faucet, turned off the water, dropped the hose on the grass, and sat on a long timber bench beside the garden I'd watered. Even being busy watering flowers was more than I needed. I needed to stop and accept that my childhood experience was what it was. I sat under the clear afternoon sky that was turning pastel shades as the sun dropped over the mountain range on our horizon, curling and uncurling my toes in the cool, wet grass and breathing calm breaths in and out.

Troy eventually walked in the side gate and sensed my quiet energy. He didn't say anything, he just sat beside me on the seat, and waited a few minutes in silence before playfully bumping my shoulder with his.

It didn't feel difficult for me to tell him about the journalling exercise, as it would have before. He asked if he could read it. I tore the page out of my notebook and brought it down from my office. He read it and looked up with red eyes. 'Honey, you've got to do this, keep writing, see Rose. It's coming up and out, let it out,' he said.

I cried that day, and quite a few more times that week. I let the tears salt up my face as they trickled down my cheeks, chin and neck. Then I'd wash myself to freshen up and let myself be quiet in the peace that follows a deep emotional release.

The following week I told Rose, who responded, 'You've never mentioned that in our past sessions'.

I said, 'I know, but that movie played in the background even as we were speaking, it just never converted from film to words'. Then I bawled my eyes out into handfuls of tissues.

Sometimes I feel like the tears in doing this healing work are packaged up in little plastic snack or sandwich-sized zip-lock bags inside of me. They're numbered or allocated to specific jobs, not all to be shed in one big messy moment.

They are waiting to be shed as each memory is given sufficient space to surface, be seen, accepted and acknowledged. Some memories are big, some small. Some are about me recognising that vision behind my eyes as the important event it had been for the little girl inside me.

Tears flowing are such a vital part of letting the past go. For me, freeing tears when feelings arise about my abuse always brings peace and new beginnings.

Let me disappear

I remember wanting to 'disappear' or become 'invisible' a lot, something that would have been quite a relief as a child. I practised but didn't get anywhere. I'd scrunch my eyes closed, focus on making my nose wiggle like Samantha the witch in Bewitched (1964); or cross my arms, close my eyes, and nod my head, with the hope to disappear into a bejewelled bottle, like the 2000-year-old genie in I Dream of Jeannie (1965). But when I opened my eyes each time, I was still there, at home, and there was no escape.

On the 'I want to disappear or become invisible' feeling, these words from Dr Therese Mascardo, CEO and Founder of

Exploring Therapy in California, a psychologist who lost her brother to suicide in 2009, rang true to me:

'The fantasy of escape is a common mechanism that superficially relieves some pressure for more difficult or complicated feelings. Running away is simply one of the ways people can respond when life gets tough. It's basically hard-wired into our survival instincts. Psychologists say that the human brain is wired to respond to stress in four basic ways—fight, freeze, fawn, or flight. The fight response involves aggressively facing perceived threats. The freeze response uses stillness to avoid danger or render people unable to act against danger. The fawn response immediately seeks to please another person to avoid conflict. And the flight response runs away from the threatening situation altogether' (Therese Mascardo, 2022).

However, as a way of getting by as an adult, disappearing and moving to Italy for a year is not practical for me, although I have been heard to say it, maybe even a few times too often! Since that is off the table for most of us, I began to ask myself, what else could be helpful to me apart from spontaneously booking a flight to Rome?

The answer arrived as more questions: What if I showed myself self-respect, acknowledged how I'm feeling, and practised giving myself some space? What if I learned how to switch off my 'on' button, and practised resting, moving, laughing, creating, or using my breathwork and meditation work?

All these options would be cheaper than flying to Italy at short notice, and less disruptive to my day, my small business, and my life with Troy and the girls. Although I would still one day love to go and live in Italy, or Tuscany to be exact, for a year—I'd like to do so from my heart. It would need to be done with loving intent for the time spent in that place that I love so much, rather than running away from myself. I like the idea of that kind of experience, as a positive choice, not as a reaction to what is distressing or overwhelming me.

Fairy tales

The stories, with all their strangeness, are needed, you see.
LUCY CAVENDISH, AUTHOR

I came across 'magic' and 'fairy tales' a few times as coping mechanisms adopted by child abuse victims to escape the reality of what was happening to them. It immediately brought back memories of getting lost in books; sharing journeys across magical lands in fairy tales.

One treasured book I picked up in 2020 was Lucy Cavendish's 'Magickal Faerytales: an enchanted collection of retold tales' (2020), in which Lucy eloquently expresses the role of fairy tales in our lives:

> 'Fairy tales are about survival. Surviving our families
> most often, and being sent out into a world which is
> hostile and navigating the new worlds in which we find
> ourselves, without bitterness or rancour... The tales
> are not only frightening, magical and enchanting, but
> hopeful too. Hopeful because there is nearly always
> a kind of transformation that occurs at a deep level,
> due to the courage displayed within the heart of the
> children, or the princess, or the girl in the tower,

wondering how she will ever turn a pile of straw into gold. This storytelling inspires us with the same courage and tells us that, no matter the hardship, we can continue to be ourselves and find our way to freedom. Often with the assistance of a magical helper, the brave characters within these wonder-tales change, they learn, and they create real, authentic lives'
(Lucy Cavendish, 2020).

The book's words, its beautiful illustrations, even the quality of the cover and the weight of it, flooded fifty-something me with memories. I remembered Wednesday evening visits to the library, filling a hand-sewn library bag with well-worn storybooks of princesses, pixies, elves, trolls, kingdoms, deep dark forests, and enchantment. I'd carry the stack of tomes to the librarian's counter, then lug my heavy bag of wonder back home to sit and read undisturbed at the table whilst the family watched television.

I'd reinvent the magic adventures of the books I read in the forest paths behind my cousin's house in Oatley, in the rickety tree house up the peach tree in our backyard, or on early morning 'sailing' voyages, anchoring offshore, midway across our above-ground pool in my blow-up boat.

Abandonment and me

I vividly recall that I'd been listening to a book for the thirty-minute drive across country to pick up my sweet little man, Biscuit the guinea pig, from the small pet vet in the hinterland of the Sunshine Coast.

The book, 'When the Body Says No: The Cost of Hidden Stress' (Dr Gabor Mate, 2019) had been recommended by a friend. Written in chapters of case studies, Dr Mate shows the correlation between people's experiences of trauma, the consequences of their coping mechanisms and the diseases they were at risk of manifesting by repressing trauma or anger, instead of addressing and transforming it.

I was listening to his words coming up to a green traffic light a few blocks away from my destination, and I was in the lane to turn right. The case studies on the audio had moved on to one of a woman with a similar history of sexual abuse to me, and as I became aware that this was relevant, I felt the triggering of acute hearing get switched on.

As far as I remember, it was the first time I heard the word 'abandonment' in the same sentence as 'repercussion of sexual abuse in childhood'.

I knew immediately that abandonment was something that had hurt me so much, so often, for so long. I just hadn't known the term to describe that hurt and confusion until I heard it said out loud in that context.

The word 'abandonment' resonated and reverberated like a boom as it was spoken. I felt only what I could explain as a rapid current of electricity zapping from the base of my spine to my head, and back down again. It was quite literally a knowing.

Chilled and rattled, I turned right at the traffic lights and immediately blinkered left to pull the car into a safe parking spot, out of the way of the afternoon traffic. I switched off the audio and the car engine, took off my seat belt to release the feeling of restriction across my chest, and sat for a few deep breaths.

I didn't try to distract myself from the sadness of the revelation. Instead, I stayed where I was, finally allowing myself the grace to acknowledge the word. I didn't break down; it didn't make me angry. I felt calm and relieved to be able to see the connection with clarity.

When I felt present enough to get back on the road to the vet, Biscuit got even more of a loving cuddle than usual when the vet handed him over after his minor procedure. I remember not rushing away, as I'd usually have done, but I asked the vet a random guinea pig mum question. It intrigues me so much that they have unique hairstyles, colours, and personalities. I asked her, 'What are guinea pigs for?' She smiled at Biscuit and said, 'Love, just love.'

I was enchanted by that simple response.

For the drive home, I chose not to put the audio back on. I didn't need to keep filling my head with any more than what it had to process already today. Instead, I listened to a bit of soul music with the driver's window down to let the fresh afternoon breeze clear the energy in the car.

That evening I mentioned my realisation to Troy when I was preparing dinner at the kitchen bench. 'I just had a big moment today. I think that Mum abandoned me.'

He looked at me quizzically and responded, 'Didn't you realise that? It's been that way for as long as I can remember.'

I thought, once again, how easily I could have chosen not to investigate the circumstances surrounding sibling sexual abuse, and not had that moment of realisation of what I'd felt, but couldn't speak about for all those years.

It was taking that first step that had led me to so much more.

I felt suddenly awake and didn't want to shy away from what I was learning. I decided it was the right time to talk with Rose about it in our next session.

Later that week, seated comfortably, I started the session shakily, 'I'm coming to terms with something; I think I have found out that Mum abandoned me. Could that be right?'

'Didn't you realise that?'

There was the same response again.

No, I hadn't.

What hadn't dawned on me in all the conversations I'd had with Mum about how abandoned she had felt due to her own life experiences, was that abandonment doesn't just happen to us alone. It becomes something we're at risk of carrying forward or passing down into other meaningful relationships and our future generations if we don't do something about it.

Whether Mum repeated the generational pattern of abandonment wholly or partly unconsciously, it didn't matter now. Still, it would take me time to accept, and longer still to think about what it meant to me—in my adult relationship with Mum and my own family.

Rose advised that processing this new knowledge would take time. For an initial period of a few months, I found myself having recurring bad dreams, and memories of unpleasant words that confused and hurt me as I grew up. Even that feeling of something having broken inside me the day I'd disclosed to Mum the first time— it was related to the feeling of being abandoned. As I explored it I uncovered many hurtful moments since, where I'd get discarded by Mum as the pest that I'd become in the happy family's life.

I was deeply rocked by this revelation, and struggled with the idea of seeing my mother at all during that time. I didn't disappear, but stayed in touch by SMS only. I tried to focus on simply taking care of myself for now. Even though it was ultimately a healing realisation, it hurt a lot and felt unfair. The wound felt like it was getting deeper before it would begin to heal.

I couldn't think what I would ever talk to Mum about when we did speak again, but when I finally did arrange a lunch date with her, the conversation came easily. Something had shifted, and

I could tell I no longer needed to fill empty spaces with small talk. I could comfortably hold quiet space and listen to what she shared, relaxed in being there at that moment. Now I didn't feel I had to find something to say if I had nothing worthwhile to contribute.

I was conscious that my energetic shift threw Mum off, and she was looking at me differently, as in giving me the up and down. She asked if I had lost weight or changed my hair colour. She asked me about the work I was doing in my training business, trying to piece together what it was she couldn't quite put her finger on just yet.

The hurt was still there in me, and it'll always be there, but the need to go on pleasing, or offering to do things from the place of feeling like a victim of our relationship, was unravelling itself little by little from around my heart.

I was gently allowing myself to come into a new place, where I would see what our time together might become. What I knew was that it would be different to how it had ever been before.

Baby steps towards thriving

*'Women who have experienced childhood trauma have a
goal to become a survivor. Is surviving really the end result
you want? Isn't thriving a much richer goal to aim for?'*
CLARISSA PINKOLA ESTES, AUTHOR

At the international launch of #SiblingsToo Day in April 2023, the event creator, Nancy Morris shared 'you can bet there would be millions of adult survivors, and abusers, not thriving in their lives right now'. I jotted that statement down in my notebook and later considered the enormity of the repercussions left in the wake of sibling sexual abuse globally. As an adult, I have referred to myself as an adult survivor, yet that day I realised I could thankfully acknowledge that I am thriving, not only surviving. That transition to thriving has taken a long time, with many baby steps forward and backwards, the most important of which was asking the right people for help.

I know that asking for help can be daunting. The kinds of rationalisations I've heard from fellow survivors about why they won't ask their doctor for a referral to see a psychologist or professional have included:

'What if the doctor thinks there's something wrong with me?'

'What if the doctor judges me?'

'What if the doctor thinks I'm crazy?'

Yes, what if?

When I hear those fears, I've responded quietly, 'and what if the doctor doesn't think or do any of those things?' My GP didn't – she was compassionate, kind and helpful. She has since left the medical practice, and the new GP I chose to continue with as my doctor is also non-judgmental and respectful.

If we look at the list of physical and mental health consequences (see Appendix 4 for a robust list of statistics and facts) that may have impacted any of us due to the early adoption of coping mechanisms and behaviours, there's a reasonably good chance that a doctor already has an inkling that child sexual abuse or something else traumatic may have happened in our past.

I know there are many other avenues to seek help through. A doctor is just one example of a professional who can hand us the keys to getting the right help. If it's about the personality of the doctor—or something else that our instincts are telling us about them—none of us is stuck with one doctor. There are plenty more doctors or health professionals in the world who will guide us.

Coping strategies

The moment a child is abused, with no one to tell about it, is the moment she understands there is no one to protect her. She will develop a variety of defences, real and imaginary, to provide a sense of safety, or she will attempt to produce a feeling of insensitivity and emotional numbness to whatever is happening to her. The ways she devises to protect herself may go unnoticed for years. When they emerge for others around her to witness, these defenses may seem bizarre or foolish to some, and immoral to others. It is important to remember that these mechanisms developed and evolved years before they emerged in the child's conscious mind. The child who was repeatedly traumatised had no hope that the assaultive behaviour would ever end, and no context within which to understand it.
STEVEN LEVENKRON, PSYCHOTHERAPIST & AUTHOR

When I started looking for coping strategies that I might have used in my younger years, the adoption of drinking heavily to numb me in my teens stood out like a sore thumb.

Humiliation was a familiar emotion I experienced in my teenage years. Everyone, including my parents, seemed to laugh at how shy twelve-year-old Alice was, and they had no qualms about helping me snap out of it.

At the teenage parties hosted at our family home, I'd get dragged out of my comfort zone by both hands, with a parental push from behind. My comfortable and safe place I'd been in felt raided. I wanted to be invisible and sit between my parents in the lounge until the party was over. But no, sometimes others decide what's best for us and apparently, that was for me to join the older kids in the backyard at the party.

When the family stopped the holiday apartment vacations at Coffs Harbour, we tried family camping trips on the NSW south coast. In the first holiday venture south, the adults, the teens below the drinking age, and the younger kids gathered around a campsite bonfire. The adults were way beyond happy hour by now, in various stages of inebriation. One or other of the men, whom I didn't know, would come and drag me up to dance way too close to him. I was fifteen, and I felt frozen inside, dying at the spectacle I thought I was, as the adults laughed and yelled, 'Alice, you can dance better than that, put a little hip action into it. Don't be shy!'

Unfortunately, in those family holiday situations, I couldn't escape into a couple of rum and cokes, like I knew the rest of the older teens were doing in the dark pockets of the dunes, and as I would have been doing if I were at a party back home without the parents. On family holidays, I didn't get to lose myself. I had to stay with the younger kids around the bonfire and take whatever was dished out by the adults.

Binge drinking

I can see now that my early drinking was interwoven with social behaviours, related to having been abused. I suffered from incredible shyness around the opposite sex, staying in the outer circle of social groups to avoid being seen. Unfortunately, that tactic often had the opposite effect and would put the spotlight on me; I seemed to attract even more comments about me than the others. What we resist persists, I guess.

I said yes to trying alcohol at thirteen, because that made me look social. After all, if I declined it, I stood out and got made fun of. I remember not wanting to get singled out for being the only straighty-one-eighty. I didn't want to be singled out again, so it was safer to blend in.

The early drinking soon turned to binge drinking. Most of the time I wasn't entirely present at parties or sometimes only just made it to a party before the night blurred. Whatever happened or was said, I would wake the next day, not only feeling incredibly sick but seeing flickers of events from the night before where I had put myself at risk of danger, and being molested.

Alcohol decreases our reaction time, so I didn't manage to dodge the groping of the older boys I had no interest in or feelings for. Girls didn't get to be at a party without being touched up at least once. Or worse. If girls were drunk, for the opportunistic men and youths, they were even more attention-grabbing!

I could see how it was a way for teenage Alice to disappear into the numbness, but I wondered why I carried on with it well beyond my teen years into adulthood.

Deciding whether I did really want to get to the truth of that ongoing choice to be numb made me feel incredibly vulnerable. It would have been much more comfortable to tuck that topic away and not bring it up. It took me naming the truth of the abuse before I could change that habit. Whatever the coping mechanism or unhealthy behaviour is, and binge drinking was my choice of poison, in order to heal we must choose to make a change to some long-held comforting habits. They are not just poor choices, but decisions that had somehow got us through some of our darkest moments.

That's a significant decision to contemplate regarding the emotional cost of choosing to change. Because, once it's gone, what would there be to replace it? How would that void be filled?

I cannot speak about how the abuse affected anyone else's life but my own. All I can do right now is to offer what I have come to understand. There *are* slivers of light through the doorway to recovery, and it's about taking one step at a time.

I thankfully let go of my habit of drinking too much, too often. To do so, I needed to make choices. Whom I was spending time with and even the time of day made a huge difference – lunch dates are wonderful. A gathering of family over lunch, with the prospect of presence in a conversation with people I love, wins over counting how many more bottles we have left, any time! I happily offer to be the driver, freeing me from friendly cajoling and raised eyebrows.

Drinking was a habit that stayed long beyond its use-by date. I know if I hadn't finally changed, it would have damaged my health, as well as my relationships.

Letting the story I was telling float to the surface allowed me to put a lot of the experiences, memories and old habits behind me. What I'd found so far had fuelled a fire that I was comfortable for now keeping alight—until I decided I'd had enough for now.

Sexuality

Another unhealthy coping mechanism I eventually recognised and let go of involved my sexuality. No oversharing here. I am already feeling naked enough by writing that one word as a sub-heading, but it must be spoken about.

Being sexualised as a child messed with my adult sexuality.

One result of being sexualised as a child is the effect it had on the openness I could (and should) have felt in a sexual relationship, especially back in my awkward earliest years of intimacy with Troy. I enjoyed sex, intimacy, and closeness with Troy—but I knew something was missing, and I wanted to be fully present for him.

I hadn't equated it with being sexualised as a child at the time, but it took a long time for me to relax fully, to learn to receive from him, and to love and be loved at a deep level. For many years I was alert and wary in moments of intimacy, and felt everything in my head rather than my heart and body.

The constant reaction of my shoulders tensing up around my ears, and feeling unsafe in moments of intimacy confused me. Yet, I wouldn't let on to Troy back in those early pre-disclosure days. He was undoubtedly worried about whether I was okay with what was happening; meanwhile I was in my own little world trying to cope and not to worry. Was this how it was meant to feel? I didn't know. Who would tell me? No one. So, keep going.

Before I met Troy, my young girl's body had been hard-wired to experience the act of sex as doing whatever was expected by the boy. In turn, I expected the boy to put up with any disconnect on my part, get what he wanted and shut up about it! Much sexual activity, but the pleasure was nowhere to be felt.

The door of intimacy opened with Troy, but to be honest, I know that it was an ongoing process over many years. I actually remained somewhat closed, even to him, until we did some work on it together in the year of our twenty-fifth wedding anniversary. It was in 2011, the same year we immersed ourselves in more profound personal and business leadership growth, and maybe in recognition of all our years of deep love, it felt right to begin exploring and discovering more about ourselves and our intimate relationship.

I wanted to know what it was we both wanted in that part of our life together. We didn't rush it. We took it slow and talked about it, and the learnings we shared showed me that I could relax and be myself fully, if I let down my guard.

A few years later, we tried a couple's relationship course for a weekend that threw my trauma triggers into overdrive. Nothing sexual was going to happen there, but the exercises creeped me out big time!

Each woman had to dance for the other men, not only me dancing in front of Troy. Most of the women had been to these things before and showed up easily and naturally as themselves. A couple of us were new and stood together in our humiliation, summoning the bravado to dance like no one was watching, but I wasn't ready to show up like that. I felt shame, and every other word I could find describing me as worthless and unattractive.

The men, like Troy, were amazing souls. They were kind and non-judgmental, giving their time to improve their intimate relationships with their present or future partners. They wanted to support we women any way they could in expressing ourselves in a safe space. Still, my body was screaming all over. The men were seated expectantly on the floor in a tight circle with their backs together waiting for the women to dance around them one by one.

I felt split between disappearing out the back door of the hall and standing ashamed with the other women, feeling terribly out of place.

I took a breath, listening to the pulse banging away in my ears, and tried to overcome my fear and dread. *How could I be the only woman not showing up like the rest of those women were doing?* The old familiar pattern rose up once more: I didn't want to stand out.

I instead prodded myself, *Come on, Alice, just be a good sport like everyone else.* Out across the floor I went dancing, not making eye contact with the men as I'd been instructed to and putting on a plastic smile. I danced like everyone was watching, feeling like a fake, shameful version of myself, which felt so bad.

That, in turn, made me feel like shrivelling up afterwards when I thought about how I did that when I didn't want to. It was like I was dirty and disrespectful of myself. I wanted to turn into dust, slip between the ancient floorboards, and blow away forever.

Note to self and Troy: I will never be going to any more group couple's classes!

I was fifty-five when I started therapy with Rose. It took many months of sessions before I could open up safely to this valuable conversation about how my childhood abuse had impacted my adult experience of sexuality.

Rose nonchalantly asked me a few questions in one of our afternoon sessions. She was setting up another deeper learning I was invited to delve into. Seemingly as an aside, Rose asked, 'So... do you enjoy sex?' I immediately responded, 'Yes, all good. I enjoy sex.' Rose had herself survived childhood sexual abuse at the hands of her stepfather. She was very aware of the repercussions abuse could have on life and family. She smiled, nodded, and stated, 'That is so good, Alice, because it is often difficult for a woman who has been abused as a child to find a partner they can trust, who has the care and patience to work through this (the trauma we were discussing) with them in the bedroom.'

I felt I was meant to have something to say, but I had nothing. I just said, 'Yes, interesting.'

Rose shared a few more pieces of information to complete the picture she was painting. Young Alice sat silently, twiddling her fingers, trying not to get in the way of hearing what adult me needed to take on board that day. My inner critic was sitting up, perched on my shoulder, back straight, scribbling notes down for later in case I missed something.

I didn't give anything further away to Rose in that session, but I knew she'd opened another closed door for me to choose to walk through—or not.

That night, even if I wasn't really thinking about anything, my mind whirred loudly! Rose's revelation may have been a seemingly obvious repercussion of being abused sexually, but it was a new understanding for me to come to terms with.

I went to bed grumpy. I told Troy I was processing what I talked about with Rose today and wasn't ready to talk with him about it yet. I needed to be alone with this myself first.

Lying in bed in the dark before Troy came in, I had an internal dialogue that the inner critic didn't even try to butt in on: *So, I believe I heard that one possible leftover impact of Darryl's sexual abuse was that it 'shocked and closed' my ability to be fully open to intimacy. Sexualising me at eight years of age, long before any girl should or is ready to be, led me to disassociate from the experience of having sex, to distance myself. I'd switch off, not on. I'd tense up and hide in my head instead of opening my heart.*

I could feel the rumble of my inner lioness' roar rising inside me, and goosebumps appeared all over my body simultaneously. I was enraged at this new knowledge.

The seeding of this new realisation in that gentle conversation with Rose upset me deeply. It rocked me to my core, and I had to give myself plenty of time to allow it to settle on me. Questions spiralled out of control inside my head, *What do I feel is good sex? What is pleasure? What was me being one hundred percent me in the bedroom? What was me being the abused me? What was anything? What if I'm sexually ruined forever? Darryl, you bastard! How dare you have done this to me!* In that moment anger arose inside me and I was not in the frame of mind to be able to blame Darryl effectively, as I'd practised some years earlier.

I was distraught that my whole adult sexual experience might be false.

The questions to myself continued: *What is fake or real? Who am I? What do I enjoy as the woman I am beneath the scared, abused young Alice? Would I ever be 100 percent me?*

I spoke to Troy about it a few days later as we watched the sunset at the river's edge. I asked him to please listen and not give me any response right now, it was enough to share some of those thoughts and questions with him. As the weeks went on, we continued the conversation. He said he understood, and let me know that we would find the answers together.

I still hadn't come back to writing the memoir at that stage. I had other projects moving forwards, completing higher-level certifications that supported my new business offerings.

Then unexpectedly one day, I pulled my notebook and book-writing journal out of my filing cabinet, re-opened the last draft of the manuscript I'd been working with on my Mac, and resolved to tell the rest of the story.

Troy poked his head in the office door when he got home that afternoon from work and asked 'What's going on here? What's spurred you on to get back to the book?'

I swung my chair around to stop looking at my computer screen for a moment and said, 'The realisation that Darryl's manipulation and sexualisation of that little girl who was me impacted my experience of sexuality and pleasure. He robbed me of my woman's right to pleasure. That is just wrong! No one should ever have that natural, personal pleasure taken away by another person. Sibling sexual abuse must be stopped, and survivors like me need to know they are not alone. The book had a purpose, and I'm back on purpose!'

It had released the lioness within me, because she roared a roar that burned with rage, truth, and fury—no one has the right to take away any other person's real sense of intimacy and completeness. No way! Not ever!

There was work for me to get on with.

The good girl – bad girl

I hadn't known that I was going to, but I found myself doing a little work to shift from calling myself a good girl or a bad girl during my gap year of travel in 2017.

It all began with Troy gifting me a book for my fiftieth birthday a few years earlier called *F**k It: The Ultimate Spiritual Way*, by John Parkin. At the back of that amusing and enlightening book, John mentioned that he and his wife, Gaia, extended an open invitation to anyone who'd like to come to a retreat with them, in Italy.

As we were planning our itinerary for the trip, I told Troy, 'Hey, we could go to one of those F**k It peoples' retreats from the book you gave me; that'd be fun.'

We had no qualms about the travel incorporating some inner work that would be healing, after our exit from our company and the past four years, that had included trauma, near death and the loss of loved ones. Where better than a F**k It retreat in an organic vineyard in Italy to heal and find a new spiritual path, before returning to our new era in Australia?

I checked the upcoming retreat dates, found one that fit in between the other countries we were visiting, filled out my registration form, emailing Troy the outline of the course and his registration form to fill out, if he was keen. We paid and added the dates to the trip planner.

I didn't give it another thought until we got out of our taxi at the beautiful vineyard's front door. I turned around, breathing in the scent of the roses creeping up the stone wall of the building, taking in an appreciation of the three-hundred and sixty-degree view of the grounds and the peaceful vista. As we were handed our room key to the Lavender Room, which we'd been allocated as our sanctuary for the next week, I remembered why I was there.

'Oh shit,' I said out loud to Troy as he walked up the stairs to our room one flight above reception. 'This retreat is going to involve internal work. What made me think this was a good idea to include in our gap year? Why didn't I find a retreat that involved cocktails, massages and facials?' Troy turned around and said, 'We're at a retreat on an organic vineyard in Italy. I think we can manage.'

Once I accepted that the book had shown up in my life for a good reason, I shook off my concerns about the hard work it would be and dropped into making the most of it. The process that John's wife Gaia was cooking up was to dissolve us. The retreat became an unforgettable and unexpected gift to me: a self-love process completed in a magic location all the way across the world!

I recall tuning into one message Gaia shared on the first morning as we sat on the floor in a large circle, sixteen participants comfortably lounging on giant cushions, our notebooks and pens ready.

It was so powerful that I scribbled down some notes in my journal. This is my take on all that Gaia shared, which I dug around and found in the journal from that year:

Up until we're two years of age, we hold the status of being sweet, of pure heart, so beautiful and only referred to by the adults in our life as being a 'good little girl' or a 'good little boy'. Around two, that sweet goodness is replaced by confusing new messages which seed in us adult words that we are naughty or bad. 'No! Stop that. That's naughty. You bad little girl. You bad little boy. That's bad. Don't do that!' Thus, our sweet innocent souls begin getting trampled and muddied with generational and societal expectations, religious and family rules and opinions.

I recall that as Gaia spoke, I recognised my feeling of being scared or thinking that I was bad had started well before the abuse at eight years old. Flashbacks don't just zoom in on the abuse but give flashes of other memories. I remember I cried a lot as a little one, almost at the drop of a hat.

I had one schoolteacher (who wasn't a nun) for my second-grade class, and the tone of her voice scared me. Short and direct, I burst into tears when she'd say my name, expecting me to read out loud or answer a question. It was embarrassing for my parents that they'd been called to the school to talk about it. When was I ever going to stop this crying thing? Eventually, one of the bribes of a toy worked. Maybe I was ready to stop crying, but I recall my grandma handing me a wind-up tin money box where the monkey threw my coin into his mouth. 'Do you think this will stop you from crying?' she asked. Like magic, the coin disappeared inside the box; and like magic, there were no further tears.

Unfortunately for me, trying to please and be a good girl, being timid, scared, ready to cry and perceived as weak, was another green light for my predatory abuser, Darryl, to know he'd selected the perfect prey.

The desired outcome of 'dissolving' at the retreat in Italy was to dissolve the hold in my mind, body and will. It was about allowing this to happen by itself rather than forcing or trying hard to let go of whatever was holding me from transformation and my true potential.

During the retreat, I experienced two incredible healing outcomes.

The one that was the most easily explicable release was in the form of a practice that let me dim the volume of the 'I am bad' soundtrack and replace it with a new one.

Gaia had us pair up with a script to go through, one person at a time. Troy and I partnered to do this one exercise together rather than with other participants.

I would say, 'I am light; that's all I am; I am light. I am not good. I am not bad. I am [insert word]. I am not [insert word].'

The words that I'd insert were one of my gifts, strengths and values. If I couldn't think of one, I'd repeat 'I am light', until I could say a positive affirmation. Those positive affirmations alternated with a list of the words that 'I am not'. Words that felt shameful and hurtful that I had called myself or had been said to me or about me in the past.

It ended simply with: 'I am only ever light'.

At arm's length, Troy and I sat opposite each other, comfortably on our cushions on the floor. We had chosen a space away from the others, over in a corner, giving ourselves a safe space to practice this together. We shared words that we'd not necessarily ever said out loud about ourselves before. It was a simple, profound and beautiful practice. Tears sprung up and quietly poured down my face, my neck and onto my shirt. I didn't try to stop them. I just followed the practice until I was out of words. Troy did the same thing. It was a vulnerable practice together that we won't forget.

'I am light' are three words I often repeat, given that I'd spent so long listening to and repeating the old soundtrack of not-so-kind words.

As a reminder of that vision from work in Italy, I have my only tattoo: a mystical lantern. It reinforces my belief that I am not good, and I am not bad. I am light. I am only ever light.

It was yet another new beginning for me.

Shame, guilt and the inner-critic

Shame is an internal experience, an internal pain. When you feel it at a toxic level, it makes you disown yourself and completely disconnect from who you are. It is the ultimate self-rejection. That self-rejection becomes the core of your identity until you heal it. The thing is you can't heal something you don't acknowledge. To heal the shame within, it is crucial that you get honest about what shame exists.
FABIENNE FREDRICKSON, AUTHOR

The practice and the mantra I found in Italy in 2017 were simple. However, I knew from all that I was reading and understanding about abuse, that the family dynamics often leave the abused person in the family feeling shamed, guilty and at fault. Sibling sexual abuse is so awkward to address within a family.

I knew I had to come to a time where I could investigate shame and guilt and my inner critic, and what I could possibly do about them. I had no idea what it would look like to be free of all the negative words of shame and guilt, or how I would go about getting rid of them. The alternative, if it seemed doubtful that I could break absolutely free, how might I begin to come to terms with them, and use them to my advantage?

Shame and guilt were part and parcel of a Catholic upbringing in the 1960s and 70s. Children were not to be conceited enough to presume we were innocent little human beings. We were taught to believe that we were born sinners, who kept on sinning, so we needed to make up somehow for all the evil deeds we did, and then one day we'd make it into heaven. Heaven was the end goal!

We were expected to self-criticise regularly. If we had nothing to be ashamed of or feel guilty about, we would quickly come up with a lie so that we didn't disappoint. If we were being hauled up to the front of the classroom or the principal's office, we soon learned to lie to avoid getting into trouble.

My mum and dad, raised by God-fearing older parents and the generations before them, also had to adhere to the Catholic faith's strict rules long before we were born. That, combined with the family's history of secrecy, makes it quite challenging to contemplate letting go absolutely of guilt, shame and self-blame.

Then add on the misplaced shame and guilt related to the sexual abuse.

My inner critic had laid the shame talk on heavily for decades, starting with the simplest yet most effective version, 'You're bad'. It was quick and easy to poke me with, like a sharp stick to the ribs before any other thought to the contrary could arise. I paid attention to that comment so long that it was easier to say, 'I'm bad', not 'You're bad'. I developed a selection of similar statements:

'I'm a bad mum. I'm a bad daughter. I'm a bad sister. I'm a bad wife. I'm a bad boss. I'm bad at everything!'

Thus, it had been a blessing to find the practice of reminding myself that 'I am light'; a powerful mantra to have in my toolkit.

When it came to self-blame, when something went wrong, even if it was an issue belonging to someone else, I could easily twist the story around to believe that whatever happened had to be my fault. I was an aficionado at this game of shame, guilt and self-blame. If any omission or oversight occurred anywhere in my life, 'It's my fault,' was my first thought—such a disempowering one-way conversation.

I found Brené Brown's audiobooks invaluable on this subject. I love that Brené narrates her own books, and the way she shares stories makes the lessons feel like I'm sitting in a room with her, and not so alone with tricky topics like vulnerability, shame and guilt.

In this journey of healing, each time they appear, it has been so valuable to find someone who resonates with me and gives me information that's so relatable that my subconscious can start making sense of it all by itself.

Mind you, early on in listening to the helpful content of those kinds of books, I would very easily find myself starting to slide down the slippery slope of shaming and guilting myself, or becoming overwhelmed at how bad I am compared to the way, for example, one of Brené's 'wholehearted people' live.

Brené described what she called 'wholehearted living' as being about engaging in life from a place of worthiness. In my heart, I wanted that, and in my mind, I'd be doubting I could own my worthiness for longer than a moment, an hour, a day. Would I be really able to climb that mountain and know that I am truly enough, just how I am?

Brené defines wholehearted living as 'cultivating courage, compassion and connection, to wake up in the morning and think, no matter what gets done, and how much is left undone, I am enough'. I am enough. I'd be hearing those words, yet my mind would drift away, and ask, *But are YOU enough, really? Who are you kidding?*

In my mind, I'd start listing all the things I should be or should do better to be more like the examples of the people Brené was sharing about. I'd stop hearing the positive words and start beating myself up again, focusing on the words of my own inner critic. Thankfully, I had some experience by this point at observing my own self-sabotage and would short-circuit the negative self-talk, redirecting it positively:

Hey, you! (me) Click the pause button for a minute. Stop calling yourself bad, you chose that book, and you chose to press play because you wanted to learn something from what you're listening to, right? You are not being judged, so stop judging yourself, stop shaming and should-ing all over yourself. Take a big deep breath, press play and listen. Please take it in and choose what you want or need to do with this good stuff you have at your fingertips! Okay? Good. I said press play!

So, although I will still fall into the trap, all the work I had done was making me much faster at recognising negative self-talk, and more effective at turning it around quickly, and getting back to what was healthy and good for me.

I have listened more than once to two of Brené's audiobooks, 'The Power of Vulnerability' and 'The Gifts of Imperfection'. They were enough to snap me out of it when I immersed myself in my guilt and self-blame. I didn't need to make this another complex project, overwhelming myself with more to contemplate that I may then feel the need to conquer. I didn't need to find more and more to read until it became yet another excuse to not deal with the real issues. I'd just cut the nonsense and use the tools I had to get back on the positive track.

I have learned to practise kindness with my inner critic voice, even finding ways to improve my situation that aren't about throwing my inner critic off the bus completely, as I used to picture would be the only way out. One day I gave my inner critic a surprise. I tried something that a friend had done when she was stuck in anxiety and couldn't move forward.

I recall that day feeling fed up with my inner critic's persecuting words. This time it was about a prospective client from the United States reaching out to work with me, my inner critic quickly bombarded me with words of self-doubt: *Who you? He must have made a mistake? Why would he want to work with you?* As I caught myself wondering who I could refer this person to when he realised I wasn't good enough, I broke the pattern of the rhetoric. I took a deep breath and looked my inner critic straight in the eyes. I walked to the hallway mirror, where I held a soft gaze at my reflection for as long as possible, and even let a small smile play on my lips. That part felt awkward and wobbly, but at the same time, it felt better than looking at myself with no smile coming back at me.

I asked out loud, 'What do you want from me? What do you want for me?'

That first time I tried it, staying present and holding my own gaze, it rattled the bully that my inner critic is. It might seem a little strange to you, but I am used to it now. I have actually become quite a fan of conversations with myself, now that my critic has been somewhat subdued. As I allowed the conversation to continue she said, *I want you to be safe. I don't want you to feel like you've failed.* No more gossip and nasty opinions, that was all. She's a timid wee thing when it comes down to it. For a week afterwards, I could feel her voice had quietened.

Around that same time, Rose suggested seeing my inner critic differently, 'Consider that she has served a purpose for a very long time and is part of you. She's not some other character playing a role in the show.' She invited me to consider that I would have had her along for the ride, whether my family had raised me, or some other, or even if I'd never been abused. We all have an inner critic, she explained, who is really just us, speaking to ourselves.

Rose suggested I thank my inner critic for what she's done to date and see how I could use her many gifts, and her extraordinary skill set to our mutual advantage. That felt good to try. It was also good to honour what she'd tried to do for me, to keep me safe, all through those earlier years.

The walk-through helped

We make sense, or fail to make sense, of our lives by
the kind of story we can, or cannot, tell about it.
JOSEPH DUNNE, AUTHOR

All healing is supported by acceptance, forgiveness and love of ourselves. To give ourselves the opportunity to free up our energy for healing, it's important to first release the negative energy of anger, guilt and shame towards ourselves. Healing begins with taking care of ourselves, and it starts with the smallest of steps.

Finding where to begin, retracing the steps of my experience of abuse, was awkward, delayed, and sometimes fumbled. I had no idea if therapy would open a bottomless, dark abyss of uncomfortable or painful discoveries.

My vision for how I would write this book, and where I was headed, lent me such a positive feeling— that it was a healthy inquiry. The therapy, the writing and what I learned all combined to make me feel more wholly held. All of it was good or better than hiding from the truths.

As difficult as it is to rake over those memories and their impact on my life, I'm so grateful that everything I have come to understand about my circumstances is possible to work on, accept or change. I've relived, acknowledged, and understood so many things. I've felt pain and deep emotions, grieved and learned from my experiences. I've built love for myself, and that love is not only for me to use, but also to give—and that feels good.

My early experiences led to adopting coping strategies and behaviours that numbed and protected me. I choose to acknowledge their good intention for me; they did help me through a lot. They allowed me to survive at a time when I felt like I had no one in my corner and didn't have more helpful tools to choose from. They did, however, have an expiry date for their effectiveness. It was the child in me who was abused who needed them, but the adult in me also has the choice of taking responsibility to change what no longer serves my present and future.

When I kept my story inside me, it put me at risk of impacting my relationships with those I love, including the one I have with myself—and at risk of dis-ease. It took me a long time, many tears, small steps, and an odd nudge (both pleasant and unpleasant) to get me on the road to recovery.

I am not my past. I am not alone. I am thankful for those nudges. I am fully empowered to create my future. I choose to heal. I heal better with support and help. Every child or adult survivor of sexual abuse deserves support and love, and professional help. We deserve to have safe places to talk about our experiences and begin the process of recovery and healing.

11

The Gift of Self-Love

As traumatised children, we always dreamed that
someone would come and save us. We never dreamed
that it would, in fact, be ourselves, as adults.
ALICE LITTLE, THE MINDS JOURNAL

At one of my later sessions with Rose, I walked into her office feeling out of sorts. I wasn't sleeping very well again. This time I couldn't identify any particular breakthrough or issue I was working on that was bringing up these feelings.

By this stage I knew quite a lot about the kinds of things that arose inside me, and this somehow felt different. I had the strong intuition that rather than old emotions or trauma being stirred up, they were somehow coming from outside of me. I was grumpy and couldn't find a way out of the feelings, so I knew I had to ask Rose if she could help me identify it and hopefully walk away from the session with it fixed.

I explained it to Rose: 'It's like I'm feeling rumbles of resentment and annoyance trying to burst out of my skin. It's weird. It's not my resentment or annoyance; it's an anger that keeps taking up space in my body like I'm breathing it in. It is so distracting, and it feels dirty.'

Rose suggested that perhaps, this time, it wasn't coming from inside. She told me that the feelings we experience could come from other people around us, their thoughts and feelings somehow intruding into our body and mind; and even if they aren't physically present, we can still feel their dark energy. She described it as being like psychic daggers being thrown at me, verbally or in the thoughts and fears of others.

I didn't need to question how Rose knew that was what it was. As she said it, I intuitively felt it was as she described. I don't need everything to be textbook proven or tested, and I knew from the start that it felt heavy on me, not heavy from inside of me.

She recommended I play around with some visualisation techniques to become good at deflecting psychic daggers so they couldn't stab my heart. I was slightly disappointed. 'So... not something that was going to be fixed by a therapist in one session?'

In the following weeks, I practised visualising the psychic daggers when I felt those dark attacks—seeing them as not my daggers felt good. I did that practice, intuitively feeling it would be more effective if I moved my body about to dodge the attacking knives. The other thing that helped was getting outside and being someplace else. I got out of the house, and looking at the sky, the river, and the birds took the pressured feeling away.

I asked Rose in another session, eager to get the resentment out of my body for good – 100 percent gone: 'How do I get rid of that feeling?' Then I moved just a touch toward dread with, 'It's going to make me ill. I know it!'

Rose guided me through the idea of attachment and detachment as a necessary understanding to move beyond the expectations of others— or resentment from others, as I was thinking of it. Likewise, it was about me releasing any expectations or resentment of others that I held onto. In my words, I needed to release my attachment to that feeling, stand outside the picture, and look back in from a different perspective.

I liked that idea, and as I explored, I learnt that somehow, we all get twisted around each other's hearts—like ribbons or contortionists at a circus—a silent movie circus act. Unwanted attachment feels like that to me, twisted up and tightened ribbons wrapped around my heart. It feels suffocating and heavy. Learning to protect myself in this way was like a whole new level of boundary setting.

Although I had done a lot of work setting boundaries, in all honesty, they were boundaries about safety, only set from a space of fear of being hurt again.

The first stage of boundary setting for me was separating my own family from potential harm by my brother in my twenties, followed by years of ongoing commitment to those choices.

In the process of recovery, boundary setting was sometimes about saying to others, 'no, that's not acceptable behaviour' or 'I feel hurt', before retreating to a safe corner to heal the hurts. I would feel guilty about the results of those actions and it was even at the risk of loneliness sometimes. In establishing boundaries, changes would be made, and others were not always completely happy about them. It was still easy for me to blame myself for everything that was uncomfortable, but Rose had, more times than once, reinforced that it's okay—if I felt hurt, I felt hurt. She reminded me to pay attention to my own emotions and take care of myself for now.

That worked, but my mind kept threading together past stories, so it didn't work for long. I'd find I'd wake up, and my first thoughts were ones of worry and feeling guilty again. I asked Rose again, how do I make all those feelings disappear forever, *finito*? Can I make them vanish easily and quickly?

It was around when I felt hurt by something Mum tried on me. We had been sitting and talking for a couple of hours in her lounge. When it was time to go, I picked up my bag, kissed her goodbye, and walked to the front door to go home. When I was halfway to the door she blurted out a random statement, still with her back to me where she was seated, sounding annoyed at me, 'What's going to make you get past all of this? You've got to stop making it hard for everyone!', which stopped me in my tracks. We hadn't spoken about what 'all of this' was in the past two hours, but I could easily guess what she was alluding to.

I turned around. I didn't react. I didn't feel angry. I headed back to the recliner chair I'd just vacated. Propped on the edge of that seat, sitting opposite Mum, I asked her, 'What brought this up now, as I'm leaving?'. Then, we talked back and forth for a while, but I could see she wasn't really in the conversation, her mind was distracted and there was something she wasn't saying. I asked, 'What is it that you want from me today, Mum?'

'You've got to accept that people aren't going to change. I only want a happy family.'

I said, 'I feel for you, Mum. It's hard. In my heart, I know I have no say about people changing and don't expect it. I know what's good, healthy and safe and what's twisted and wrong. I just chose not to be a part of something that doesn't make me feel safe anymore. I would love it if you had a happy family too.'

She smiled and nodded sadly, sagging a little in her lounge, not saying anything further but I could see in her eyes I hadn't given her the answers she wanted. I leaned down and we said 'I love you' to each other, then I kissed her forehead. It felt unfinished, but also like we were getting through these conversations faster, more calmly, and with much less energy and words consumed. It was nice to leave without the bruised heart and overwhelm from rehashing past hurts like we used to.

However, before I arrived home, and it was only a five-minute drive, I heard the ding of a text message notification that I read in my garage. Ah, so that's what it was. Mum asking me to change my ways translated into, 'Don't come around for the next week, I've got Sydney coming'. She hadn't mentioned Darryl was coming to stay in our conversation. That would have let me get home far earlier than I did if she had.

Ding! Like that, I felt my trust fall through the floor again, and the creeper safety alert switch on. I sat quietly and questioned every word we'd shared in our chat before I'd left, to find clues about where I'd gone wrong. If I'd said 'Okay, Mum I am past all of this', what would tomorrow look like for me? Would I have shown up to take her to her doctor's appointment, and Darryl would have been there? Would she even tell me that part if the conversation had gone differently? What had I missed? I know it must break Mum's heart every day that her family is estranged.

Rose and I talked more deeply about the newness of my realisation about my abandonment, as well as attachment and detachment. I had to accept that this work was not about quick fixes because I couldn't control what others would say or do—and they would do whatever they wanted to—without forewarning.

Rose gave me a one-page 'law of detachment' statement, including instructions to follow, reinforcing that it would take time. In my heart, I knew I needed to believe in what she offered me, as I had already come so far with her help. I knew what I'd worked through and felt released from already, and that had taken time. So I chose to respect myself, setting a longer timeline to allow this new learning to settle on me, and see what else might intuitively come to me to help me resolve my feelings.

Saltwater and my attachment releasing visualisation

I left the therapy session with the printed page in one hand and the idea of sourcing a spiritual healer or some healing process to help me disentangle myself.

At yoga class that night, the teacher gave us poses aimed specifically at helping us open up regarding trauma. It was soothing, I felt something was moving inside me, and slept restlessly. The following day, I tuned into a morning meditation hypnosis titled 'Letting go of the past and negative emotions', and tears rolled off the side of my face and onto my pillow. They didn't stop.

I got out of bed and found Troy downstairs, asking him if he'd like to come with me to the ocean before he went to work. I knew intuitively I needed the healing power of saltwater. We arrived at sunrise, and I floated quietly in the gentle swell. As we sat for a takeaway coffee on a park bench afterwards, the tears floated to the surface again and poured down my face. Troy eventually suggested we return to the car. I couldn't stop the flow, and my tissues had become small sodden balls. I had nowhere to look to avoid the prying, curious eyes of the early-bird locals as they walked past.

Back in the car, I blurted out all my feelings about the hurt of abandonment and the confusion around attachment and de-tachment. As saltwater is healing for me, I realised I needed to find my own ritual to release what I was experiencing. Strangely enough, I knew exactly what I needed the ceremony to include, or the first few steps of it anyway.

I booked myself an hour in the saltwater float pool of a local spa. Before I left home, I read through Rose's law of detachment sheet and journalled everything I could until my pen ran out of words. I padded along the paths I knew at the spa, almost like that walk was part of the ritual. The attendant led me into the warm float pool room and set the door signs as occupied. I put in my earplugs to block the water and used the timed three minutes until the ceiling of twinkling lights would fade to darkness to lay down on my back in the shallow water, floating fully stretched out, with my hands open, facing upward, ready to receive. I closed my eyes as the lights went out completely for the hour that was my time to use just for me.

Drawing on a visualisation practice I vaguely recalled listening to years ago, I pictured myself as a sovereign, seated on a large stone bench looking across the bountiful gardens of my personal realm. The gardens spread out into the distance, with the most beautiful glittering mosaiced walls, and the gates and a moat down at the far bottom left corner of the garden. On the stone terrace to the right where I was seated, Troy, my daughters, loved ones and friends were laughing, setting a long table for a celebratory evening feast. There was a hearth with a fire burning over in that direction.

My personal realm was full of heart, soul, music, art, beautiful colourful fabrics, and flowers—all good, creative and loving elements filled the space. I felt clearly that this realm was my life. I wasn't renting it from anyone, I could pour into it whatever I chose and leave out of it anything that no longer served me.

As the sovereign, I visualised my heart beating and thought about the list of all the people in my life who were entangled, via red ribbons, around my heart. I'd written that list down in my journal at home, and I knew it was healthy to include all relationships, including Troy, and anyone's name who came up, be it close or extended family, people I used to work with, or had met overseas; if a name popped up, it was added to the list.

The point of the exercise is that no one should be entangled tightly around anyone else's heart. We love, give and grow beside each other, and it doesn't serve us to twist ourselves up with each other to make one entangled mess.

I took a deep breath in through my nose and breathing out, I inserted the list of people's names into the two spaces of the following statement:

'I fully and freely forgive and release [names] and
let them go to their own and best happiness, and
[names] fully and freely forgive and release me
and let me go to my own and best happiness'.

Repeating the statement four more times in my mind, one by one, I could see the red ribbons loosen and fall away from my heart with every slow breath in and out. Released, everyone from the list drifted out to the distant gardens, happily chatting away amongst themselves. They did so aware that they were all welcome and loved inside the walls of my personal realm, my life, if love-based emotions such as compassion, integrity, kindness and openness were respected.

The realm's guards collected all the untethered ribbons and placed them in a basket beside the fireplace. I decided I needed to rest and enjoy the beautiful surroundings of what was present in my life for a moment. I floated without thought for a while in the salty pool, replenishing my energy just for me.

The sovereign, re-energised, stood by the fire and tipped the loose ribbons in, watching them disintegrate into ash. If any of those ribbons had been secretly concealing psychic daggers, I didn't want any of those within the gardens of my life, at risk of piercing my heart. I felt my strength increasing and my heart opening, free. I looked up and smiled at those now meandering back up from the gardens with the sun setting behind them to be seated at my table.

Creativity and childhood joy merged. The realm was now floating on fluffy white clouds, one of the clouds that sat above the 'Magic Faraway Tree' that Young Alice had cherished the stories of, and I'd read to each of our girls over and over when they were little.

I invited Young Alice, and all the magical folk she loved, to join us at the celebration because the realm and the table we would be seated at were safe, loving and full of joy, laughter and hope. I hugged her, and she felt safe now to trust and embrace me. She knew she was safe, that my life was a sanctuary and that I wasn't going to compromise her or me again.

I got up from the pool at the end of that hour, feeling like I'd rested for a day, and the words 'bombs away' came to me as I lifted my first foot from the water onto the dry sandstone beside the pool. *How odd,* I thought. *Is that the title of the book?* At that stage, I was still working on the title of this book. *Was that it?* I couldn't be sure.

I walked quietly back to my car, and before heading up the long tree-lined driveway to head home, I switched on my streaming service and found the band Sheppard's playlist to put on the song 'Geronimo', which had 'bombs away' in the lyrics. The playlist defaulted to another song, 'Find Someone' which I'd never heard before, also by Sheppard, and as I listened to the lyrics, I started to laugh. It was a sign! I laughed and smiled, then played it on repeat for the fifteen-minute drive home. I felt like the process was done.

The realisation was clear: I only needed to look inside of myself, and be the person who loves me the most. Begin there with self-love, kindness and self-respect. It was a theme song for that day, not beyond, but it was a theme song nonetheless! I felt lighter, quieter and more peaceful, and my mind felt crystal clear.

Rose and I spoke to debrief over the phone, and she recommended that kind of release needed rest afterwards. My old me would have just moved on with what was next, but I heeded that advice and did rest as prescribed.

I felt peace and contentment in a way I'd never felt before. So simple a practice to gift myself, healthy, happy boundaries with a hell of a lot of love, joy and creativity wrapped up in them.

Everything that came up during my time in sessions with Rose was my journey, from what I experienced as a child and adult. I cannot speak to all that therapy would bring up for any other person. Finding the resolve to heal showed me the answer to my coach, Leanne's, question back in 2011, 'and you've dealt with that?', in response to my mentioning the abuse.

No, I had not dealt with it, and that had made everything good I was trying to do that little bit harder, dragging the heavy weight of the past along until I was ready to let it go.

I hadn't wanted to crack open at the seams because I was approaching my past and the idea of therapy from a place of fear. In reality, therapy has been a conversation connecting my head and heart, stopping me from doubting my resolve to stand apart from the mainstream, empowering me to ask more questions about myself and in relation to the bigger picture of abuse.

With a skilled, caring professional, I felt safe unpacking what I needed to look at until I was done with it. Each step forward has been about forgiving others and myself, forgetting what I don't need to bring back up to the surface any more times than I already have, and replacing old habits, thoughts and self-talk that haven't served me, with healthy practices that do.

Interweaving threads

Being around inspired, visionary, enthusiastic people who are living their truths is one of the fastest ways to massively transform your life.
JEN SINCERO, AUTHOR

I signed up for a webinar in 2018 called 'Stop Rescuing Start Coaching', hosted by Donna Zajonc MCC and David Emerald, author of The Power of TED* (*The Empowerment Dynamic) and I got the most wonderful surprise!

The title caught my attention because the word 'rescuing' rang a bell with me. It reminded me of the drama triangle roles I'd been introduced to years earlier through Helene. The webinar for coaches opened with an image of an upside-down triangle balancing on its tip on the screen, and I knew it as soon as I saw it.

Busy as I was back in 2005, I didn't forget about Dr. Karpman's drama triangle. I just put it aside to look at another time. The drama triangle has a knack of staying in our mind, as once we have seen it, it is impossible to unsee it in ourselves or our interpersonal relationships, in life and at work.

So, this new information I received in 2018 was like a beacon of light. I couldn't believe that someone was reintroducing me to this topic I'd found so fascinating all those years earlier.

After the introduction refresher on the drama triangle roles of victim, persecutor and rescuer, what Donna shared made me exclaim out loud, 'Woohoo! You've got to be kidding me!'

Luckily, my audio was set to mute.

I heard these words, '...and the antidote to the Dreaded Drama Triangle is TED* (*The Empowerment Dynamic), a framework created by David Emerald. TED* is a triangle of empowering roles: creator, challenger and coach. The role that describes the opposite of playing the Dreaded Drama Triangle's victim role is the creator role' (Zajonc & Emerald, 2018).

Creator! Now that word had sparkle, and it resonated so fully with me.

I was thankful for coming across the antidote to the drama triangle that day and told Troy what I'd discovered when he arrived home. I knew it was a vital lesson that had crossed my path for a reason.

In weeks to come, I couldn't help but smile at the stacking

of 'creator' messages through my journey I'd previously not put together. In recruiting and supplying healthcare staff, our previous company let me trial personality, behavioural and strengths assessment tools regularly, and 'creator' or similar descriptions appeared in my personal test results.

That said, I wasn't going to pretend I knew how to magically shift from my long-lived drama roles to these more empowering alternatives I'd just been introduced to, but I was incredibly inspired to dive in deep and learn more.

In 2018, this book was a bundle of thoughts not yet articulated on paper. Both it and the therapy would only begin to take shape in 2019, but I could feel that good magic was beginning to interweave somehow, and I didn't even need to know how specifically; I just knew they would.

In 2021 I became a certified facilitator, joining The Center for The Empowerment Dynamic's global community of trainers and coaches, whom I'm incredibly honoured to learn and grow with as we deliver this life-changing work.

Four simple gifts

Let me fall…. For I will be caught by who I am becoming.
CIRQUE DU SOLEI - QUIDAM

I am a work in progress. I'd never profess I've fully got it all together. You'll probably have guessed that by now. I am, however, the most willing, motivated and respectful participant in my recovery and in choosing to live a fulfilling and loving existence.

In 2020 I chose to get creative, and granted myself some simple gifts that supported me outside of therapy, helping me to sculpt the more authentic expression of myself that was slowly taking shape.

Before I go further, I'll share a humbling experience I've not spoken of before.

We came away from selling our company in 2016, able to release ourselves from company and personal debt. We could put funds aside for retirement and what was left into a comfortable, small, quirky 1940s home for Troy and I, and we took our first long overseas holiday together just for us.

Like high school graduates, we played and celebrated our freedom to travel, giving ourselves a gift of a gap year. We travelled broadly, slept in more than forty different beds, focused on seeing wonders and bucket-list items, all on a lean daily budget. I was glad to slip into my comfortable bed when we returned home after all those twenty-dollar-a-night lodgings, and I never wanted to see scrambled eggs again—our staple room-cooked dinner for many nights of that trip.

While we were travelling, we both dreamt up new business plans. Troy needed the feel of cash and coins jingling in his pockets, so he started a business that took him back to his earlier passion for being in nature and sharing his knowledge of all things botanical. He started the cash slowly rolling in, whilst I gained my certification as a professional coach and trainer, ready to open my practice the following year.

Together, we have been thoroughly humbled by the experience of starting over again in our fifties! This time felt completely different from setting up an in-demand service in a niche industry. This was us delivering 100 percent ourselves and what we love to the world. We devised simple business plans, did the start-up research, attained the necessary licences and tools of the trade, and then put ourselves out there to get the two businesses growing.

We both came to this round of starting new businesses a little more battle-worn, older and wearier than we had when we started that first business. At times I lay awake with worry, wondering, *Where are we going wrong? Why is it taking this long? What am I not seeing?*

I had to remind myself that the earlier business didn't take a week to get to the magnitude we took it to. Organic growth and our desire to draw word-of-mouth referrals would take time. We had to be patient and keep moving forward toward our business outcomes.

The four gifts are a handful of self-love opportunities I decided to embrace for myself. They all were accessed when Troy and I looked at our bank account, shaking our heads in frustration 'Wow, is that the lowest amount of money we've ever had? Oh no, now it's lower!'

We had two small businesses with limited cash flow, and one or all clients would be delaying their payment for services in any given week. Anyone in a small business will have experienced that Friday afternoon silence of no notifications of deposits landing in the business bank account. They were crazy times, followed by the strangeness of COVID-19 and all the changes it brought. Our appreciation for the small things—good people; living the quiet life; budgeted simple menus cooked and served with love—became amplified as the most important things.

We stuck with our mutual resolve to give things a go and face our fears until we made it happen, and that's working now for us. It took time, and it did take putting our respective hands up for help.

These four gifts are about the present moment—each a simple and pleasing ingredient mixed into a feeling of completeness. Initially, I listed seven gifts and then felt, *Where is the simplest place to start, if I were beginning this journey?* So, I shortlisted those seven to the four most meaningful ones.

They are gifts that helped me heighten a sense of peace and contentment and helped me see myself more fully. I share them with the hope they may seed the idea there is something we can each do today that will help us come back to ourselves more fully.

We've all got to start someplace!

Gift #1 creativity

*Using your creativity to solve your problems
brings confidence and joy, brings openness
and generosity of spirit and thought.*
NIKKI DAVIES, WRITER

I feel that creativity has always been part of the roles I have played in my adult life, in how I went about day-to-day life, including that of being a business owner. Life would be incredibly dull if we didn't have creativity and variety in how we go about making things happen.

The creativity I'd loved as a child, in making small handicrafts— immersed in the pages of library books that set out instructions for making felt puppets, crochet rugs, crepe paper flowers and the like—had disappeared through the years my brother abused me. I sewed and did textiles and design at school and was good at it, but it was more of a practical step-by-step kind of skill. It didn't fill my heart with joy.

I recall creating vision boards in the early days of finding personal development, and gluing down the business card of a local mosaic art teacher. In early 2019, I allowed that creativity out and booked into a series of three beginner's mosaic classes. All I had to do was choose something simple to work on, and even that was a wonderful feeling to consider what it was that I'd create. I settled on a house number on a rectangle board and just got started, gluing down the colourful tiles around the border. Simple, basic skills to begin with, no cutting, just me, the piece of board, a pile of colourful square tiles and the glue. Peacefully I stood there in the first class and rolled out lines of adhesive, placing one tile beside the other, leaving enough space for grout that I'd learn how to apply by the time the three sessions were up.

I fell in love with the mindfulness, the colours, and the choices open to be explored, and I still love mosaic work today. I lose myself in it. It lets me bring colour, magic and light into my creations. I even wake up at night and wonder about the current project I might be working on, how to balance shadows and light, which colour will work best as the border, or combine with gold mirror glass. I'd rather wake up to consider those options than other reasons to wake up that I've now left behind me.

Imperfection and the freedom to create whatever I wanted were unleashed. You cannot fail creativity. You cannot fail art.

When I'm in the present moment of creating, it fills me up and re-energises me. It's quite a beautiful shifting of energy to experience. Creating for me involves intuition, and it is a moment in time that requires commitment. At some stage of the day, it is time to glue down that glass or those tiles onto the board. Then there are the moments when I can stand back to see the work-in-progress and smile that it's all coming together.

Giving myself creative respite soothes and positively uses my energy. When I'm done, be it for two, three or four hours, I can feel when I've had enough, and I'm ready to do whatever else is in my plan for the day.

The added benefit of having creativity as part of my weekly routine is surrounding myself with like-minded, creatively inspired budding artists. We meet, drink coffee and get all our news—good, bad, or otherwise—out of our minds first. Then we set up to sketch, or snip, glue and chip away at our glass and tiles, chatting away on light topics or listening to music, finding that three hours go by in an instant when lost in using our creative hearts and minds entirely.

I encourage any person attempting to heal from trauma to seek out a creative outlet. The great thing is that it's also okay to accept when it's time to try something else, find something new to learn, and let creativity flow.

Gift #2 practice gratitude

The more we believe there's something to
celebrate, the more we'll see it everywhere.
DEWITT JONES, WRITER & PROFESSIONAL PHOTOGRAPHER

The gift of gratitude soothes the soul, whether done by using a gratitude journal or online apps, or through meditation and visualisation practices. Gratitude is more than an exercise in improving and maintaining my mental health; it has been a liberating experience. The practice of gratitude has given me greater resilience to those things that would have previously triggered the feeling of being alone or that would set me off into a shame and self-blame spiral.

For me, it's been about having some fun and getting creative with gratitude. I came across a YouTube video by Dewitt Jones, the National Geographic photographer, titled "Celebrate What's Right with the World!" that opened me up to see the practice of gratitude is much more than writing three things I am grateful for today before switching out the bedside light; and before I get bored with, or forget about that daily routine.

By incorporating into my daily moments taking a few photos

of my own—of say, the sweet pea flowers I planted as they first start to unfold in my flower pots, or the bees humming in the ends of our trumpet flowers that have the most incredible heady scent when the evening air cools—that is enough to bring me to gratitude.

Early in the morning, I'll stand with my feet in the sand out in waist-deep water at our beach, looking through the crystal-clear water at the sand, conscious that no other human being has stood in that place yet today. As the fishes move in to see who I am, I'll stand still, then do a slow 360-degree turn looking out at the ocean, possibly see a dolphin breaking the surface or watch the sea mist floating up into the trees of the National Park above the beach at the south end. I'll watch the sun slowly spread up to brighten the day along the coast as it peeps over the top of the hill.

Simple, beautiful, and I didn't create any of that; it's there to lift my gaze and see anytime I need to get out of my head and remind myself how lucky I am to be alive. It takes self-love, creativity and developing a consistent routine of practice. A personal practice that suits us alone.

Gift #3 inner peace and self-awareness

Be so still inside (yet vibrant) that you can listen
at every moment to what life is offering you.
BROTHER DAVID STEINDL-RAST, AUTHOR

Mindfulness, meditation, breathwork and yoga became key elements in the healing process for me. Beyond my own experience, I found in reading other peoples' research that they are incredibly helpful in healing for trauma survivors.

I've been meditating, sometimes twice daily, for nearly two decades now and can feel the days when I've skipped it first thing in the morning. There are plenty of hours in the day to find twenty minutes to lay down, breathe, relax in silence, or try other options like listening to one meditation instructor or another share their lesson, or incorporate hypnosis into their visualisations on YouTube.

I didn't know until reading about abuse that for some of us who've experienced trauma, lying down and closing our eyes to meditate may trigger the feeling of being unsafe. That made me sad, but it was good to understand. Meditation, with a softening of the gaze, also works just as well as closing the eyes completely.

Breathwork in the form of pranayama is something I came across in India in 2017. Part of the daily ritual at an ayurvedic wellness centre where I stayed was one hour each of yoga, meditation, and pranayama. At first, I misheard that I was expected to attend all three, so I opted just for yoga and meditation. One day the yoga master came to me and asked why I wasn't attending the pranayama session, suggesting it would be excellent for me to try it.

I attended the next day, and honestly, it was the first time in all my adult years that my mind went completely quiet for a whole hour. What a gift that breathwork is to give ourselves. I have a mobile phone recorded video from India that I brought home to guide me at first, however there are plenty of sources of pranayama or breathwork practices on YouTube or through yoga or meditation schools face-to-face.

In India, the instructors would explain before introducing each type of breathwork what it was and for whom it was suitable. If anyone had a health condition or symptoms of one kind or another, there were breathwork practices that were either beneficial to try, or better to avoid.

I had never liked yoga, but I found out along the way that it is powerful. It's taken a long time, and many different yoga studios, to move beyond wanting to stand up halfway through the class and walk out of the room.

I know I don't bend well. I swear under my breath whilst doing so-called flow poses and thinking about what to have for dinner, before smiling into my favourite pose, which also happens to be the final one: Savasana.

Yoga is a gift for all trauma survivors, something Bessel van der Kolk ('The Body Keeps the Score', 2014) shared: 'Yoga's inherent focus on the breath, moving with each inhale and exhale, noticing whether your breath is fast or slow, and counting breaths in certain poses... strengthens the capacity to be present, at the moment and not in my mind elsewhere.'

I found a yoga practice that met my needs by trial and error. At a gym I was going to, we were shown the most wonderful Yin and Restorative yoga, and I immediately fell in love with it! Because who said we must do yoga someone else's way—the style other people love, and think is easy? It's entirely about ourselves and what we need.

I also appreciated the feeling of being let off the hook at a yoga class run by a yoga instructor from Scotland. I remember thinking, *Thank you universe!*, one morning when we began our class at six am sharp. She shared that all our bodies are different. She realised early on that she didn't like other yoga classes where she felt bad that she wasn't as flexible as other participants. 'I'm from Scotland; my heritage is more about having strong, thick wee legs to walk the moors and climb mountains. My legs do not bend the way someone else's legs do. Be okay with doing what you can. Do not do something that makes you feel pain.'

Her words reminded me that I was one of those awkward children who, when told to sit on the floor with their legs crossed, couldn't do that, or if I did, my knees would be up in front of my chest.

I'd easily sink to the floor, but my knees slid together out front, my feet turned back at my sides, tucked close to my hips, and I could sit that way comfortably and gracefully as a bird folding its wings as long as I liked. The other kids would laugh at me, and I had to wear that, because sitting with my legs crossed felt worse than sitting the way I could. I remember the teacher would look at me, perplexed that I'd got the 'sit on the ground with your legs crossed' command wrong.

I feel I'm never going to twist those legs the other way around, no matter how much I try. My body and I are trying to get along with what we've got.

Yin and Restorative yoga are gentle approaches that suit me. They are deeper stretching, a lot of resting, some easing back, and then releasing a little more into the pose. I get to settle there for three to ten minutes in each posture. I am appreciative of the opportunity to quieten the mind, body and nervous system. I feel restored, nurtured, safe and peaceful in every class I attend. I'm amazed and keep saying to myself, *So who'd have thought you do like yoga after all?*

Others shared that, like me, they'd cried during or after a yoga class. That's a good thing, releasing the pain and old experiences from the body is one of the main reasons to do yoga. It's also both kind to ourselves, and interesting to understand what parts of our body relate to our particular trauma.

I think it's all about finding an experienced yoga instructor whose practice is focused on a room of individuals. That builds trust and safety, and it was worth getting to the class early to talk to the instructor about my trialling yoga as a therapy to heal from trauma. How would she know to share her knowledge on whether to use or avoid a pose, change the posture so it isn't overwhelming for me, or give me a pose that is just right for me today?

Yoga has been a gift I'm still finding love for, but I can see the benefits in continuing. It was just about finding what was suitable for me at that moment.

Namaste!

Gift #4 forget the old programs of pleasure

What lies before us, what lies behind us, is
nothing compared to what lies within us.
RALPH WALDO EMERSON, ESSAYIST & PHILOSOPHER

This gift nearly got cut due to shyness, and then I knew it was such an essential part of this journey to have made me resume my writing, so I could not take it out.

It is hard to share because of the vulnerability involved. I know that intimacy and sexuality are one area of my life that was greatly affected by childhood sexual abuse, and I won't let bashfulness make me put my pen down now.

Given that my own creeper alert is probably as fine-tuned as any other abuse survivor, I will not be oversharing here! My daughters will even feel safe reading this section.

I remember once meeting a woman in her mid-eighties as we went through the process of making a cup of tea from the same urn of boiled water. Over this ostensibly polite and short interaction, she shared quite openly, 'I love sex. I always want sex!'

I looked up and realised she was talking to me. I was surprised and said, bemused, 'Hi, I'm Alice. Sorry, I didn't catch your name. Good for you!' then moved away before she shared more.

What I'm sharing here I feel is worthwhile to share; to consider in the safe space held within this book for adult survivors and those who love us.

I don't know about you, but I wasn't aware that there are

sex and intimacy practices that help release trauma, and we can de-armour our vaginas from the trauma and numbness caused by sexual abuse. I'm not going to discuss that now, but it was yet one more piece of information that I found helpful to contemplate. It made me wonder what else was there for me to learn about.

Before being introduced to all that, the simple gift of seeing myself wholly for the first time in my life was an act of self-love that opened doors for me.

After the shock of finding out how being sexualised as a child affects the sexual experience of teen and then adult survivors, I resolved that this would not impact me for life. Not if I could do something about it. Finding out was better than not finding out.

Having enjoyment in sexual intimacy with a partner is something I had experienced with Troy, but I remained shy to ever talk about it, not to him or myself or anyone. I imagine I'm not alone here in that the private details of sex and intimacy weren't something I had talked about at any stage of my development as a teen or adult.

Now it was time to change the old soundtracks and programs, to reframe what I had running through my body and mind in terms of guilt, shame and numbness about sexuality and intimacy. I chose to be open to learning things I did not know about sexuality and pleasure, with the small hope that I wasn't truly irreparably damaged in some way. Yes, another research project!

Where better to start anew and become fully alive about all things intimacy and sexuality—than with an expert's professional care and guidance?

I investigated a few sex and intimacy coaches and chose one who resonated with me, ticking off all the boxes. I didn't even know I had boxes to tick, but as I investigated I realised they were: that I felt safe in her space; depth of knowledge and openness on the topic; and she had also experienced and was recovering from sexual abuse. Alex is a coach passionate about intimacy, creating a safe space first, and sharing her healthy public message about sex.

Rose had told me way back when we first spoke about the sexual experience being tainted by the abuse, that it takes a very patient, kind and loving partner to help with this work.

So, my first thought was that I'd be doing this thing for Troy and me, and then I breathed a sigh of relief at being advised that the priority was to attend solely for myself first. There was plenty I could learn anew without worrying about homework with Troy or whether I'd remember everything, and what if I couldn't get that homework right? The communication with Troy would come next.

Troy and I had discussed that I would explore this, and he fully supported the plan, yes for himself, but first for me. It did have to start with me.

The coach made it clear she was not a sex therapist and asked me questions, pleased Rose was in the wings should anything trauma-related arise.

I began an incredibly open and enlightening conversation with this jewel of a woman. I could go deep and ask any question I had ever (or never!) thought to ask anyone. We talked about me, Troy, the abuse and the book, and many more things. I immersed myself in a six-week coaching course, including self-love practices, both journalled and lived. I opened my awareness of how I receive, and how I make myself feel safe outside of the bedroom, let alone inside it.

Her course description felt welcoming, too: 'My Voice, My Body, My Pleasure: a six-week journey to awaken your sensuality, connect to your sexuality, discover your voice and love your body so you can feel worthy of pleasure and love.'

In one of the first practices, I realised I'd never stood in front of a full-length mirror naked for more than a moment of drying myself after a shower or applying body lotion. There wasn't even a moment I can recall where I'd stop, with interest or curiosity, to give myself a full inspection, let alone open admiration!

I'd come from a childhood where I'd always had to have my knickers on since it was naughty to be naked, even in bed at night. We didn't ever see our parents naked. During the abuse years though, I saw a lot I didn't want to see that didn't exactly help me to feel comfortable about nudity or my own body.

At some stage, I chose not to see myself as fully physically feminine. Perhaps I never had.

As an awkward and post-abuse teenager not yet healed, feelings about my body and sexuality were shrouded with shame. As a busy young wife and mum three times over, perhaps almost ready to look at my physical being, there was no time, privacy, or full-length mirrors!

I became roles; a body called Alice moved about the place, not really me. It's common for an abuse survivor to disconnect their head from the body, a comment I'd heard numerous times over the years in physical therapies, like massage and chiropractic treatments. Now I have full cognisance of what that disconnect means.

The practice: To stand naked in front of a full-length mirror.

I followed the instructions, and slowly scanned every single part of my body, starting with the top of my head, my hairline, forehead, eyebrows, spots and lashes, every single detail as slowly as possible. It was awkward but purposeful, taking that time to look. If I didn't like it for some reason, I had to write the body part or area and reason down on my notepad before moving on.

Whichever area I wrote down, I was to check if there was a feeling or emotion within my heart and body about it. I had to ask myself whether someone had ever said something to make me feel that way, whether I could recall if it was abuse related, and examine what my self-talk, that inner critic, had to say about it.

Afterwards, I went back through the list and wrote down three reasons to be grateful for that part of me. My list took up the full notebook page, and I was okay with that. Thankfully I had found 'Embrace: the documentary', and 'Embrace Yourself', the audiobook by Taryn Brumfitt about the same time, and I loved what Taryn was sharing about our long-held limiting beliefs around body image. I know that I'd held onto many unkind words that I said to myself far too often about my teenage and adult woman's body, my post-birth body, my weight, and my sexual prowess.

Alex shared that such beliefs are all too common, and that made this exercise that little bit more hopeful—that it wasn't just me who had a whole page of data to work with, following such a simple exercise.

I felt confident that I was on a very empowering path I'd never stepped onto before. It felt good to have written all those words out of my body, to read and do something about.

The list became a starting point. I recall one message:

'We cannot love only 90 percent of our bodies.
That other 10 percent we don't love will be
the one part we focus on that takes us out
of the moments of pleasure in intimacy.'

We must love ourselves 100 percent: lumps, bumps, wobbly bits and all!

I knew the course wasn't therapy, and it felt wholly nurturing and safe.

As abuse survivors, it is easy and understandable to remain stuck in the *What if something is wrong with me?* and *Is it just me?* feeling, because we don't know how to move forwards. Besides, intimacy and sexuality are awkward to discuss.

It was a movement toward loving myself first, about what I

enjoy, what I still might not feel, or what I do feel, how and when. It was also powerful for my body and vagina, to know that they can trust me to protect them from harm. To let them know that they are safe with me. I never thought to reflect on that before. Then, after that, finding the strength and confidence to communicate better with my partner would find its time, without a hurry.

Wouldn't it be kind to acknowledge that none of us is born with an inbuilt knowledge or the skills to have great sex and intimacy straight off the bat?

Our earliest lessons or practices of our first attempt at intimacy are a fumble in the dark at best. And for abuse survivors starting from the most negative of sexual experiences, we come at it from a screwed-up standpoint, and yes, that's just my opinion.

Imagine if we all chose to forget our old programs of sex.

What if it was possible to learn what we were never taught or to allow adolescents to have that kind of education to normalise the conversation around healthy sexuality?

I'm not dismissing the long-term trauma effects of abuse on sexuality and intimacy and would never presume to speak on behalf of all survivors. I'm hypothesising there are possibilities surrounding pleasure, intimacy and loving ourselves more.

Even if the outcome was the simple ability to physically wrap our arms around ourselves and give ourselves a hug to connect with our own body for three minutes before we get out of bed each morning to start our day, a simple and tiny step that begins the process of reprogramming our minds and bodies? Alex assured me our body is happy to receive a self-hug any day. It's a huge step forward for any sexual abuse survivor, and the idea of that three-minute gift of a self-love hug daily was the starting point on Day One of the six-week course I chose.

It is a lovely, gentle and safe practice to hold ourselves in an embrace, and lovingly talk to ourselves before the day begins.

When we look ourselves in the eyes, and see the change between the first time we practised that self-love and several weeks and months down the track, when we see that smile sparkling in our eyes—it's hard not to smile back at ourselves!

12

The Way Forward

Don't forget that while you're busy doubting
yourself, someone else admires your strength.
KRISTEN BUTLER, CEO, POWER OF POSITIVITY

Forcing change to happen because we're supposed to want it is exhausting and soul-destroying. Personal development or healing work is a dance to a beat that only we can hear.

For me, my way forward will probably always involve splashing around in the mud puddles of my imperfections and my not-quite-there-yets, and owning that I do screw up here and there along the way (and probably always will).

The good work comes from giving ourselves the grace to turn inward first, to wipe away the grime that the abuse left behind so we can let our inner light shine through. We are incredible beings. Whether we were abused or not, we each have powerful resources we've developed along this life journey. They include our values, unique gifts and strengths, our use of creativity and our imagination, love and hope.

Forgive by repairing

You can have compassion without forgiving.
There are many ways to move on, and pretending
to feel a certain way isn't one of them.
LORI GOTTLIEB, PSYCHOTHERAPIST &
AUTHOR

'It includes forgiving, doesn't it?' That is a common question I have been asked regularly by non-abused people.

'Yes, I've found my way to forgive. Forgiveness comes in a variety of forms,' is my response.

When I first practised forgiveness in hypnosis, where I cut the visualised cords of attachment between myself and Mum and with Darryl, I had not yet explored how to go about releasing myself from the shackles of misplaced guilt, shame and self-blame, nor done the work of recovery that I have now.

Forgiveness had a heavier connotation to me because, born into the Catholic faith, sins, guilt and forgiveness were spoken about regularly. However, my parents and grandparents didn't model terribly well what we were meant to be or do. I wondered if forgiveness was a farce in regards to forgiving sexual abuse.

Dr Scott Eilers permitted me to share these words of his that I found made me smile. Dr Scott was the only psychologist I didn't feel like deleting from my Instagram feed during the years I was writing. His daily posts kept me going, and helped me feel sane when I got wrapped up in the process of writing or felt lost in all the emotions and thoughts that arose:

Has anyone ever told you where the 'forgive' button
is located in your brain? No?
It's probably because there isn't one.
I hear a lot of people talk about forgiveness
like it's a simple decision.
Just decide to forgive and magic happens
and forgiveness occurs.
If you say that you forgive someone,
but your feelings don't change,
have you actually forgiven them?
And, as we know, you don't get
to choose your feelings.
They're outcomes of interactions of processes.
So how do you actually forgive?
I've only found one way. I forgive by repairing.
Once I've mended the damage someone has caused
in my life, it takes a fair amount of conscious effort
for me to stay angry at them.
Mostly, I just stop thinking about them at that point,
which I think is a form of forgiveness.
Personally, I've found it impossible to forgive
until I can repair.
I think forgiveness happens near the end of moving on,
not at the beginning.
And, by the way, it's okay not to forgive.
It should always be your choice.

SCOTT EILERS, PSYCHOLOGIST & AUTHOR

Forgive by repairing. I understand that.

All we can do is the healing work that is beneficial to ourselves and show up for those we love honestly from that place.

I have shared my story and placed all those thoughts and memories onto paper. To do that, I chose to take one final walk through the abuse years. I felt and saw it again and released other memories that I hadn't let surface before, which I'm incredibly grateful to have happened. I tried to find other memories, and then I let that idea go because enough was enough.

In my everyday life, I rarely give Darryl a thought. I chose to write because the abuse had left a dirty stain on my body, mind and soul. Darryl's abuse was the starting point. Many repercussions and complications followed, adding more difficulties of their own to the actual realities of the abuse.

My focus is now on creating a life full of creativity, growth, contribution, adventure, love and good health, and making magic with friends and family. It brings me great joy and freedom to know I have done what was right for me. I said I would contribute to breaking the silence of the sibling sexual abuse taboo for my family: myself, my husband, my daughters and our future generations. It brings me peace and strength to know I'm not pretending to be anything but the whole of me. I just had to learn to start with me first.

Choosing the path of dealing with buried hurts, melting away the ice layer that concealed my suppressed emotions, and seeking recovery with a spirit of curiosity has given me so much. It has given me the ability to navigate drama with clear focus and good grace and helped me to re-access my childlike wonder, magic-making and creativity, which I sprinkle liberally into my daily life, relationships and work. Doing this work has moved me to become humbler and a little wiser, and comfortable enough in myself to gently lift away the shield that once protected my mischievous and loving heart.

It's about knowing that we truly do matter and that we are important too. We count more than the opinions or fears of anyone else—especially those who won't or cannot understand, or want to keep what happened to us quietly hidden to avoid family or societal shame.

I realise I will not change the world, but I can contribute to change. I can contribute to a widening reach of the ripple effect that touches each survivor, our intimate partners, our children, siblings, nephews and nieces and generations of grandchildren and great-grandchildren. Hopefully, it will ripple out to potential abusers of tomorrow and the abusers of today and yesterday.

If I had a magic wand, I would love to wave it and cast a binding spell for abusers, one that would spur them to choose an alternative pastime that doesn't involve harming their siblings' lives. I would wish that they feel remorse, as I'm sure many do, but not only so they can be released from their deeds. I would also want them to own up to what they did, and consider what they could do now to contribute to the positive ripple effect of change.

Possibly there is or will be a hotline established just for that purpose. For abusers of siblings, specifically. Not mushing it in together with adult abusers of children. Give this matter its necessary focus and resources from a broader, more understanding perspective, to allow whole families to come through experiences like our family went through together—happier, healthier and faster than they would otherwise.

No one deserves to go through this—much less so alone. If by writing this book I am able to relieve the suffering of even one person and help them to gain the support they need better and faster, it will have been worth the difficult journey and literally thousands of hours I have invested.

Enough for now

Your trauma is valid. Even if other people have experienced 'worse'. Even if someone else who went through the same experience doesn't feel debilitated by it. Even if it 'could have been avoided'. Even if it happened a long time ago, even if no one knows, your trauma is real and valid, and you deserve a space to talk about it... Your pain matters.
DANIELL KOEPKE, AUTHOR

I came to this journey of recovery and writing with a limited understanding of the repercussions of sibling sexual abuse: the coping mechanisms, the PTSD, and the consequences on our adult relationships, dis-ease and health conditions. I have not just recorded my experiences but have explored sibling sexual abuse through background reading of published papers and the writings of experts in the field. I have learned much about its origins, and how it presents in many different cases, and how society chooses to remain silent on the topic, across multiple generations.

I found validation from the numerous statistics and facts I have pulled together from the many organisations that support survivors of sibling and child sexual abuse. Some of it made me audibly breathe out a sigh of relief, or shed a few quiet tears.

All this newfound knowledge has been enlightening and validating, and at times, I had to put the reading and writing away when it made my heart heavy and my mind unable to switch off. I now understand fully how the words, *enough for now*, have been integral to my journey of recovery from the abuse.

Those three words have risen to the surface of my mind many times since I first successfully disclosed the abuse to Troy.

When people have chosen to disclose their stories to me, I hold confidential and non-judgmental space for that sharing. I don't pretend to have the answers for them, because sibling sexual abuse and the trauma each of us suffers comes about with many variations, and I am not a therapist. I wish I could wave a magic wand for that, too, to make it all right and ease their pain.

The stories each of us bears may be relatable, but no two stories are alike—from how we were first groomed or approached by our abuser to how the abuse is delivered, when and for how long—it will all be a different story to mine. It may be in a chaotic family such as mine, or there may have been only you and a brother, or you and a sister (I read case studies of both scenarios). I've also heard and read about situations where the abused child felt truly loved by their abuser, or that it was an act of love or enjoyment, or they were confused about what it was because they'd orgasmed.

The facts and information I've gathered that was shared in the earlier chapters showed that disclosure is often not made for many reasons: thinking it is too late to heal, from confusion and guilt or a culture that makes silence seem the best approach, or even wondering whether the perpetrator's actions were really sibling sexual abuse.

The only comment I would give is—if it were me who was still thinking about it, or if my subconscious randomly threw memories of it into my days or nights, my thoughts and dreams— then whatever story might be replaying in your mind, seeking your attention: it has always been more helpful than not, to talk it through with a professional.

Whilst I often lean towards alternative therapies, which help unlock the mysteries and emotional pain held within our bodies, I found it was working with a therapist that really let me unwrap and examine questions that kept replaying in my mind.

I hear people's stories on a regular basis, because I work helping people understand the drama triangle and its effects on their lives. Sometimes, they have experienced one form of sexual abuse, childhood trauma, or other traumas that have shown up throughout their lifetime. To me, any conversation related to abuse that one can practice feeling safe having, is one more important step forward for that courageous human being. Even if it is a very small opening, or conversation, that may be enough for them now until they're ready to brave the next step ahead.

In my experience, I now know it would have been foolishly optimistic to book in to see a therapist, ask for a six-session package, and expect to be miraculously healed. Healing takes patience and love. Just like we'd allow someone else, why would we not apply that same patience and love for ourselves in healing too?

When I started to share, even with an experienced trauma-informed therapist I did click with, I was concerned that I might very well crack open right down the middle, and it'd be hard to zip me closed again! Guess what? I cracked open. However, it wasn't as messy or dramatic as I'd pictured. It did at times take lots of tissues to dry up the flow of tears that had waited a long time to surface and be released, but the fear of becoming broken by opening up that had held me back for so long never came true.

Life, work or business still go on, while the therapy is finding its place in our busy schedules. Sometimes, doing nothing towards healing was necessary when other matters needed my full attention.

When I experienced breakthroughs in healing or coming to terms with one thing or another, I often didn't see those break-throughs coming. However, I am so grateful to have kept walking forward through the murky emotions, or I wouldn't have experi-enced those breakthroughs happening for me, and I would have risked never seeing the brilliant blue sky beyond those dark clouds.

I laugh now, thinking how I would walk into Rose's rooms, babble a million words a minute at her, all the while fiddling with the hem of my dress, wringing my hands or throwing one arm over the back of the couch. Then I would see her watching me do that, quietly nodding back at me, having not yet gotten a word in edgewise. I'd be thinking, *Ooh, what's she watching? Oh no, she's onto something!* Then, when I ran out of words and came up for air, I'd calm and quieten, and be astonished to find a truth had surfaced from within me to address, maybe grieve, or heal from.

Any breakthrough, be it the first or one of many more to follow along the journey of healing, eventually will close a door to the past. In allowing that to happen, I find that I am giving myself more space for what's most essential for me now—and in the future.

I hope that wherever you are in your journey, if you are a survivor of abuse, or if you are a person who loves or cares about someone who has been abused, this book has served as a healthy inquiry for you, and has helped you find some answers to what was on your mind. Possibly, like me, you may not have thought to ask certain questions before, or to investigate your history and family dynamics to see how the abuse could have been possible.

I hope it's given you at least enough of a shake to fizz up the oxygen in your blood, to create an awakening to what might be your next steps if the time is right for steps to be taken. Or maybe for you reading this has been enough for now.

From me, with love to you—may your healing journey be gentle, curious, and empowering, and your future one where love and creativity blossom.

Appendices

APPENDIX 1

This table from the Australian Institute of Family Studies (Stathopoulos, 2012) sets out developmentally inappropriate sexual behaviours in the age bracket of 0 to 18.

Age Group	Developmentally INAPPROPRIATE sexual behaviours
0-5 years of age	Curiosity about sexual behaviour becomes an obsessive preoccupation Exploration becomes re-enactment of specific adult activity Behaviour involves injury to self Childrens' behaviour involves coercion, threats, secrecy, violence or aggression
6-10 years of age	Sexual penetration Genital kissing Oral copulation Simulated intercourse
11-12 years of age	Any sexual play which involves children younger than themselves
13-18 years of age	Compulsive masturbation Attempt to touch or expose other's genitals, especially without permission Sexual contact with animals or younger children Using sexual themes to degrade others or themselves Chronic preoccupation with sex and pornography

APPENDIX 2

Details of the different forms of sibling sexual behaviours

Normative sexual interactions between siblings

As with children generally, young siblings may engage in exploratory sexual interactions and sexual play with each other. This is relatively common and harmless and serves a developmental function: it helps children to learn about their own bodies and the bodies of those around them. Curiosity about other people's bodies is expected among young children, and may often involve looking at each other's genitals through games such as 'you show me yours, I'll show you mine' and playing 'doctors and nurses' (Allardyce and Yates, 2018).

Johnson (2015) describes this kind of behaviour as an information-gathering process between children of a similar age, size and developmental status, provided it meets all these criteria:

- It is voluntary, light-hearted and playful.
  It diminishes if the children are told to stop by an adult.
- It is balanced by a curiosity to explore all sorts of other things in the child's world.

The more the behaviour varies from this description, the more that concerns should be raised and professional advice sought by the family.

Examples of normative sexual interactions between siblings include the following:

- A mother comes across her five-year-old son and his four-year-old sister laughing and showing their genitals to each other. She tells them off and has not seen them doing it again. There are no other reasons to be concerned.
- A seven-year-old girl tells her father that she plans to marry her five-year-old brother when they grow up and that they will have babies together.

Inappropriate or problematic sexual behaviour involving siblings

Inappropriate or problematic sexual behaviour involving similar-age siblings of any age is behaviour that falls outside developmental norms and can be developmentally or emotionally harmful to either or both of the siblings involved. Inappropriate behaviours are generally those where context is misjudged and are typically single instances. Problematic behaviours tend to emerge when the behaviour becomes more repeated and patterned, or where issues concerning consent and reciprocity are unclear (Hackett, 2010).

Even when mutually initiated, sexual behaviour outside developmental norms between similar-age siblings can be developmentally harmful to them. Partly for this reason, it is widely accepted that older siblings should not engage in sexual behaviour with each other. Evidence from a large survey suggests that non-abusive sibling sexual behaviour that falls outside developmental norms may be associated with depression and hyper-eroticisation of those involved (Stroebel et al., 2013).

Sibling sexual abuse

Although there are no universally accepted criteria for defining sibling sexual abuse, it is a type of child sexual abuse, which is defined by the UK Government as behaviour that:

'... involves forcing or enticing a child or young person to take part in sexual activities, not necessarily involving a high level of violence, whether or not the child is aware of what is happening. The activities may involve physical contact, including assault by penetration (for example, rape or oral sex) or non-penetrative acts such as masturbation, kissing, rubbing and touching outside of clothing. They may also include non-contact activities, such as involving children in looking at, or in the production of, sexual images, watching sexual activities, encouraging children to behave in sexually inappropriate ways, or grooming a child in preparation for abuse. Sexual abuse can take place online, and technology can be used to facilitate offline abuse. Sexual abuse is not solely perpetrated by adult males. Women can also commit acts of sexual abuse, as can other children (Department for Education, 2018).

All of these typical indicators of child sexual abuse can apply to interactions between siblings. Where any of the following factors are present, the sibling sexual behaviour can be regarded as abusive:

- There are large age gaps between the children. While an age gap of five years is commonly accepted as large, some authors suggest that three or even two years between the children should raise concerns (Carlson et al., 2006).
- The behaviour involves the use of threats or force, or other forms of coercion such as bribes, trickery and manipulation—for example, the giving or withholding of affection.

- There are significant power imbalances—due, for example, to size, strength, intellectual ability or position of authority.

Sexually abusive behaviour can be initiated by children of any age. Sexual behaviour between siblings close in age, or with no coercion evident, may still be abusive. Both large and small studies have identified incidents of sibling sexual abuse that have not involved the use of force or other overt coercion. Likewise, large and small studies have identified abuse where age gaps between the siblings were small, or even where the abuse was carried out by the younger sibling (e.g. Cyr et al., 2002; Krienert and Walsh, 2011; Pierce and Pierce, 1990; Russell, 1986).

The factor that primarily characterises sibling sexual behaviour as abusive is the exploitation of power for sexual objectives. In the absence of large age gaps or obvious use of coercion, the dynamics of the sibling relationship within the context of the family culture need to be explored in order to inform an assessment of the sexual behaviour (Allardyce and Yates, 2013).

The exercise of power and control is often a feature of sibling relationships, and such relationships may be characterised by significant dependency and power imbalances, even where age differences are small. Understanding the dynamics of power will require exploration of factors such as birth order, age, sex, cognitive ability and gendered power relations within the immediate family and the wider culture in which the sibling relationship exists. Brother-brother, sister-brother, sister-sister and multiple sibling sexual abuse (including involving extended family members such as cousins) can and do occur, but the most commonly known pairing is a brother abusing a sister.

Shared with permission: Extract from 'Sibling Sexual Abuse: A Knowledge and Practice Overview', S. Allardyce & P. Yates, Centre of Expertise on Child Sexual Abuse (January 2021).

APPENDIX 3

Help for parents of children who have been sexually abused by family members

If you find out or suspect that your child has been sexually abused by a family member, it can take a toll on you as a parent. It's important to find a way to manage your feelings, so you can focus on creating a safe environment for your child that is free from harm, judgment, and blame. It is imperative that when your child discloses to you, you continue to repeat the following messages through both your words and your actions:

- I love you
- What happened is not your fault
- I will do everything I can to keep you safe

How am I supposed to react?

There is no 'right' reaction to hearing that your child has been abused. You may experience a wide range of reactions and feelings that may impact different aspects of your life. Some common reactions from parents include:

- **Anger:** You may feel angry at the abuser for hurting your child or even frustrated with your child for not telling you. It's also possible to feel angry at your child for disclosing the abuse. It's not easy news to hear, but it's important to remember it is not your child's fault.
- **Anxiety:** You might be anxious about responding in the 'right' way to your child or navigating the other relationships in your life, especially if you have a relationship with the abuser.
- **Fear:** Depending on your family circumstances, you may be afraid that the abuser will find a way to harm your child

again or be concerned about taking care of your family on your own.

- **Sadness:** You may feel sad for your child, for your family, or for yourself. When a child discloses sexual abuse, it will cause changes in your life. It's okay to be upset over the changes in your life that may result from this disclosure.
- **Shock:** If you had no idea that the harm was occurring, you may be very surprised to hear what has happened.

It is important to keep in mind that there is no one 'right' reaction, and that all reactions and responses are normal. Having both you and your child talk to a professional about these thoughts and feelings can help sort through these issues. Professional support can also result in healthier long- and short-term results for both you and your child.

How do I manage these feelings?

Your child is counting on you for support. In order to put your child's safety first, it's important to take care of yourself. That means finding a way to work through your feelings and reactions to the abuse that doesn't interfere with your child's welfare. It may not be easy, but with the right support it is possible.

- Consider talking to a counsellor one-on-one. Individual counselling gives you the chance to focus entirely on you and your concerns, without needing to worry about how your child will react to those thoughts.
- Develop your support system. It might be family and friends you trust, or it might be a support group that you didn't have a connection with before.
- Set limits. Dealing with these emotions can be time-consuming and draining. Set aside time for activities that don't revolve around the abuse.
- Practice self-care to keep your mind and body in healthy shape.

What if the perpetrator is part of my family?

Finding out that your child was hurt by someone you know and trust can present some additional challenges as a parent. You may be faced with a range of emotions specific to this situation that others can't relate to. No one has the right to invalidate the way you feel, but it's important to find a way to manage these emotions in order to prioritise the safety of your child. Some experiences of non-offending parents may include:

- Anger towards the child for disrupting your family, especially if the perpetrator is your partner
- Anger towards the perpetrator for hurting your child and betraying your trust
- Guilt that you didn't know the abuse was occurring or for still having feelings for the person who hurt your child
- If the person who harmed your child was another one of your children, you may feel conflicted about how to provide support to the child who was harmed while still trying to protect your other child
- Losing faith in your judgement or abilities as a parent
- Practical fears about finances and day-to-day life that may change when the family member who caused harm is removed from the family circle
- Sense of loss for the family member who hurt your child as you begin to cut ties.

What can I expect from my child?

The effects of sexual assault and abuse vary from person to person. The process of healing from sexual abuse can take a long time, and it's understandable to feel frustrated as a parent. Survivors of child sexual abuse can react in a wide variety of ways. Some of these reactions could cause you discomfort or take you by surprise:

- Being angry at you for not protecting them
- Being angry at you for removing the perpetrator from the home
- Confiding in someone who isn't you
- Not talking about it at all
- Talking about the abuse all the time.

To speak with someone who is trained to help:

If you are in the USA, call the National Sexual Assault Hotline at: 800.656.HOPE (4673) or chat online at hotline.rainn.org/

If you live in Australia, speak with one of the trained counsellors at: 1800RESPECT.

Shared with the permission of RAINN.org

APPENDIX 4

Common long-term physical and mental health consequences of child sexual abuse

Whilst the following statistics and facts are probably not eye-opening, they acknowledge what we might wish to close our eyes to, yet intuitively know to be true.

According to the well-referenced and researched 'Darkness to Light' report (2017), not only do survivors of childhood sexual abuse have more minor health conditions, but they are also at greater risk for more serious conditions as well:

- Adults with a history of childhood sexual abuse are 30% more likely than their non-abused peers to have a serious medical condition such as diabetes, cancer, heart problems, stroke or hypertension.
- Male sexual abuse survivors have twice the HIV-infection rate of non-abused males, with 41% of HIV-infected twelve to twenty-year-olds reporting a sexual abuse history.

Mental health problems are also a common long-term consequence of child sexual abuse:

- Adult women who were sexually abused as a child are more than twice as likely to suffer from depression as women who were not sexually abused.
- Adults with a history of child sexual abuse are more than twice as likely to report a suicide attempt.

- Females who are sexually abused are three times more likely to develop psychiatric disorders than females who are not sexually abused.
- Among male survivors, more than 70% seek psychological treatment for issues such as substance abuse, suicidal thoughts and attempted suicide.

Adult survivors of childhood sexual abuse are at greater risk of a wide range of conditions that are non-life threatening and potentially psychosomatic in nature, including:

- fibromyalgia
- severe premenstrual syndrome
- chronic headaches
- irritable bowel syndrome
- a wide range of reproductive and sexual health complaints, including excessive bleeding, amenorrhea, pain during intercourse and menstrual irregularity.

Substance abuse problems are also a common consequence for adult survivors of child sexual abuse:

- Female adult survivors of child sexual abuse are nearly three times more likely to report substance use problems (40.5% versus 14% in the general population).
- Male adult childhood sexual abuse survivors are 2.6 times more likely to report substance use problems (65% versus 25% in the general population).

Obesity and eating disorders are more common in women who have a history of child sexual abuse:

- 24-year-old women who were sexually abused as children were four times more likely than their non-abused peers to be diagnosed with an eating disorder.
- Middle-aged women who were sexually abused as children were twice as likely to be obese compared to their non-abused peers.

Shared with permission of Darkness to Light (2017)

REFERENCE LIST

Allardyce. S. & Yates, P. (2021) Sibling sexual abuse: a knowledge and practice overview, Centre of Expertise on Child Sexual Abuse. Retrieved from: https://www.csacentre.org.uk/knowledge-in-practice/practice-improvement/sibling-sexual-abuse/

Allardyce, S. & Yates. P. (2022) Abuse at the Heart of the Family: The Challenges and Complexities of Sibling Sexual Abuse, Springer Nature Switzerland. Retrieved from: https://doi.org/10.1007/978-3-030-80212-7_4

Asher, J. (2017). Thirteen Reasons Why. New York: Razorbill Publishing.

Babbell, A. (7 February 2013). Trauma: Incest. Retrieved from www.psychologytoday.com/au/blog/somatic-psychology/201302/trauma-incest

Ballantine, M. and Soine, L. (Nov/Dec 2012). Sibling Sexual Abuse – Uncovering the Secret. Social Work Today. 12(6) p18. Retrieved from https://www.socialworktoday.com/archive/111312p18.shtml

Blyton, E. and Hargreaves, G. (1984). The Magic Faraway Tree. Melbourne: Budget Books.

Bravehearts Foundation Ltd. Child Sexual Assault Facts and Statistics, Retrieved January 2021, from https://bravehearts.org.au/research-lobbying/stats-facts/

Brown, B. (2012). The Power of Vulnerability: Teachings on Authenticity, Connection, & Courage. [Audiobook]. Boulder, CO: Sounds True.

Brown, B. (2020). The Gifts of Imperfection. London: Vermilion.

Caffaro, J. V. and Conn-Caffaro, A. (1998). Sibling abuse trauma: Assessment and intervention strategies for children, families and adults. The Haworth Maltreatment and Trauma Press. Binghamton, New York.

Caffaro, J. V. and Conn-Caffaro, A. (2005). Treating sibling sexual abuse families. Aggression and Violent Behaviour. 10(5) 604-623.

Cavendish, L. (2020). Magical Faerytales: an enchanted connection of retold tales. Glen Waverly VIC: Blue Angel Publishing.

Crisma, M., Bascelli, E., Paci, D., and Romito, P. (2004). Adolescents who experienced sexual abuse: Fears, needs and impediments to disclosure. Child Abuse and Neglect. 28, 1035-1048

Darkness to Light. (2017). Child Sexual Abuse Statistics Report. Retrieved from http://www.d2l.org/wp-content/uploads/2017/01/all_statistics_20150619.pdf

Doty, J.R. (2016). Into the Magic Shop: A Neurosurgeon's True Story of the Life-Changing Magic of Compassion and Mindfulness. London: Yellow Kite.

Dympna House Collective (Haberfield NSW). (1990). Facing the unthinkable: a survival guide for mothers whose children have been sexually abused. Haberfield, NSW: Dympna House Inc.

Eilers, S. (2021). For When Everything Is Burning. Amazon.

Emerald, D. (2015), The Power of TED* (*The Empowerment Dynamic). Bainbridge Island WA: Polaris Publishing

Fontes, L. and Plummer, C. (2010) Cultural issues in disclosures of child sexual abuse. Journal of Child Sexual Abuse, 19(5):491–518, as cited in Yates & Allardyce (2022).

Fredrickson, F. (2014) *Embrace Your Magnificence*. New York: Balboa Press.

Freyd, JJ. (1996) Betrayal Trauma: The Logic of Forgetting Childhood Abuse. Cambridge, MA: Harvard University Press.

Hanson, K. Source: TODAY, 15 Nov 2021.

Hatch, J., & Hayman-White, K. (2001). Adolescents who sexually abuse their siblings: An overview of the literature and issues for research attention. 8th Australasian Conference on Child Sexual Abuse and Neglect, Melbourne, as cited in Stathopoulos, October 2012.

Karpman, S. (2015). Karpman Drama Triangle. Retrieved from www. KarpmanDramaTriangle.com.

Kluft, R. (12 January 2011). Ramifications of Incest, *Psychiatric Times, 27(12)*. Retrieved from https://www.psychiatrictimes.com/view/ramifications-incest

Levenkron, S. (2007). Stolen Tomorrows: Understanding and treating women's childhood sexual abuse. New York: Lion's Crown Ltd.

Maroutian, E. (2018). *In Case Nobody Told You.* (New York: Maroutian Entertainment)

Mascardo, T. (2022). In Santos, R. 'I want to disappear or become invisible'. Retrieved from: https://www.vice.com/en/article/m7g9xq/escape-disappear-feeling-psychology-tiktok

Martin, R.M. (2018). The Brave Art of Motherhood: Fight Fear, Gain Confidence, and Find Yourself Again. Colorado: Waterbrook Press.

Mate, G. (2019). When the Body Says No: The Cost of Hidden Stress. London: Vermilion.

McVeigh, M. J. (2003). "But she didn't say no": An exploration of sibling sexual abuse. Australian Social Work, 56(2), 116–126, as cited in Stathopoulos, October 2012).

Morin, A. (2022). Sibling sexual abuse facts parents should know. https://www.verywellmind.com/facts-about-sibling-sexual-abuse-2610456

Morrill, M. (2014). Sibling sexual abuse: an exploratory study of long-term consequences for self-esteem and counselling considerations. Journal of Family Violence. 29(2), 205-213.

O'Brien, M. J. (1991). Taking sibling incest seriously. In M. Patton (Ed.), Family sexual abuse: Frontline research and evaluation. Newbury Park: Sage Publications, as cited in Stathopoulos, October 2012.

Pasco, A. H. (1995). "Lovers of self": Incest in the romantic novel. In L. G. Stheeman & H. Li (Eds.), Cincinatti romance review (Vol. 14). Cincinatti: Department of Romance Languages and Literature, as cited in Stathopoulos, October 2012.

Perez, D. (2021). Clarity and Connection. Missouri: Andrews McMeel Publishing.

RAINN https://www.rainn.org/articles/help-parents-children-who-have-been-sexually-abused-family-members

Robbins, A. (2011). Date With Destiny, Robbins Research International, Inc. San Diego.

Rowntree, M. (2007). Responses to sibling sexual abuse: Are they as harmful as the abuse? Australian Social Work, 60(3), 347–361, as cited in Stathopoulos, October 2012.

Selye, H. (1956). The Stress of Life. New York: McGraw-Hill Book Company Inc.

Sheppard, G.J., Bovino, J., Sheppard, A.L. (2014). *Find Someone*. On *Bombs Away*. Empire of Song.

Stathopoulos, M. (2012). Sibling sexual abuse (ACSSA Research Summary). Melbourne: Australian Centre for the Study of Sexual Assault, Australian Institute of Family Studies. © Commonwealth of Australia. Retrieved from: https://aifs.gov.au/sites/default/files/publication-documents/ressum3_0.pdf.

Stroebel, S., O'Keefe, S., Beard, K., Kuo, S., Swindell, S. and Stroupe, W. (2013). Brother-Sister incest: Data from anonymous computer-assisted self-interviews. Journal of Child Sexual Abuse. 22(3):255-276. https://doi.org/10.1080/10538 712.2013.743952.

van der Kolk, B. (2014). The Body Keeps the Score: Brain, Mind and Body in the Healing of Trauma. New York City, Penguin Press.

Welfare, A. (2008). How qualitative research can inform clinical interventions in families recovering from sibling sexual abuse. Australia and New Zealand Journal of Family Therapy, 29(3), 139–147, as cited in Stathopoulos, October 2012.

Welfare, A. (2010). Sibling Sexual Abuse: understanding all family members' experiences in the aftermath of disclosure. (Doctor of Philosophy Degree, La Trobe University, Bundoora) , as cited in Stathopoulos, October 2012.

Wright, K., Swain, S. and McPhillips, K. (December 2017). Royal Commission into Institutional Responses of Child Sexual Abuse. Child Abuse & Neglect 74, 1-9. Retrieved from https://www.sciencedirect.com/science/article/pii/S0145213417303678

Zajonc, D. and Emerald, D. (2018). Stop Rescuing: Start Coaching. ICF Australasia, Nov 28, 2018. Power of TED* and Donna Zajonc, MCC.

Acknowledgements

The idea of this book was, for a long while, held close to my heart, a solo journey that began as a handwritten mission. There is a saying that it takes a village to raise a child. Likewise, it took a village to get this book to publication. I am thankful for so many people who stepped forward and let me know they had my back and supported me in sharing my story for the purpose it is written.

Thank you to my close circle of family, friends and professional peers for your friendship, kind ear and guidance. Thank you for your quiet, solid support and gentle nudges to focus on what I said I wanted to create.

To Mel Uys, thank you for sifting through 500 pages of the first draft of the manuscript and making some sense of it. My courage grew from having had you, the first person to ever read my written story, not doubt it as a story worth sharing.

To the many experts I read from: Dr Gabor Mate, Dr Steven Levenkron and more; the local and international organisations supporting victims and survivors, and the hundreds of researchers who have poured their lives into studying, understanding and finding solutions relating to sibling sexual abuse. I will forever be grateful for your published work and the changes you are making to aid prevention, inform communities and support recovery.

To Farrah Motley and Micaela Diaz at Prosper Law, for your comprehensive review of the manuscript, reported findings and counsel that allowed the book to be published in its current form to do good in the world.

To book designer, Nada Backovic, I appreciate your patience in interpreting my creative thoughts on the design and professionally delivering a book I am so proud of. The day I saw your final cover was the first time I felt a buzz of confidence; and I walked into a bookstore with a smile, knowing this book has power.

To Leigh Robshaw at Stellar Words, my heartfelt thanks for your professional, critical editing input and self-publishing consulting.

To editor, Matt Earsman, I deeply appreciate your editing and writing talent. I had never anticipated that I would need to dig so deep in showing, not just telling my story, and you challenged me to do that. Thank you, not only from myself but on behalf of any other person who benefits from the words in this book, now and in the future.

To therapist, Rose, thank you for creating the safe space I needed to begin to trust that I wasn't nuts and for allowing me to open up slowly at my own pace. Your love, experience and compassion helped me see, feel and hear what I had feared would split me open at the seams for all those years. I'm so grateful to have you in my corner. Young Alice and adult me got to let down our guard. We'd never experienced the safety and benefit of doing that before. I owe you a lifetime supply of tissues. Thank you.

To the three human beings I was blessed to bring into this world, I love you with all my heart. Thank you for letting me find my way through this; for not rescuing me; for believing in me as capable of resolving my trauma my way. I love you and those you've chosen to love and bring into our lives.

To my husband, you are the most honourable, kind, and thoughtful man with whom I could have been blessed to unite. Writing this let me see how often you guided me to take another step forward, prompting me not just to find the path but to go use my gifts and create my own path. I cannot imagine where I would have been without your love and willingness to believe that what we had from the beginning was strong. Thank you for giving me time and space to heal for me first. I love you now and will love you forever.

Author's Page

The author is the former CEO of a successful healthcare organisation and a qualified coach and trainer, specialising in self-leadership and personal development. A loving wife, mother of three, and devoted grandmother, she lives with her husband in South-East Queensland, Australia, on the beautiful Sunshine Coast.

To avoid any negative personal repercussions and protect the privacy of her family and loved ones, she has chosen for the purposes of this book to use the pseudonym Alice Perle.

Alice signifies truth, graciousness, and reality, while Perle—an original form of pearl—represents innocence, elegance, and wisdom acquired through experience.

Through patience and love, even the most negative experiences can be transformed into valuable treasure.

Ingram Content Group Australia Pty Ltd
Printed in Australia
AUHW011232090623
379349AU00001B/1

9 780645 749700